Advanced French

Edited by

Shaina Malkin and Cindy Hazelton

LIVING LANGUAGE®

Published in the United States by Living Language, an imprint of Random House, Inc.

www.livinglanguage.com

Editor: Shaina Malkin
Production Editor: Carolyn Roth
Production Manager: Tom Marshall
Interior Design: Sophie Chin
Illustrations: Sophie Chin

First Edition

ISBN: 978-0-307-97155-5

This book is available at special discounts for bulk purchases for sales promotions or premiums. Special editions, including personalized covers, excerpts of existing books, and corporate imprints, can be created in large quantities for special needs. For more information, write to Special Markets/ Premium Sales, 1745 Broadway, MD 3-1, New York, New York 10019 or e-mail specialmarkets@ randomhouse.com.

PRINTED IN THE UNITED STATES OF AMERICA

10 9 8 7

Acknowledgments

Thanks to the Living Language team: Amanda D'Acierno, Christopher Warnasch, Suzanne McQuade, Shaina Malkin, Erin Quirk, Laura Riggio, Amanda Munoz, Fabrizio La Rocca, Siobhan O'Hare, Sophie Chin, Sue Daulton, Alison Skrabek, Carolyn Roth, Ciara Robinson, and Tom Marshall.

How to Use This Course 9

UNIT 1: Shopping 14

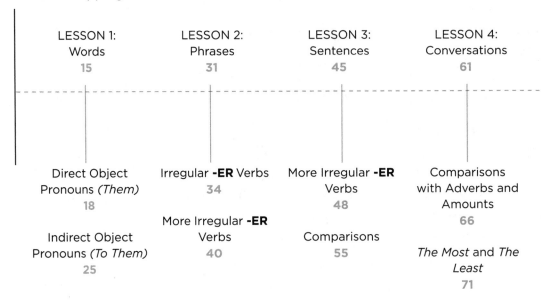

LESSON 1:
Words
15

LESSON 2:
Phrases
31

LESSON 3:
Sentences
45

LESSON 4:
Conversations
61

Direct Object
Pronouns *(Them)*
18

Indirect Object
Pronouns *(To Them)*
25

Irregular **-ER** Verbs
34

More Irregular **-ER**
Verbs
40

More Irregular **-ER**
Verbs
48

Comparisons
55

Comparisons
with Adverbs and
Amounts
66

The Most and *The
Least*
71

COURSE

UNIT 2: Work and School 90

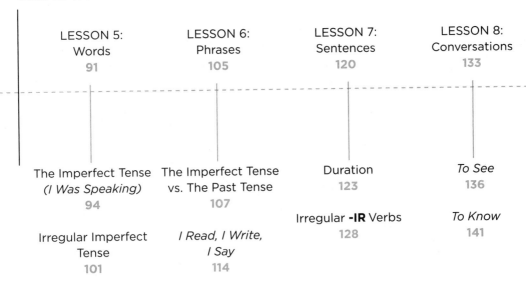

LESSON 5:
Words
91

LESSON 6:
Phrases
105

LESSON 7:
Sentences
120

LESSON 8:
Conversations
133

The Imperfect Tense
(I Was Speaking)
94

Irregular Imperfect
Tense
101

The Imperfect Tense
vs. The Past Tense
107

I Read, I Write,
I Say
114

Duration
123

Irregular **-IR** Verbs
128

To See
136

To Know
141

OUTLINE

UNIT 3: Sports and Leisure 159

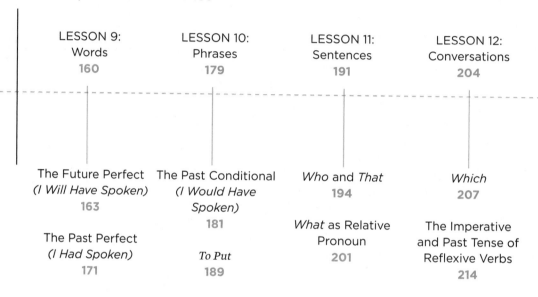

LESSON 9:
Words
160

LESSON 10:
Phrases
179

LESSON 11:
Sentences
191

LESSON 12:
Conversations
204

The Future Perfect
(I Will Have Spoken)
163

The Past Perfect
(I Had Spoken)
171

The Past Conditional
*(I Would Have
Spoken)*
181

To Put
189

Who and *That*
194

What as Relative
Pronoun
201

Which
207

The Imperative
and Past Tense of
Reflexive Verbs
214

COURSE

UNIT 4: Doctors and Health **233**

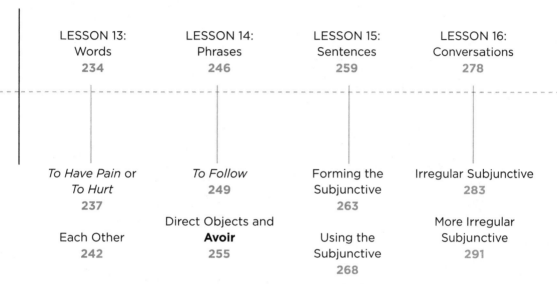

LESSON 13:
Words
234

LESSON 14:
Phrases
246

LESSON 15:
Sentences
259

LESSON 16:
Conversations
278

To Have Pain or
To Hurt
237

Each Other
242

To Follow
249

Direct Objects and
Avoir
255

Forming the
Subjunctive
263

Using the
Subjunctive
268

Irregular Subjunctive
283

More Irregular
Subjunctive
291

Pronunciation Guide 314
Grammar Summary 321
Glossary 336

How to Use This Course

Bienvenue à *Living Language Advanced French*!

Before we begin, let's take a quick look at what you'll see in this course.

CONTENT

Advanced French is a continuation of *Intermediate French*.

Now that you've mastered the basics with *Essential* and *Intermediate French*, you'll take your French even further with a comprehensive look at irregular verbs, advanced verb tenses, and complex sentences.

UNITS

There are four units in this course. Each unit has four lessons arranged in a "building block" structure: the first lesson will present essential *words*, the second will introduce longer *phrases*, the third will teach *sentences*, and the fourth will show how everything works together in everyday *conversations*.

At the beginning of each unit is an introduction highlighting what you will learn in that unit. At the end of each unit you'll find the Unit Essentials, which review the key information from that unit, and a self-graded Unit Quiz, which tests what you've learned.

LESSONS

There are four lessons per unit for a total of 16 lessons in the course. Each lesson has the following components:

- **Introduction** outlining what you will cover in the lesson.

- **Word Builder 1** (first lesson of the unit) presenting key words and phrases.

- **Phrase Builder 1** (second lesson of the unit) introducing longer phrases and expressions.

- **Sentence Builder 1** (third lesson of the unit) teaching sentences.

- **Conversation 1** (fourth lesson of the unit) for a natural dialogue that brings together important vocabulary and grammar from the unit.

- **Take It Further** providing extra information about the new vocabulary you just saw, expanding on certain grammar points, or introducing additional words and phrases.

- **Word / Phrase / Sentence / Conversation Practice 1** practicing what you learned in Word Builder 1, Phrase Builder 1, Sentence Builder 1, or Conversation 1.

- **Word Recall** reviewing important vocabulary and grammar from any of the previous lessons in *Essential, Intermediate,* or *Advanced French.*

- **Grammar Builder 1** guiding you through important French grammar that you need to know.

- **Work Out 1** for a comprehensive practice of what you saw in Grammar Builder 1.

- **Word Builder 2 / Phrase Builder 2 / Sentence Builder 2 / Conversation 2** for more key words, phrases, or sentences, or a second dialogue.

- **Take It Further** for expansion on what you've seen so far and additional vocabulary.

- **Word / Phrase / Sentence / Conversation Practice 2** practicing what you learned in Word Builder 2, Phrase Builder 2, Sentence Builder 2, or Conversation 2.

- **Word Recall** reviewing important vocabulary and grammar from any of the previous lessons in *Essential*, *Intermediate*, or *Advanced French*.

- **Grammar Builder 2** for more information on French grammar.

- **Work Out 2** for a comprehensive practice of what you saw in Grammar Builder 2.

- **Drive It Home** ingraining an important point of French grammar for the long term.

- **Tip or Culture Note** for a helpful language tip or useful cultural information related to the lesson or unit.

- **How Did You Do?** outlining what you learned in the lesson.

UNIT ESSENTIALS

You will see the **Unit Essentials** at the end of every unit. This section summarizes and reviews key grammar from the unit, and tests your knowledge of vocabulary by allowing you to fill in your very own "cheat sheet," with hints directing you back to the vocabulary in the lessons. Once you complete the blanks with the missing vocabulary, the Unit Essentials will serve as your very own reference for the most essential vocabulary and grammar from each unit.

UNIT QUIZ

After each Unit Essentials, you'll see a **Unit Quiz** testing your progress. Your quiz results will allow you to see which sections, if any, you need to review before moving on to the next unit.

PROGRESS BAR

You will see a **Progress Bar** on each page that has course material. It indicates your current position within each unit and lets you know how much progress you're making. Each line in the bar represents a Grammar Builder section.

AUDIO

Look for this symbol ▶ to help guide you through the audio as you're reading the book. It will tell you which track to listen to for each section that has audio. When you see the symbol, select the indicated track and start listening! If you don't see the symbol, then there isn't any audio for that section. You'll also see ⊍, which will tell you where that track ends.

The audio can be used on its own—in other words, without the book—when you're on the go. Whether in your car or at the gym, you can listen to the audio on its own to brush up on your pronunciation or review what you've learned in the book.

PHONETICS

Phonetics will occasionally be used in this course (in other words, [eh-truh] in addition to être), usually in order to highlight a point about French pronunciation. Remember that phonetics are not exact—they're just a general approximation of sounds—and so you should rely most on the audio, **_not_** the phonetics, to further your pronunciation skills.

For a guide to our phonetics system, see the **Pronunciation Guide** at the end of the course.

PRONUNCIATION GUIDE, GRAMMAR SUMMARY, GLOSSARY

At the back of this book you will find a **Pronunciation Guide**, **Grammar Summary**, and **Glossary**. The Pronunciation Guide provides information on French pronunciation and the phonetics system used in this course. The Grammar Summary contains a brief overview of key French grammar from *Essential, Intermediate,* and *Advanced French*. The Glossary (French-English and English-French) includes all of the important words from *Essential, Intermediate,* and *Advanced French,* as well as additional vocabulary.

FREE ONLINE TOOLS

Go to *www.livinglanguage.com/languagelab* to access your free online tools. The tools are organized around the units in this course, with audiovisual flashcards, and interactive games and quizzes. These tools will help you to review and practice the vocabulary and grammar that you've seen in the units, as well as provide some bonus words and phrases related to the unit's topic.

Unit 1:
Shopping

Welcome to *Advanced French*! In this course, you'll learn how to form complex sentences and use more advanced verb tenses. By the end of the course, you'll have all the skills and knowledge necessary to speak and understand conversational French.

There are four units in *Advanced French*, and four lessons in each unit. As in *Intermediate French*, each unit will gradually build from words to conversations.

Ready to get started?

By the end of this unit, you should be able to:

☐ Name different types of clothing

☐ Say *I understand them*

☐ Name different types of accessories

☐ Say *I speak to them*

☐ Talk about hundreds, thousands, or millions of something

☐ Discuss what to *throw out* and what to *buy*

☐ Name items you might find at a French market

☐ Discuss what you *prefer*

☐ Talk about price and size when you go shopping

☐ Discuss what you *use* and who is *paying*

☐ Make comparisons

☐ Say whether something was done *more slowly* or *less quickly*

☐ Talk about *the most* and *the least*

Lesson 1: Words

By the end of this lesson, you will be able to:

☐ Name different types of clothing

☐ Say *I understand them*

☐ Name different types of accessories

☐ Say *I speak to them*

Word Builder 1

Let's get started with different types of vêtements *(m.)* *(clothes, clothing)*.

▶ 1A Lesson 1 Word Builder 1 (CD 7, Track 1)

(man's) suit	le complet
pants	le pantalon
jacket	le veston
coat	le manteau
(fashion) scarf	le foulard
hat	le chapeau
sweater	le pull(-over), le tricot
raincoat	l'imperméable *(m.)*
glove	le gant
shirt (usually button)	la chemise

skirt	la jupe
blouse	la blouse*, le chemisier
sock	la chaussette
shoes	les chaussures (*f.*)

* Note that blouse can also mean *coat*. For example, a doctor might wear une blouse blanche (*a white coat*).

Take It Further

In these sections, we'll expand on what you've seen so far or introduce additional grammar and vocabulary.

For instance, let's talk more about scarves. Scarves are very popular in France, so it's important to know the difference between the two words for *scarf*:

fashion scarf	le foulard
winter scarf	l'écharpe (*f.*)

Un foulard is often made out of silk. It is worn as a fashion accessory, not as a way to keep warm. However, une écharpe could be made of other fabric such as wool when it's cold outside, or worn as a belt or around the shoulders.

Also, you learned that le complet means *suit*. However, there are actually multiple words for *suit* in French. Here are the others:

man's suit	le costume
woman's suit	le tailleur

Le complet is more of a formal word for a man's suit and is often used when referring to a three-piece suit or complet-veston.

✎ Word Practice 1

Identify the following items by filling in the blanks with the correct French word. Make sure to include le, la, l', or les before each word.

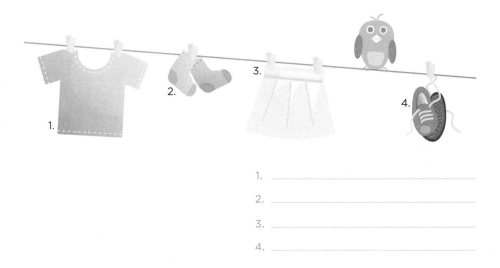

1. _____

2. _____

3. _____

4. _____

ANSWER KEY:
1. la chemise; 2. la chaussette; 3. la jupe; 4. les chaussures

✎ Word Recall

Remember that these exercises will review important vocabulary and grammar from any of the previous lessons in the program, from the first lesson of *Essential French* through *Intermediate French* up to your current point in *Advanced French*. The exercises will reinforce what you've learned so far and help you retain the information for the long term.

Match the French question words on the left to the correct English translations on the right.

1. quand	a. *how much, how many*
2. combien	b. *when*
3. quel/quelle/quels/quelles	c. *where*
4. où	d. *what, which*

ANSWER KEY:
1. b; 2. a; 3. d; 4. c

Grammar Builder 1
DIRECT OBJECT PRONOUNS (*THEM*)

▶ 1B Lesson 1 Grammar Builder 1 (CD 7, Track 2)

In *Advanced French*, you're going to learn how to form more complex sentences in French. To start, let's talk about "direct object pronouns."

Take a look at the following sentence:

Je prends le livre.
I take the book.

In technical terms, je (*I*) is the subject of that sentence, prends (*take*) is the verb, and le livre (*the book*) is what's known as the "direct object." A direct object is a noun that receives the action of a verb. In this case, it is the "thing that is taken."

However, in English, you know that it is also possible to say *I take **it*** instead of *I take **the book***. In other words, you replace the noun *the book* with the pronoun *it*. In this example, *it* is therefore the "direct object pronoun" that replaces the "direct object" noun *the book*. Simply put, direct object pronouns take the place of direct object nouns in sentences.

Here are the direct object pronouns in French:

me (m')	*me*	nous	*us*
te (t')	*you*	vous	*you*
le (l')	*him, it (m.)*	les	*them (m.)**
la (l')	*her, it (f.)*	les	*them (f.)**

* Note that les can also mean *it* when replacing certain French plural nouns, like les fruits (*fruit*) and les vacances (*vacation*), that are singular in English. You'll see an example of this below.

As you can see, in French, direct object pronouns must agree in number and gender with the nouns they replace. So if you want to replace la porte (*the door*), you must use la (*it, f.*) and not le (*it, m.*). If you want to replace les portes (*the doors*), you must use les (*them*). Notice that *them* has the same form in both the masculine and feminine.

While the direct object pronoun comes after the verb in English (*I take it*), it always comes **before** the verb in French. Here are a few examples, the first one using the verb fermer (*to close*):

Elle ferme la porte. Elle la ferme.
She closes the door. She closes it.

Il aime le film. Il l'aime.
He likes the movie. He likes it.

Aimez-vous les fruits ? Non, je ne les aime pas.
Do you like fruit? No, I don't like it.

Direct object pronouns can also replace the proper names of people, places, etc. So instead of saying *I understand Sophie*, you can say *I understand her*.

Here are some examples:

Je vous comprends.
I understand you.

Je la comprends.
I understand her./I understand it.

Je le comprends.
I understand him./I understand it.

Je les comprends.
I understand them. (I understand it [pl.].)

Il ne me comprend pas.
He doesn't understand me.

Me comprends-tu ?
Do you understand me?

In some sentences, a verb may be followed by a verb in the infinitive. For example: vous pouvez aider (*you can help*). If you want to use a direct object pronoun in this type of sentence, place the pronoun ***directly before the verb it is referring to***, which is usually the verb in the infinitive.

Vous pouvez nous aider ?
Can you help us?

In this case, you put the direct object pronoun nous (*us*) directly before aider (*lit., to help*) and not pouvez (*can*). This is because you're saying *help us*, and not *can us*, which of course wouldn't make sense.

Finally, note that, in the positive imperative, the direct object pronouns me and te become moi and toi. Also, the pronoun normally comes after the verb in the positive imperative. For example: Vous me quittez. Quittez-moi ! (*You're leaving me. Leave me!*). This only applies to the positive imperative, not the negative imperative: Ne me quittez pas. (*Don't leave me.*)

✎ Work Out 1

Rewrite the following sentences in French by replacing the direct object nouns with direct object pronouns.

1. Nous chantons une chanson. (*We sing a song.*)

2. Elle prépare le déjeuner. (*She prepares lunch.*)

3. Il vend les fruits. (*He sells fruit.*)

4. Est-ce que vous aimez les foulards ? (*Do you like scarves?*)

5. Ils prennent la voiture. (*They take the car.*)

6. **Je n'aime pas le poulet.** (*I don't like chicken.*)

ANSWER KEY:

1. **Nous la chantons.** (*We sing it.*) 2. **Elle le prépare.** (*She prepares it.*) 3. **Il les vend.** (*He sells it.*) 4. **Est-ce que vous les aimez ?** (*Do you like them?*) 5. **Ils la prennent.** (*They take it.*) 6. **Je ne l'aime pas.** (*I don't like it.*)

Word Builder 2

Now let's look at **les accessoires** (*m.*) (*accessories*).

1C Lesson 1 Word Builder 2 (CD 7, Track 3)

handkerchief (tissue)	le mouchoir
purse, bag	le sac
stocking (hose)	le bas
bathing suit	le maillot (de bain)
pajamas	le pyjama
jewelry	les bijoux (*m.*)
watch	la montre
earring	la boucle d'oreille
ring	la bague
bracelet	le bracelet
umbrella	le parapluie
tie	la cravate
cap	la casquette
glasses	les lunettes (*f.*)
sunglasses	les lunettes (*f.*) de soleil
briefcase	la serviette*

* **La serviette** can mean *briefcase*, *towel*, or *napkin* depending on the context.

Take It Further

Note that la bague can only refer to a *ring* that you wear on your finger and that usually has a gem or other design element on it. The word anneau (m.), on the other hand, means almost any kind of *ring*, not just jewelry. When referring to jewelry, anneau usually means a basic band without a setting.

Here are some more French words and phrases related to rings:

wedding ring	l'alliance (*f.*)
engagement ring	la bague de fiançailles
diamond ring	la bague en diamant
diamond	le diamant
gold	l'or (*m.*)
silver	l'argent (*m.*)*

* Remember that argent can also mean *money* or *cash*.

Finally, here are some other words and phrases related to shopping that will be helpful to know:

salesman/saleswoman	le vendeur/la vendeuse
merchant, vendor, dealer	le marchand/la marchande
to wear	porter
outfit	l'ensemble (*m.*), la tenue
clothing size	la taille
shoe size	la pointure
tennis shoes, sneakers	les baskets (*f.*), les chaussures (*f.*) de basket/tennis
t-shirt	le T-shirt*

* Pronounced [tee-shehrt].

jeans	le jean**
dress	la robe
belt	la ceinture
necklace	le collier
well-dressed	bien habillé/bien habillée
casual	décontracté/décontractée
formal, in formal dress/attire	en tenue de soirée
dress code	le code vestimentaire

** Pronounced just as in English: [dzheen].

Est-ce qu'il y a un code vestimentaire ?
Is there a dress code?

✎ Word Practice 2

Fill in the blanks with the appropriate French word.

1. Il fait du soleil ce matin. J'ai besoin de mes _____ (*sunglasses*).

   (*It's sunny this morning. I need my sunglasses.*)

2. Elle a beaucoup de _____ (*jewelry*). (*She has a lot of jewelry.*)

3. Martine a vendu son _____ (*bag*) et sa _____ (*watch*).

   (*Martine sold her bag and her watch.*)

4. Il pleut. Est-ce que vous avez votre _____ (*umbrella*) ?

   (*It's raining. Do you have your umbrella?*)

5. Gérard n'a pas de _____ (*ties*). (*Gérard doesn't have any ties.*)

   ANSWER KEY
   1. lunettes de soleil; 2. bijoux; 3. sac, montre; 4. parapluie; 5. cravates

✎ Word Recall

Write out the following numbers in French.

1. *eleven* _____

2. *four* _____

3. *seventy-three* _____

4. *forty* _____

5. *fifty-seven* _____

ANSWER KEY
1. onze; 2. quatre; 3. soixante-treize; 4. quarante; 5. cinquante-sept

Grammar Builder 2
INDIRECT OBJECT PRONOUNS (*TO THEM*)

▶ 1D Lesson1 Grammar Builder 2 (CD 7, Track 4)

In Grammar Builder 1, you learned that direct objects receive the action of a verb, and direct object pronouns replace direct objects in sentences.

As opposed to direct objects, **indirect** objects receive the action of a verb indirectly and are usually separated from the verb by a preposition like *to, at, for*, etc.

For example, compare the following two sentences:

I understand Mark.
I speak to Mark.

In the first sentence, *Mark* is a **direct** object. However, in the second sentence, *Mark* is an **indirect** object because it is separated from the verb *speak* by the preposition *to*. As a result, if you said *I speak to him* instead of *I speak to Mark*, the word *him* would be an indirect object pronoun, not a direct object pronoun.

The same is true in French. Indirect objects in French are usually preceded by a preposition like à (*to*). Note, however, that indirect object pronouns in French replace both the indirect object **and** the preposition in the sentence. So they don't just mean *me, you, him, her*, etc.; they mean *to me, to you, to him, to her*, and so on, depending on the preposition.

Here are the French indirect object pronouns, using the preposition *to* as an example:

me (m')	*to me*	nous	*to us*
te (t')	*to you*	vous	*to you*
lui	*to him/her/it*	leur	*to them**

* **Leur** can also mean *to it* when replacing certain French plural nouns that are singular in English.

Keep in mind that if, for instance, the pronoun is replacing the preposition pour (*for*) and not à (*to*), then the pronouns would translate as *for me, for you*, etc. The same is true for any other preposition.

Also note that there is only one pronoun for *to him, to her*, and *to it*: lui. Similarly, there is only one pronoun for *to them (m.)* and *to them (f.)*: leur.

Like direct object pronouns, indirect object pronouns are placed immediately before the verb.

Je parle à Luc. Je lui parle.
I speak to Luc. I speak to him.

Je parle à ma fille. Je lui parle.
I speak to my daughter. I speak to her.

Il me parle.
He speaks to me.

Il te parle.
He speaks to you.

Il lui parle.
He speaks to him./He speaks to her. (He speaks to it.)

Il nous parle.
He speaks to us.

Il vous parle.
He speaks to you.

Il leur parle.
He speaks to them. (He speaks to it [pl.].)

Note that in a sentence where a verb is followed by a verb in the infinitive, indirect object pronouns behave in the same way as direct object pronouns: je vais te parler (*I'm going to talk to you*).

Finally, as with direct object pronouns, the indirect object pronouns me and te become moi and toi in the positive imperative. Also, the pronoun normally comes after the verb in the positive imperative. For example: Vous me parlez. Parlez-moi ! (*You speak to me. Speak to me!*). Again, this doesn't apply to the negative imperative: Ne me parlez pas. (*Don't speak to me.*)

✎ Work Out 2

Rewrite the following French sentences by replacing the underlined indirect objects with indirect object pronouns.

1. Suzanne parle à ses amis. (*Suzanne speaks to her friends.*)

   _____

2. Nous parlons à toi et à Claude. (*We speak to you and to Claude.*)

   _____

3. Ils donnent les livres à leurs enfants. (*They give the books to their children.*)

   _____

4. Vous parlez à votre ami. (*You speak to your friend.*)

   _____

ANSWER KEY:
1. Suzanne leur parle. (*Suzanne speaks to them.*) 2. Nous vous parlons. (*We speak to you.*) 3. Ils leur donnent les livres. (*They give them the books.*) 4. Vous lui parlez. (*You speak to him.*)

✎ Drive It Home

Remember that this exercise is designed to instill key information about French grammar. Although it may seem repetitive, it is **very** important that you read through each question carefully, write out each response, and then read the whole question out loud. It will help you to retain the information beyond just this lesson and course.

A. Fill in the blanks with the correct direct object pronoun.

1. Je _____ aide. (*I help her.*)

2. Tu _____ aides. (*You help me.*)

3. Elle _____ aide. (*She helps him.*)

4. Nous _____ aidons. *(We help you, infml.)*

5. Vous _____ aidez. *(You help them, m.)*

6. Elles _____ aident. *(They help us.)*

7. Ils _____ aident. *(They help you, pl./fml.)*

8. Il _____ aide. *(He helps them, f.)*

B. Now fill in the blanks with the correct indirect object pronoun.

1. Je _____ donne la bague. *(I give the ring to her.)*

2. Tu _____ donnes la bague. *(You give the ring to me.)*

3. Elle _____ donne la bague. *(She gives the ring to him.)*

4. Nous _____ donnons la bague. *(We give the ring to you, infml.)*

5. Vous _____ donnez la bague. *(You give the ring to them, m.)*

6. Elles _____ donnent la bague. *(They give the ring to us.)*

7. Ils _____ donnent la bague. *(They give the ring to you, pl./fml.)*

8. Il _____ donne la bague. *(He gives the ring to them, f.)*

ANSWER KEY:

A. 1. l'; 2. m'; 3. l'; 4. t'; 5. les; 6. nous; 7. vous; 8. les

B. 1. lui; 2. me; 3. lui; 4. te; 5. leur; 6. nous; 7. vous; 8. leur

Tip

It's important to note that there are some verbs that are followed by **_indirect_** objects in English, but by **_direct_** objects in French. Here are two of the most common ones:

attendre*	*to wait for*
regarder*	*to look at*

* Attendre can also simply mean *to wait* and regarder can also mean *to watch*, depending on the context.

In other words, attendre and regarder should be followed by direct objects and direct object pronouns in French, even though they would be followed by indirect objects and indirect object pronouns in English. This is because the English verbs contain a preposition (*to wait **for***, *to look **at***), while their French equivalents are not followed by a preposition.

J'attends ma femme. Je l'attends.
I'm waiting for my wife. I'm waiting for her.

Je regarde la porte. Je la regarde.
I'm looking at the door. I'm looking at it.

The opposite is also true. There are some verbs that take direct objects in English, but require indirect objects in French. Here are three common ones:

obéir à	*to obey*
répondre à	*to answer*
téléphoner à	*to call*

So, for example, you would follow *to obey* with a direct object in English: *I obey the teacher. I obey him.* However, you would use an indirect object in French because obéir is usually followed by the preposition à. You literally say *I obey to the teacher. I obey to him.* in French.

Il obéit à son père. Il lui obéit.
He obeys his father. He obeys him. (lit., He obeys to his father. He obeys to him.)

Je réponds à mon ami. Je lui réponds.
I answer my friend. I answer him.

Je téléphone à mon amie. Je lui téléphone.
I call my friend. I call her.

How Did You Do?

Let's see how you did! By now, you should be able to:

☐ Name different types of clothing
(Still unsure? Jump back to page 15)

☐ Say *I understand them*
(Still unsure? Jump back to page 18)

☐ Name different types of accessories
(Still unsure? Jump back to page 22)

☐ Say *I speak to them*
(Still unsure? Jump back to page 25)

Lesson 2: Phrases

By the end of this lesson, you will be able to:

☐ Talk about hundreds, thousands, or millions of something

☐ Discuss what to *throw out* and what to *buy*

☐ Name items you might find at a French market

☐ Discuss what you *prefer*

Phrase Builder 1

Let's review numbers higher than 100.

▶ 2A Lesson 2 Phrase Builder 1 (CD 7, Track 5)

one hundred one	cent un
two hundred	deux cents

two hundred six	deux cent six
one thousand	mille
one thousand one	mille un
one million	un million

Take It Further

Multiples of cent (*one hundred*) are written with a final s:

trois cents
three hundred

However, that final s is dropped when it is followed by a number:

trois cent quatorze
three hundred fourteen

Multiples of mille (*one thousand*), on the other hand, do not add a final s:

deux mille
two thousand

Note that, unlike un million (*one million*), mille (*one thousand*) and cent (*one hundred*) are never preceded by un or une in order to say *one thousand* or *one hundred*.

If million is followed by a noun, then you need to place de in between million and the noun:

un million de dollars
a million dollars

However, if million is followed by other numbers and then the noun, you don't add de:

trois millions cinq cents personnes
three million five hundred people

Finally, un milliard is *one billion* and un trillion is *a trillion*. If you're *a billionaire*, you're un/une milliardaire. If you're *a millionaire*, you're un/une millionnaire.

✎ Phrase Practice 1

Translate the following numbers into English.

1. cent un _____

2. mille six cents _____

3. deux mille dix _____

4. trois cent cinquante _____

5. deux millions huit cent soixante-six _____

ANSWER KEY:
1. *one hundred one;* 2. *one thousand six hundred;* 3. *two thousand (and) ten;* 4. *three hundred (and) fifty;* 5. *two million eight hundred (and) sixty-six*

✎ Word Recall

Fill in the blanks with the correct family member in French.

1. La sœur de mon père est ma _____ .

2. Le père de ma mère est mon _____ .

3. **Les filles de ma tante sont mes** _____ .

4. **Le frère de mon père est mon** _____ .

5. **Le fils de ma sœur est mon** _____ .

ANSWER KEY:
1. tante (*The sister of my father is my aunt.*) 2. grand-père (*The father of my mother is my grandfather.*) 3. cousines (*The daughters of my aunt are my female cousins.*) 4. oncle (*The brother of my father is my uncle.*) 5. neveu (*The son of my sister is my nephew.*)

Grammar Builder 1
IRREGULAR -ER VERBS

▶ 2B Lesson 2 Grammar Builder 1 (CD 7, Track 6)

You know that most -er verbs follow the same pattern: je parle, tu marches, il/elle dîne, nous jouons, vous lavez, ils/elles demandent.

However, you also know that some -er verbs are slightly irregular, such as manger (*to eat*) and appeler (*to call*). Manger adds an e in the nous form and appeler doubles the l in every form except for the nous and vous forms.

Let's review the full conjugation of appeler in the present tense:

APPELER (*TO CALL*) - **PRESENT**			
j'appelle	*I call*	nous appelons	*we call*
tu appelles	*you call*	vous appelez	*you call*
il appelle	*he calls*	ils appellent	*they call*
elle appelle	*she calls*	elles appellent	*they call*

Notice the difference in pronunciation between appelle and appelons/appelez in the audio. The first e in appelle is pronounced [eh], while the first e in appelons/appelez (and in the infinitive form appeler) is pronounced [uh].

The verb jeter (*to throw, to throw out/away*) is conjugated and pronounced in a very similar way.

JETER (*TO THROW, TO THROW OUT/AWAY*) - **PRESENT**			
je jette	*I throw*	**nous jetons**	*we throw*
tu jettes	*you throw*	**vous jetez**	*you throw*
il jette	*he throws*	**ils jettent**	*they throw*
elle jette	*she throws*	**elles jettent**	*they throw*

As you can see, the t is doubled in every form except for the nous and vous forms. Also, the first e in jette is pronounced [eh], while the first e in jetons/jetez (and in the infinitive form jeter) is pronounced [uh].

However, it is important to note that, in the future and conditional tenses, both appeler and jeter double their respective letters for *all* forms, including nous and vous.

Tu appelleras ton ami demain.
You will call your friend tomorrow.

Nous jetterons les papiers dans la poubelle.
We will throw the papers in the garbage.

Notice the new words le papier (*paper*) and la poubelle (*garbage, trash can*) in the sentence above.

Other verbs like appeler and jeter include:

rappeler	*to call back*
projeter	*to plan*
rejeter	*to reject*

Another -er verb that is slightly irregular is acheter (*to buy*).

ACHETER *(TO BUY)* - **PRESENT**			
j'achète	*I buy*	nous achetons	*we buy*
tu achètes	*you buy*	vous achetez	*you buy*
il achète	*he buys*	ils achètent	*they buy*
elle achète	*she buys*	elles achètent	*they buy*

In this case, instead of doubling a letter, the first e is changed to an è in every form except for nous and vous. But, conveniently enough, the pronunciation is just like appeler and jeter. The è in achète is pronounced [eh], while the first e in achetons/achetez (and acheter) is pronounced [uh].

Again similar to appeler and jeter, the è is used for ***all*** forms of acheter in the future and conditional tenses.

ACHETER *(TO BUY)* - **FUTURE**			
j'achèterai	*I will buy*	nous achèterons	*we will buy*
tu achèteras	*you will buy*	vous achèterez	*you will buy*
il achètera	*he will buy*	ils achèteront	*they will buy*
elle achètera	*she will buy*	elles achèteront	*they will buy*

Other verbs conjugated like acheter include:

lever	*to lift, to raise, to pick up*
enlever	*to remove, to take off*
mener	*to lead*
emmener	*to take (someone)*
promener	*to walk (to take someone or something for a walk)*
peser	*to weigh*

Marie achète des bijoux au grand magasin.
Marie buys some jewelry at the department store.

Jean emmène ses amis au restaurant.
Jean takes his friends to the restaurant.

Ils enlèvent leurs manteaux.
They take off their coats.

✎ Work Out 1

Fill in the blanks with the correct present tense form of the verb in parentheses.

1. Elle _____ (acheter) des chaussures. *(She is buying shoes.)*

2. _____ -ils (jeter) les chaussettes ? *(Are they throwing out the socks?)*

3. Tu _____ (jeter) tes vêtements sur le lit. *(You throw your clothes on the bed.)*

4. Vous _____ (acheter) des blouses. *(You buy some blouses.)*

5. Ils _____ (acheter) des bijoux. *(They buy jewelry.)*

6. Nous _____ (appeler) nos amis. *(We call our friends.)*

7. Est-ce qu'il _____ (acheter) un costume ? *(Is he buying a suit?)*

8. Comment t'_____-tu (appeler) ? *(What's your name?)*

ANSWER KEY:
1. achète; 2. Jettent; 3. jettes; 4. achetez; 5. achètent; 6. appelons; 7. achète; 8. appelles

Phrase Builder 2

Here is some vocabulary for specialty foods that you might find at un marché (*a market*).

▶ 2C Lesson 2 Phrase Builder 2 (CD 7, Track 7)

Dijon mustard	la moutarde de Dijon
a piece of cheese	un morceau de fromage
chestnut paste	la crème de marrons
a box of sugar-coated chestnuts	une boîte de marrons glacés
black currant syrup	le sirop de cassis
a basket of strawberries	un panier de fraises
a bunch of asparagus	une botte d'asperges*
waffles	les gaufres (*f.*)

⏸ * Botte can also mean *bundle*, as in, *a bundle of leeks or straw.*

Take It Further

Les marrons (*m.*) (*chestnuts*) are popular in France. La crème de marrons (*chestnut paste*) is often used to create spreads, desserts, or fillings for pastries. Les marrons glacés (*sugar-coated chestnuts*) are sweet, candy-coated chestnuts that are served as candy or with dessert. You'll frequently see them in chocolate and candy stores.

Another popular nut is la noisette (*hazelnut*). You will also find hazelnut paste in many spreads, desserts, and pastry fillings. Furthermore, hazelnut is frequently added to chocolate in France. If a piece of chocolate is labeled as praliné, for example, that usually means it's filled with a noisette or amande (*f.*) (*almond*) ganache.

✏ Phrase Practice 2

Match the English words on the left to the correct French translations on the right.

1. *bunch*	a. **panier**
2. *box*	b. **morceau**
3. *mustard*	c. **botte**
4. *basket*	d. **boîte**
5. *piece*	e. **moutarde**

ANSWER KEY:
1. c; 2. d; 3. e; 4. a; 5. b

✏ Word Recall

Fill in the blanks with the correct French word.

1. **Je fais du** _____. *(I play sports.)*

2. **Je fais la** _____. *(I'm waiting in line.)*

3. **Je fais des** _____. *(I'm shopping.)*

4. **Je fais des** _____. *(I'm running errands.)*

5. **Je fais le** _____. *(I'm cleaning the house.)*

ANSWER KEY:
1. **sport**; 2. **queue**; 3. **courses**; 4. **achats**; 5. **ménage**

Grammar Builder 2
MORE IRREGULAR -ER VERBS

▶ 2D Lesson 2 Grammar Builder 2 (CD 7, Track 8)

Another irregular -er verb is préférer (*to prefer*). Here is its full conjugation:

PRÉFÉRER (*TO PREFER*) - **PRESENT**			
je préfère	*I prefer*	nous préférons	*we prefer*
tu préfères	*you prefer*	vous préférez	*you prefer*
il préfère	*he prefers*	ils préfèrent	*they prefer*
elle préfère	*she prefers*	elles préfèrent	*they prefer*

Notice that the last é changes to an è in all forms except for nous and vous.

Qu'est-ce que vous préférez, le café ou le thé ?
Which (What) do you prefer, coffee or tea?

Je préfère l'eau.
I prefer water.

In the future and conditional, the last é doesn't change for any form.

Vous préférerez le chocolat.
You will prefer chocolate.

Vous préféreriez le chocolat.
You would prefer chocolate.

Other verbs that conjugate like préférer include:

célébrer	to celebrate
compléter	to complete
espérer	to hope
posséder	to own
protéger	to protect
répéter	to repeat

Il espère aller en France.
He hopes to go to France.

Nous célébrons les fêtes avec notre famille.
We celebrate the holidays with our family.

The verb suggérer (*to suggest*) is also formed like préférer: je suggère d'aller (*I suggest going*).

Work Out 2

Fill in the blanks with the correct present tense form of the verb préférer.

1. Elle _____ la blouse blanche. (*She prefers the white blouse.*)

2. Je _____ les croissants. (*I prefer croissants.*)

3. Elles _____ les robes. (*They prefer dresses.*)

4. Il _____ la cravate rouge. (*He prefers the red tie.*)

5. Nous _____ les gants noirs. (*We prefer black gloves.*)

ANSWER KEY:
1. préfère; 2. préfère; 3. préfèrent; 4. préfère; 5. préférons

✎ Drive It Home

A. Fill in the blanks with the correct present tense form of the verb jeter.

1. Nous _____ nos vêtements sur la chaise.

   (We throw our clothes on the chair.)

2. Tu _____ tes vêtements sur la chaise.

   (You throw your clothes on the chair.)

3. Elle _____ ses vêtements sur la chaise.

   (She throws her clothes on the chair.)

4. Ils _____ leurs vêtements sur la chaise.

   (They throw their clothes on the chair.)

5. Je _____ mes vêtements sur la chaise.

   (I throw my clothes on the chair.)

6. Vous _____ vos vêtements sur la chaise.

   (You throw your clothes on the chair.)

7. Elles _____ leurs vêtements sur la chaise.

   (They throw their clothes on the chair.)

8. Il _____ ses vêtements sur la chaise.

   (He throws his clothes on the chair.)

B. Now fill in the blanks with the correct present tense form of the verb acheter.

1. Vous _____ des chaussures au grand magasin.

   (You buy some shoes at the department store.)

2. Il _____ des chaussures au grand magasin.

   (He buys some shoes at the department store.)

3. J' _____ des chaussures au grand magasin.

   (I buy some shoes at the department store.)

4. Elles _____ des chaussures au grand magasin.

   (They buy some shoes at the department store.)

5. Tu _____ des chaussures au grand magasin.

   (You buy some shoes at the department store.)

6. Elle _____ des chaussures au grand magasin.

   (She buys some shoes at the department store.)

7. Nous _____ des chaussures au grand magasin.

   (We buy some shoes at the department store.)

8. Ils _____ des chaussures au grand magasin.

   (They buy some shoes at the department store.)

C. Finally, fill in the blanks with the correct present tense form of the verb **préférer**.

1. Je _____ le thé. *(I prefer tea.)*

2. Tu _____ le thé. *(You prefer tea.)*

3. Nous _____ le thé. *(We prefer tea.)*

4. Elle _____ le thé. *(She prefers tea.)*

5. Elles _____ le thé. *(They prefer tea.)*

6. Vous _____ le thé. *(You prefer tea.)*

7. Ils _____ le thé. (*They prefer tea.*)

8. Il _____ le thé. (*He prefers tea.*)

ANSWER KEY:

A. 1. jetons; 2. jettes; 3. jette; 4. jettent; 5. jette; 6. jetez; 7. jettent; 8. jette

B. 1. achetez; 2. achète; 3. achète; 4. achètent; 5. achètes; 6. achète; 7. achetons; 8. achètent

C. 1. préfère; 2. préfères; 3. préférons; 4. préfère; 5. préfèrent; 6. préférez; 7. préfèrent; 8. préfère

 ## Tip

Let's go back to numbers for a second. Now that you know how to talk about *thousands* of something, you actually also know how to talk about the year in French.

To say a year in French, spell out the entire number using mille (*thousand*):

deux mille dix	2010 (*lit., two thousand ten*)
mille neuf cents	1900 (*lit., one thousand nine hundred*)
mille neuf cent quatre-vingt-dix	1990 (*lit., one thousand nine hundred ninety*)
mille sept cent soixante-seize	1776 (*lit., one thousand seven hundred seventy-six*)

How Did You Do?

Let's see how you did! By now, you should be able to:

☐ Talk about hundreds, thousands, or millions of something
(Still unsure? Jump back to page 31)

☐ Discuss what to *throw out* and what to *buy*
(Still unsure? Jump back to page 34)

☐ Name items you might find at a French market
(Still unsure? Jump back to page 38)

☐ Discuss what you *prefer*
(Still unsure? Jump back to page 40)

Lesson 3: Sentences

By the end of this lesson, you will be able to:

☐ Talk about price and size when you go shopping

☐ Discuss what you *use* and who is *paying*

☐ Make comparisons

Sentence Builder 1

▶ 3A Lesson 3 Sentence Builder 1 (CD 7, Track 9)

I would like to buy some clothes.	Je voudrais acheter des vêtements.
What do you have?	Qu'est-ce que vous avez ?
It's how much? (How much is it?)	C'est combien ?
It's too expensive.	C'est trop cher.
That's inexpensive./It's a good buy. (lit., It's good market.)	C'est bon marché.
Is there a discount?	Y a-t-il une remise ? (Il y a une remise ?)
May I try it on? (Can I try it on?)	Est-ce que je peux l'essayer ?
Where are the dressing rooms?	Où sont les cabines d'essayage ?
What size? (clothing)	Quelle taille ?
It's a good choice.	C'est un bon choix.
It's on sale.	Il/Elle est en solde.
I'll take it. (I'm going to take it.)	Je vais le/la prendre.

Take It Further

Let's review *this* and *that*, also known as the "demonstratives." They're very useful words to know when shopping.

DEMONSTRATIVES		
Masculine Singular	ce	*this, that*
Masculine Singular (before a vowel or silent h*)*	cet	*this, that*
Feminine Singular	cette	*this, that*
Masculine Plural	ces	*these, those*
Feminine Plural	ces	*these, those*

Notice that the plural form is the same for both the masculine and feminine.

Ce pull est jaune.
This sweater is yellow./That sweater is yellow.

Cet imperméable est joli.
This raincoat is pretty./That raincoat is pretty.

Ces chaussures sont marron.
These shoes are brown./Those shoes are brown.

If you want to specify that you mean *this* or *that*, remember that you can add -ci (*here*) and -là (*there*) after the noun. For example:

Vous voudriez ce manteau-ci ou ce manteau-là ?
Do you want this coat or that coat? (lit., Do you want this coat here or that coat there?)

J'achète cette robe-ci. Je n'aime pas cette robe-là.
I'm buying this dress. I don't like that dress.

You can do the same thing with *these* and *those*:

Ces chaussettes-ci ou ces chaussettes-là ?
These socks or those socks?

Finally, if you want to say *this one* or *that one* in French, use the following words:

celui-ci/celle-ci	*this one, this one here (m./f.)*
celui-là/celle-là	*that one, that one there (m./f.)*
ceux-ci/celles-ci	*these ones, these ones here (m./f.)*
ceux-là/celles-là	*those ones, those ones there (m./f.)*

Notice the different forms depending on gender.

Vous voulez quel chapeau ? Celui-ci.
Which hat do you want? This one.

Je préfère celui-là.
I prefer that one.

Je n'aime pas ces chaussures-ci. J'aime celles-là.
I don't like these shoes. I like those (ones).

✎ Sentence Practice 1

Translate the following words and phrases into French.

1. *the (clothing) size* _____

2. *the dressing rooms* _____

3. *a discount* _____

4. *on sale* _____

5. *inexpensive* _____

ANSWER KEY:
1. la taille; 2. les cabines d'essayage; 3. une remise; 4. en solde; 5. bon marché

✎ Word Recall

Let's review some more question words. Match the French words on the left to the correct English translations on the right.

1. qu'est-ce que	a. *why*
2. comment	b. *who*
3. pourquoi	c. *what*
4. qui	d. *how*

ANSWER KEY:
1. c; 2. d; 3. a; 4. b

Grammar Builder 1
MORE IRREGULAR **-ER** VERBS

▶ 3B Lesson 3 Grammar Builder 1 (CD 7, Track 10)

Let's look at the full conjugation of the verb **employer** (*to use, to employ*).

EMPLOYER *(TO USE, TO EMPLOY)* - **PRESENT**			
j'emploie	*I use*	**nous employons**	*we use*
tu emploies	*you use*	**vous employez**	*you use*
il emploie	*he uses*	**ils emploient**	*they use*
elle emploie	*she uses*	**elles emploient**	*they use*

As you can see, the **y** in the verb changes to an **i** for every form except **nous** and **vous**.

In the future and conditional, the **y** in **employer** changes to an **i** for *all* forms, including **nous** and **vous**. For example: **nous emploierons** (*we will employ*), **vous emploieriez** (*you would employ*).

Here are two other verbs like **employer**:

ennuyer	*to bore, to annoy*
nettoyer	*to clean*

Estelle emploie le téléphone pour son travail.
Estelle uses the phone for her work.

Le jeudi, je nettoie la maison.
On Thursdays, I clean the house.

Verbs in **-yer** are conjugated in the future and conditional using the third person singular form of the present tense rather than the infinitive as the stem.

The verb **envoyer** (*to send, to throw*) is also conjugated like **employer** in the present tense: **j'envoie**, **nous envoyons**, etc. However, it is irregular in the future and conditional. Those tenses are formed with **enverr-** + ending for all forms: **j'enverrai** (*I will send*), **nous enverrions** (*we would send*), and so on.

Now let's look at another verb that ends in -yer: payer (*to pay, to pay for*).

Interestingly, payer can actually be conjugated with or without the i change. In other words, you can change the y to i for the forms that change, or just keep the y as is. Either one is fine, and you will see both ways used.

PAYER *(TO PAY, TO PAY FOR)* - **PRESENT**			
je paye/je paie	*I pay*	nous payons	*we pay*
tu payes/tu paies	*you pay*	vous payez	*you pay*
il paye/il paie	*he pays*	ils payent/ils paient	*they pay*
elle paye/elle paie	*she pays*	elles payent/elles paient	*they pay*

Notice that nous and vous only have one possible form.

Also note that payer is one of those verbs that takes a direct object in French even when it would take an indirect object in English.

Je paye/paie les billets.
I pay for the tickets.

Or: Je les paye/paie. (*I pay for them.*)

In the future and conditional, either all forms of verbs like payer keep the y or all forms change the y to i. Both ways are correct.

The verb essayer (*to try, to try on/out*) is formed like payer:

J'essaie/essaye de parler français.
I'm trying to speak French.

✎ Work Out 1

Complete the sentences by filling in the correct present tense forms of the verbs in parentheses.

1. Il _____ (employer) l'ordinateur. (*He's using the computer.*)

2. Nous _____ (nettoyer) la maison. (*We're cleaning the house.*)

3. Est-ce que tu _____ (payer) l'addition ? (*Are you paying the bill?*)

4. Vous _____ (essayer) le pantalon. (*You're trying on the pants.*)

ANSWER KEY:
1. emploie; 2. nettoyons; 3. payes/paies; 4. essayez

Sentence Builder 2

▶ 3C Lesson 3 Sentence Builder 2 (CD 7, Track 11)

I would like to buy some souvenirs.	Je voudrais acheter des souvenirs.
I'd like to buy some perfume for my girlfriend.	Je voudrais acheter du parfum pour ma petite amie.
I'd like to buy some cologne for my boyfriend.	Je voudrais acheter de l'eau de cologne pour mon petit ami.
I would like to buy a (fashion) scarf.	Je voudrais acheter un foulard.
You don't have anything else?	Vous n'avez rien d'autre ?
Do you have something less expensive?	Avez-vous quelque chose de moins cher ?
Do you have something of the same kind ? (lit., Do you have something in the same kind/type?)	Avez-vous quelque chose dans le même genre ?
That costs a lot. (That costs dearly.)	Ça coûte cher.

That's three euros per pair. (lit., It/That costs three euros the pair.)	Ça coûte trois euros la paire.
Excuse me, but where is the register?	Excusez-moi, mais où est la caisse ?
You must pay at the register.	Il faut payer à la caisse.

Take It Further

Quelque chose (*something*) is what's known as an "indefinite pronoun." Indefinite pronouns are used to talk generally, referring to nothing or no one specific. You actually already know a few of them. Here's a list of the most common indefinite pronouns:

something	quelque chose
someone, somebody	quelqu'un
each (one)	chacun
another, another one	un/une autre
several	plusieurs
nothing, anything	ne... rien
no one, anyone, nobody, anybody	ne... personne
whatever/whoever/wherever, anything/anyone/anywhere/anytime	n'importe quoi/qui/où/quand

On can also be used as an indefinite pronoun when it means *one, people in general,* or a non-specific *you/they.*

Comment va-t-on au musée ?
How does one get to the museum?

Quelqu'un t'a téléphoné.
Somebody called you.

Il n'y a personne ici.
There's no one here./There's nobody here.

Il fait n'importe quoi pour gagner de l'argent.
He does anything to make money.

You can use **d'autre** or **autre** with some of the indefinite pronouns to mean *else*:
quelqu'un d'autre (*someone else*), **ne... rien d'autre** (*nothing else, anything else*),
etc. If you want to say *something else*, use **autre chose**. **Autre chose** can also mean
anything else.

And here are some of the other words you saw in Sentence Builder 2. You already
knew **le parfum**, which can mean *perfume, fragrance,* or *flavor.*

(cash) register	**la caisse**
souvenir, memory	**le souvenir**
cologne	**l'eau** *(f.)* **de cologne**
pair	**la paire**
same, even	**même**
kind, type, genre	**le genre**

Finally, you saw that you can use a definite article (**le, la**) when you want to say
per something: **trois euros la paire** (*three euros per pair*). Another, more general
way is to use **par** (*per*):

trois euros par jour
thirty euros per day

par personne
per person

✎ Sentence Practice 2

Translate the following conversation into English.

- Je voudrais acheter quelque chose pour ma petite amie.

_____

- Qu'est-ce que tu veux acheter ?

_____

- Un foulard ?

_____

- Voici un foulard.

_____

- C'est combien ?

_____

- Ça coûte 60 euros.

_____

- C'est bon marché. Où est la caisse ?

_____

ANSWER KEY:
- *I would like to buy something for my girlfriend.*
- *What do you want to buy?*
- *A scarf?*
- *Here's a scarf.*
- *How much is it?/It's how much?*
- *It's sixty euros./It costs sixty euros. or That's sixty euros./That costs sixty euros.*
- *That's inexpensive./It's a good buy. Where is the (cash) register?*

Word Recall

Match these expressions.

1. **C'est vrai !**	a. *Okay!*
2. **Pas de chance !**	b. *It's true!*
3. **Formidable !**	c. *Of course!*
4. **D'accord !**	d. *No luck!*
5. **Bien sûr !**	e. *Fantastic!*

ANSWER KEY:
1. b; 2. d; 3. e; 4. a; 5. c

Grammar Builder 2
COMPARISONS

 3D Lesson 3 Grammar Builder 2 (CD 7, Track 12)

You've learned how to form and use adjectives in basic sentences. Now let's look at how to use them in comparisons.

For example, you may want to say that someone or something has *more* or *less* of a characteristic *than* someone or something else. Or you may want to say that they have the same degree of it.

It's very easy to do this in French. Just use the following constructions:

plus + adjective + **que**	*more ... than*
moins + adjective + **que**	*less ... than (not as ... as)*
aussi + adjective + **que**	*as ... as*

Il est plus actif que moi.
He is more active than I am. (He is more active than me.)

Il est moins actif que moi.

He is less active than I am. (He is less active than me./He is not as active as me.)

Il est aussi actif que moi.

He is as active as I am. (He is as active as me.)

Note that "plus + adjective + que" can also be translated as:

-er form of the adjective ... *than*

In other words: *shorter than, taller than,* etc.

Robert est plus grand que Michel.

Robert is taller than Michel.

Don't forget that the adjective must agree with the noun it is describing in gender and number.

Jeanne est plus grande que Robert.

Jeanne is taller than Robert.

Les robes sont plus jolies que les jupes.

The dresses are prettier than the skirts.

Les adultes sont moins actifs que les enfants.

Adults are less active than children. (Adults are not as active as children.)

Les garçons sont aussi grands que les filles.

The boys are as tall as the girls.

In French, you can also use "plus/moins/aussi + adjective" without the que. This is like saying *the dress is longer* instead of *the dress is longer than the skirt* in English.

La robe est plus longue.
The dress is longer.

Les parents sont plus gentils.
The parents are kinder.

L'appartement est aussi cher.
The apartment is just as expensive.

Notice that, in this case, "aussi + adjective" translates as *just as ... .*

The adjectives bon/bonne (*good*) and mauvais/mauvaise (*bad*) are irregular when used to make comparisons, just as they are in English.

For example, you wouldn't say plus bon/bonne (*lit., more good*) in French or in English. That's incorrect. Instead, you would use the word meilleur/meilleure (*better*):

Le vin est bon, mais le champagne est meilleur.
The wine good, but the champagne is better.

To say that something is *worse*, change the adjective mauvais/mauvaise (*bad*) to plus mauvais/mauvaise (*worse*) or use the irregular form pire (*worse*). The two forms are interchangeable.

Ce restaurant est pire/plus mauvais que l'autre.
This restaurant is worse than the other.

If you want to say something is *as good* or *as bad,* just use aussi always: Le vin est bon, mais le champagne est aussi bon. (*The wine is good, but the champagne is just as good*). Ce restaurant est aussi mauvais que l'autre. (*This restaurant is as bad as the other.*)

Moins can also be used normally with those two adjectives: **moins bon/bonne** (*not as good*), **moins mauvais/mauvaise** (*not as bad*).

Finally, if you're using **beaucoup de** (*many, much, a lot of*) as an adjective, you don't use **aussi beaucoup de** if you want to make an equal comparison. Instead, you use **autant de**:

Il a beaucoup de problèmes.
He has many problems.

Il a autant de problèmes que nous.
He has as many problems as we do. (lit., He has as many problems as us.)

Work Out 2

Complete the sentences by filling in the blanks with the correct French words.

1. **Le livre est** _____ **intéressant** _____ **le film.** (*as ... as*)

2. **André est** _____ **intelligent** _____ **Gérard.** (*less ... than*)

3. **Les gants sont** _____ **beaux** _____ **les sacs.** (*more ... than*)

4. **Le manteau est** _____ **long** _____ **l'imperméable.** (*as ... as*)

ANSWER KEY:
1. **aussi... que** (*The book is as interesting as the movie.*) 2. **moins... que** (*André is less intelligent than Gérard./André is not as intelligent as Gérard.*) 3. **plus... que** (*The gloves are more beautiful than the bags.*) 4. **aussi... que** (*The coat is as long as the raincoat.*)

Drive It Home

A. Fill in the blanks with the correct present tense form of the verb **employer**.

1. **J'** _____ **l'ordinateur.** (*I'm using the computer.*)

2. Vous _____ l'ordinateur. *(You're using the computer.)*

3. Elle _____ l'ordinateur. *(She's using the computer.)*

4. Tu _____ l'ordinateur. *(You're using the computer.)*

5. Ils _____ l'ordinateur. *(They're using the computer.)*

6. Il _____ l'ordinateur. *(He's using the computer.)*

7. Nous _____ l'ordinateur. *(We're using the computer.)*

8. Elles _____ l'ordinateur. *(They're using the computer.)*

B. Now complete the sentences by filling in the blanks with plus... que. Make sure to read each sentence out loud once you're done.

1. Elle est _____ petite _____ moi.

   (She is shorter than me.)

2. Il est _____ petit _____ moi.

   (He is shorter than me.)

3. Vous êtes _____ petit(e)(s) _____ moi.

   (You are shorter than me.)

4. Tu es _____ petit(e) _____ moi.

   (You are shorter than me.)

5. Ils sont _____ petits _____ moi.

   (They are shorter than me.)

ANSWER KEY:
A. 1. emploie; 2. employez; 3. emploie; 4. emploies; 5. emploient; 6. emploie; 7. employons;
8. emploient
B. all plus... que

⊕ Culture Note

Paris has a reputation for being one of the centers of the fashion world. And, in fact, fashion is one of the most important industries in France. French **haute couture** (*high fashion*) includes many famous names of **couturiers** (*designers*) from the past and present, including Coco Chanel, Yves Saint Laurent, Christian Dior, and so on.

If you're interested in high fashion, the **rive droite** (*right bank*), between **Opéra** and **Place Charles de Gaulle**, or the neighborhood near **Saint-Germain-des-Prés** on the **rive gauche** (*left bank*), is where you need to go in Paris. There are also many small boutiques scattered throughout Paris, as well as famous department stores like **Galeries Lafayette**, **Printemps**, and **Le Bon Marché**. There are various shopping malls scattered throughout the city as well.

How Did You Do?

Let's see how you did! By now, you should be able to:

☐ Talk about price and size when you go shopping
(Still unsure? Jump back to page 45)

☐ Discuss what you *use* and who is *paying*
(Still unsure? Jump back to page 48)

☐ Make comparisons
(Still unsure? Jump back to page 55)

Lesson 4: Conversations

By the end of this lesson, you will be able to:

☐ Say whether something was done *more slowly* or *less quickly*

☐ Talk about *the most* and *the least*

Conversation 1

Mme Martin is at the marché (*market*) shopping for the items she needs to make a soup containing poireaux (*m.*) (*leeks*) and pommes (*f.*) de terre (*potatoes*).

▶ 4A Lesson 4 Conversation 1 (CD 7, Track 13)

Mme Martin : Bonjour monsieur. Est-ce que vous avez des poireaux aujourd'hui ?

Le marchand : Bien sûr, madame, combien en voulez-vous ?

Mme Martin : Combien coûtent les poireaux ?

Le marchand : Deux euros la livre.

Mme Martin : Donnez-moi une livre, s'il vous plaît.

Le marchand : Voilà. Il vous faut autre chose, madame ?

Mme Martin : Ah, oui. Je fais une bonne soupe ce soir—aux poireaux et aux pommes de terre—donc il me faut des pommes de terre.

Le marchand : Combien en voulez-vous, madame ?

Mme Martin : Je voudrais trois livres, s'il vous plaît.

Le marchand : Et voilà, de belles pommes de terre. Et avec ça ?

Mme Martin : Ça suffit, pour le moment. Je vous dois combien, monsieur ?

Le marchand : Ça fait cinq euros, madame.

Ms. Martin: *Hello sir. Do you have leeks today?*

Merchant: *Of course, ma'am, how many of them do you want?*

Ms. Martin: *How much do the leeks cost?*

Merchant:	*Two euros per pound.*
Ms. Martin:	*Give me one pound, please.*
Merchant:	*Here it is. Do you need anything else, ma'am?*
Ms. Martin:	*Oh, yes. I'm making a good soup tonight—leek (and) potatoes—so I need some potatoes.*
Merchant:	*How many of them do you want, ma'am?*
Ms. Martin:	*I would like three pounds, please.*
Merchant:	*And here they are, beautiful potatoes. And with that?*
Ms. Martin:	*That's enough, for the moment. How much do I owe you, sir?*
Merchant:	*That's five euros, ma'am.*

Take It Further

You know that the word **en** can be used to mean *in, on,* or *to.*

Je vais en vacances.
I'm going on vacation.

Il est allé en France.
He went to France.

Je suis en France.
I'm in France.

However, **en** can also be used as a pronoun. Like the pronoun **y** (*there*), it is used to replace a phrase.

En is used to replace "**de/du/de la/de l'/des** + noun." As a result, it can mean *some, of it, of them, from it,* etc. For example, instead of saying:

Combien voulez-vous de poireaux ?
How many leeks do you want?

You could say:

Combien en voulez-vous ?
How many of them do you want?

Notice that, like **y**, **en** comes before the verb.

Here are some more examples:

Nous buvons du thé.
We drink tea.

Nous en buvons.
We drink some (of it)./We drink it.

J'ai besoin de deux pommes de terre.
I need two potatoes.

J'en ai besoin.
I need some (of them)./I need them.

When **en** is used with a quantity expression like **beaucoup de** (*a lot of*) or **une livre de** (*a pound of*), the **de** is removed but the quantity (**beaucoup, une livre**) remains. Notice that English works the same way.

Je voudrais une livre et demie de champignons.
I would like a pound and (a) half of mushrooms.

J'en voudrais une livre et demie.
I would like a pound and (a) half of them.

Je mange beaucoup de fromage.
I eat a lot of cheese.

J'en mange beaucoup.
I eat a lot of it.

In Conversation 1, you also saw that you can use a form of **il faut** to mean *I need,*
she needs, etc. instead of the general *you need to* or *it's necessary to.* Just insert the
appropriate *indirect* object pronoun between **il** and **faut**:

il faut	it's necessary to, you have to, you need to, you must
il me faut	I need
il vous faut	you need
il lui faut	he needs, she needs

Finally, you saw the very helpful phrase **Ça suffit**, which means *That's it* or *That's*
enough. A related phrase is **C'est tout**, which means *That's all.* So if the clerk in a
store asks you if **C'est tout ?** (*Is that all?*), you can respond **Oui, c'est tout.** (*Yes,*
that's all.)

✎ Conversation Practice 1

Re-read Conversation 1. Then say whether each sentence below is **vrai** (*true*) or
faux (*false*). Next to each sentence, write down V for **vrai** or F for **faux**.

1. **Mme Martin voudrait faire une soupe.** _____

2. **Mme Martin voudrait trois livres de poireaux.** _____

3. **Mme Martin voudrait une livre de pommes de terre.** _____

4. **Les poireaux coûtent cinq euros la livre.** _____

5. **Mme Martin doit cinq euros.** _____

ANSWER KEY:

1. V (*Yes, she does want to make a soup.*) 2. F (*No, Mme Martin would like one pound of leeks.*) 3. F (*No, Mme Martin would like three pounds of potatoes.*) 4. F (*No, the leeks cost two euros per pound.*) 5. V (*Yes, she does owe five euros.*)

✎ Word Recall

Translate the following avoir expressions into English.

1. **avoir froid** _____

2. **avoir soif** _____

3. **avoir besoin de** _____

4. **avoir tort** _____

5. **avoir faim** _____

6. **avoir envie de** _____

7. **avoir raison** _____

ANSWER KEY:

1. *to be cold*; 2. *to be thirsty*; 3. *to need*; 4. *to be wrong*; 5. *to be hungry*; 6. *to feel like*; 7. *to be right*

Grammar Builder 1
COMPARISONS WITH ADVERBS AND AMOUNTS

▶ 4B Lesson 4 Grammar Builder 1 (CD 7, Track 14)

You can also make comparisons with adverbs.

For example, here are the three ways you can make a comparison using poliment (*politely*):

plus poliment que	*more politely than*
moins poliment que	*less politely than (not as politely as)*
aussi poliment que	*as politely as*

Here are some more examples of comparisons with adverbs:

Marc parle plus lentement que Joseph.
Marc speaks more slowly than Joseph.

Le train va moins vite que l'avion.
The train goes less quickly than the plane. (The train does not go as quickly as the plane.)

L'autobus va aussi vite que la voiture.
The bus goes as quickly as the car.

Like the adjective bon (*good*), the adverb bien (*well*) has an irregular comparative form when talking about more. Instead of plus bien (*lit., more well*), which is incorrect, you say mieux (*better*).

Marie parle bien, mais Jean parle mieux.
Marie speaks well, but Jean speaks better.

And like the adjective **mauvais** (*bad*), the adverb **mal** (*bad, badly*) has two possible comparative forms when talking about *more*: **plus mal** (*worse*) or **pire** (*worse*). However, **pire** is mainly used in informal conversation and is generally not considered correct in writing or formal speech.

When used as adverbs, **beaucoup** (*many, a lot, much*) and **peu** (*little*) also have some irregular comparative forms. Instead of **plus beaucoup**, you simply say **plus** (*more*). And instead of **plus peu**, you say **moins** (*less*). In equal comparisons, **beaucoup** becomes **autant**.

Je travaille beaucoup.
I work a lot.

Je travaille autant que toi.
I work as much as you do. (I work as much as you.)

You can also compare amounts of things. Just use "**plus de** + noun + **que**" (*more ... than*) or "**moins de** + noun + **que**" (*less ... than*).

Il y a plus de baguettes dans la boulangerie que dans la pâtisserie.
There are more baguettes in the bakery than in the pastry shop.

(II)

✎ Work Out 1

Complete the following sentences with the correct missing words.

1. **Paul parle** _____ **Christine.** (*Paul speaks better than Christine.*)

2. **Il conduit** _____ **moi.** (*He drives worse than me.*)

3. **Elle travaille** _____ **lui.** (*She works as much as him.*)

4. Nos parents conduisent _____ vous.

   (*Our parents drive as slowly as you.*)

5. Tu parles _____ moi. (*You speak more quickly than me.*)

   ANSWER KEY:

   1. mieux que; 2. plus mal que/pire que; 3. autant que; 4. aussi lentement que; 5. plus vite que

꩜ Conversation 2

Cheyann and Jeanne are shopping for a special event next Saturday evening.

▶ 4C Lesson 4 Conversation 2 (CD 7, Track 15)

Cheyann :	Je voudrais acheter une nouvelle paire de chaussures pour la soirée de samedi prochain.
Jeanne :	Et moi, je vais regarder les robes.
Cheyann :	Regarde ces belles chaussures rouges ! Je les aime ! Qu'est-ce que tu penses ?
Jeanne :	Elles sont très belles, mais je pense que les chaussures noires sont plus belles et plus chic. Essaye-les.
Cheyann :	Voici ma pointure… Je les aime beaucoup ! Tu as raison. Les chaussures noires sont les plus belles.
Jeanne :	Et maintenant, qu'est-ce que tu penses, la robe bleue ou la robe noire ?
Cheyann :	La robe bleue est la plus jolie. J'adore la couleur. Essaye-la.
Jeanne :	Regarde cette belle robe que je porte !
Cheyann :	Oh là là ! Elle te va à ravir.
Jeanne :	À mon avis, nous serons les plus jolies femmes à la soirée.
Cheyann :	De toute façon, nous serons bien habillées !

Cheyann:	I'd like to buy a new pair of shoes for the party next Saturday (lit., of next Saturday).
Jeanne:	And me, I'm going to look at dresses.
Cheyann:	Look at these beautiful red shoes! I like them! What do you think?
Jeanne:	They're very beautiful, but I think that the black shoes are more beautiful and more stylish. Try them on.
Cheyann:	Here's my (shoe) size ... I like them a lot! You're right. The black shoes are the most beautiful.
Jeanne:	And now, what do you think, the blue dress or the black dress?
Cheyann:	The blue dress is the prettiest. I love the color. Try it on.
Jeanne:	Look at this beautiful dress that I'm wearing!
Cheyann:	Wow! It looks great on you.
Jeanne:	In my opinion, we'll be the most beautiful women at the party.
Cheyann:	At any rate, we'll be well-dressed!

Take It Further

You just saw some good expressions to use in conversation. Let's review:

in my opinion	à mon avis
at any rate, in any case, anyhow	de toute façon
to look great on someone, to suit someone well	aller à ravir à quelqu'un

La jupe va à ravir à Sophie. Elle lui va à ravir.
The skirt looks great on Sophie. It looks great on her.

Also notice the use of que to mean *that* in je pense que... (*I think that ...*) and cette belle robe que je porte (*this beautiful dress that I'm wearing*). You'll learn more about how to use que in Unit 3.

Finally, here are some new words you'll see in Grammar Builder 2:

student, pupil	un/une élève
class, grade, classroom	la classe
famous	célèbre

✎ Conversation Practice 2

Translate the following sentences into English.

1. Je les aime ! _____

2. Essaye-les. _____

3. Essaye-la. _____

4. Elle te va à ravir. _____

ANSWER KEY:
1. *I like them!* 2. *Try them on.* 3. *Try it on.* 4. *It looks great on you.*

✎ Word Recall

Fill in the blanks with the correct French word.

1. Il me faut une _____. (*I need a fork.*)

2. Il me faut un _____. (*I need a knife.*)

3. Il me faut une _____. (*I need a napkin.*)

4. Il me faut une _____. (*I need a spoon.*)

5. Il me faut du _____. (*I need salt.*)

6. Il me faut du _____. (*I need pepper.*)

ANSWER KEY:
1. **fourchette**; 2. **couteau**; 3. **serviette**; 4. **cuiller/cuillère**; 5. **sel**; 6. **poivre**

Grammar Builder 2
THE MOST AND THE LEAST

▶ 4D Lesson 4 Grammar Builder 2 (CD 7, Track 16)

If you want to talk about *the most* or *the least* of something, then you need to use the "superlative" form of the adjective.

In French, the superlative is formed by using:

le/la/les + **plus** + adjective	*the most …*
le/la/les + **moins** + adjective	*the least …*

Don't forget that the adjective has to agree in gender and number with the noun. Here are some examples with *the most*:

le plus beau
the most handsome

la plus belle
the most beautiful

les plus beaux
the most handsome

les plus belles
the most beautiful

Note that the **plus** superlative can also be translated as the *-est* form of an adjective: *the tallest, the smallest,* etc. For example: **le plus joli** (*the prettiest*).

Now here are some examples with *the least*:

le moins joli
the least pretty

la moins jolie
the least pretty

les moins jolis
the least pretty

les moins jolies
the least pretty

Now let's look at how to use the superlative in sentences. Remember that most adjectives in French follow the noun. As a result, their superlatives also follow the noun. Note that the definite article (le, la, l', les) appears twice as a result.

Où est le restaurant le plus cher ?
Where is the most expensive restaurant? (lit., Where is the restaurant the most expensive?)

Les restaurants les plus célèbres sont à New York.
The most famous restaurants are in New York. (lit., The restaurants the most famous are in New York.)

In French, the word *in* is translated by the partitive (du, de la, etc.) when it follows the superlative:

C'est la ville la plus riche du monde.
It's the richest city in the world. (lit., It's the city the richest of the world.)

Keep in mind, however, that some adjectives come before the noun in French. For those adjectives, you usually put their superlatives before the noun as well. In this case, the definite article only appears once.

Henri est le meilleur élève de la classe.
Henri is the best pupil in the class.

As you can see, the plus superlative of bon/bonne (*good*) is irregular. So, if you want to say *the best*, use le/la/les + meilleur(s)/meilleure(s). Not surprisingly, the plus superlative of mauvais/mauvaise (*bad*) is irregular as well. If you want to say *the worst*, use le/la/les + pire(s) or le/la/les + plus mauvais/mauvaise(s).

✎ Work Out 2

Translate the following sentences into English.

1. C'est la plus jolie maison. _____

2. C'est la jupe la moins chère. _____

_____

3. Elle est la plus belle femme. _____

_____

4. Elle est la meilleure amie de Sophie. _____

5. Il est l'homme le plus heureux du monde. _____

_____

ANSWER KEY:
1. *This is/That is/It is the prettiest house/home.* 2. *This is/That is/It is the least expensive skirt.* 3. *She is the most beautiful woman.* 4. *She is Sophie's best friend./She is the best friend of Sophie.* 5. *He is the happiest man in the world.*

✎ Drive It Home

A. Complete the sentences by filling in the blanks with **moins... que**.

1. **Elle marche** _____ vite _____ **lui.**

   (She does not walk as quickly as him.)

2. **Tu marches** _____ vite _____ **lui.**

   (You do not walk as quickly as him.)

3. **Je marche** _____ vite _____ **lui.**

   (I do not walk as quickly as him.)

4. **Nous marchons** _____ vite _____ **lui.**

   (We do not walk as quickly as him.)

5. **Ils marchent** _____ vite _____ **lui.**

   (They do not walk as quickly as him.)

B. Now complete the following sentences by filling in the blanks with **le plus**.

1. **C'est** _____ **grand restaurant.** *(It's the biggest restaurant.)*

2. **C'est le livre** _____ **cher.** *(It's the most expensive book.)*

3. **C'est** _____ **long film.** *(It's the longest movie.)*

4. **C'est le grand magasin** _____ **célèbre.**

   (It's the most famous department store.)

5. **C'est** _____ **joli magasin.** *(It's the prettiest store.)*

   ANSWER KEY:
   A. all **moins... que**
   B. all **le plus**

Tip

You know a lot about French pronouns by now. You've learned about subject pronouns, direct object pronouns, indirect object pronouns, y, en, etc.

You've also learned that they all come before the verb in French.

Elle la ferme.
She closes it.

Il me parle.
He speaks to me.

J'y vais.
I'm going there.

Nous en buvons.
We drink some.

However, what do you do when you need to use more than one of those pronouns in a sentence? Well, there's a specific order for that as well. In sentences, place the pronouns in the following order:

ORDER OF PRONOUNS IN SENTENCES						
subject pronouns	me (m')	le	lui	y	en	verb
	te (t')	la	leur			
	se (s')	l'				
	nous	les				
	vous					

Il me le donne.
He gives it to me.

Il le lui donne.
He gives it to him/her/it.

Il y en a trois.
There are three of them.

Je leur en parlerai.
I'll speak to them about it. (lit., I'll speak to them of it.)

How Did You Do?

Let's see how you did! By now, you should be able to:

☐ Say whether something was done *more slowly* or *less quickly*
(Still unsure? Jump back to page 66)

☐ Talk about *the most* and *the least*
(Still unsure? Jump back to page 71)

Unit 1 Essentials

Test your knowledge of the materials in Unit 1 by filling in the blanks in the following charts and sentences. Once you've completed these pages, you'll have your very own reference for the most essential vocabulary and grammar from this unit.

Don't forget to go to **www.livinglanguage.com/languagelab** to access your free online tools for this lesson: audiovisual flashcards, and interactive games and quizzes.

Vocabulary Essentials

CLOTHING

clothing		raincoat	
(man's) suit		glove	
pants		shirt	
jacket		skirt	
coat		blouse	
(fashion) scarf		sock	
hat		shoes	
sweater			

[Pg. 15] (If you're stuck, visit this page to review!)

ACCESSORIES

accessories		ring	
purse, bag		umbrella	
bathing suit		tie	

pajamas		glasses	
jewelry		sunglasses	
watch		briefcase	

[Pg. 22]

NUMBERS ABOVE 100

one hundred one		one thousand	
two hundred		one thousand one	
two hundred six		one million	

[Pg. 31]

SPECIALTY FOODS

Dijon mustard	
a piece of cheese	
a box of sugar-coated chestnuts	
a basket of strawberries	

[Pg. 38]

SHOPPING EXPRESSIONS

It's how much?/How much is it?	
It's too expensive.	
That's inexpensive./It's a good buy.	
Is there a discount?	
May I try it on?/Can I try it on?	
Where are the dressing rooms?	
What size? (clothing)	

It's on sale.	
I'll take it./I'm going to take it.	

[Pg. 45]

MORE SHOPPING EXPRESSIONS

Do you have something less expensive?	
Excuse me, but where is the register?	
You must pay at the register.	

[Pg. 51]

IRREGULAR -ER VERBS

to eat		*to buy*	
to call		*to lift, to raise, to pick up*	
to call back		*to take (someone)*	
to throw, to throw out, to throw away		*to walk, to take someone or something for a walk*	

[Pgs. 34–36]

MORE IRREGULAR -ER VERBS

to prefer		*to repeat*	
to celebrate		*to suggest*	
to hope			

[Pgs. 40 & 41]

MORE IRREGULAR -ER VERBS

to use, to employ		to send	
to bore, to annoy		to pay, to pay for	
to clean		to try, to try on, to try out	

[Pgs. 49 & 50]

Grammar Essentials

DIRECT OBJECT PRONOUNS

1. Direct object pronouns in French always come before the verb in a sentence.

2. If a verb is followed by another verb in the infinitive, place the direct object pronoun directly before the verb it is referring to, which is usually the verb in the infinitive.

3. The direct object pronouns me and te become moi and toi in the positive imperative. Also, the pronoun normally comes after the verb in the positive imperative.

DIRECT OBJECT PRONOUNS			
me	me (m')	us	nous
you	te (t')	you	vous
him, it (m.)	le (l')	them (m.), it (m. pl.)	les
her, it (f.)	la (l')	them (f.), it (f. pl.)	les

INDIRECT OBJECT PRONOUNS

1. Indirect objects in French are usually preceded by a preposition like à (to).

2. Indirect object pronouns in French replace both the indirect object **and** the preposition in the sentence.

3. Indirect object pronouns are placed immediately before the verb.

4. The indirect object pronouns **me** and **te** become **moi** and **toi** in the positive imperative. Also, the pronoun normally comes after the verb in the positive imperative.

INDIRECT OBJECT PRONOUNS			
to me	me (m')	*to us*	nous
to you	te (t')	*to you*	vous
to him/her/it	lui	*to them, to it*	leur

COMPARISONS WITH ADJECTIVES

more ... than, -er ... than	plus + adjective + que
less ... than, not as ... as	moins + adjective + que
as ... as	aussi + adjective + que

IRREGULAR COMPARISONS WITH ADJECTIVES

better	meilleur/meilleure
worse	plus mauvais/mauvaise, pire
as many, as much	autant de

COMPARISONS WITH ADVERBS

more ... than	plus + adverb + que
less ... than, not as ... as	moins + adverb + que
as ... as	aussi + adverb + que

IRREGULAR COMPARISONS WITH ADVERBS

better	mieux
worse	plus mal, pire
more	plus
less	moins
as much	autant

COMPARISONS WITH AMOUNTS

more ... than	plus de + noun + que
less ... than	moins de + noun + que

THE SUPERLATIVE

1. If an adjective normally follows the noun, then its superlative follows the noun.
2. If the adjective normally comes before the noun, then its superlative comes before the noun.

The superlative is formed by using:

the most ... , the -est	le/la/les + plus + adjective
the least ...	le/la/les + moins + adjective

IRREGULAR SUPERLATIVES

the best	le/la/les + meilleur(s)/meilleure(s)
the worst	le/la/les + pire(s), le/la/les + plus mauvais/mauvaise(s)

VERBS

ACHETER (*TO BUY*) **- PRESENT**

I buy	j'achète	*we buy*	nous achetons
you buy (infml.)	tu achètes	*you buy (pl./fml.)*	vous achetez
he buys	il achète	*they buy (m.)*	ils achètent
she buys	elle achète	*they buy (f.)*	elles achètent

ACHETER (*TO BUY*) **- FUTURE**

I will buy	j'achèterai	*we will buy*	nous achèterons
you will buy (infml.)	tu achèteras	*you will buy (pl./fml.)*	vous achèterez
he will buy	il achètera	*they will buy (m.)*	ils achèteront
she will buy	elle achètera	*they will buy (f.)*	elles achèteront

APPELER (*TO CALL*) **- PRESENT**

I call	j'appelle	*we call*	nous appelons
you call (infml.)	tu appelles	*you call (pl./fml.)*	vous appelez
he calls	il appelle	*they call (m.)*	ils appellent
she calls	elle appelle	*they call (f.)*	elles appellent

EMPLOYER (*TO USE, TO EMPLOY*) **- PRESENT**

I use	j'emploie	*we use*	nous employons
you use (infml.)	tu emploies	*you use (pl./fml.)*	vous employez
he uses	il emploie	*they use (m.)*	ils emploient
she uses	elle emploie	*they use (f.)*	elles emploient

JETER *(TO THROW, TO THROW OUT/AWAY)* - **PRESENT**			
I throw	je jette	*we throw*	nous jetons
you throw (infml.)	tu jettes	*you throw (pl./fml.)*	vous jetez
he throws	il jette	*they throw (m.)*	ils jettent
she throws	elle jette	*they throw (f.)*	elles jettent

JETER *(TO THROW, TO THROW OUT, TO THROW AWAY)* - **FUTURE**			
I will throw	je jetterai	*we will throw*	nous jetterons
you will throw (infml.)	tu jetteras	*you will throw (pl./fml.)*	vous jetterez
he will throw	il jettera	*they will throw (m.)*	ils jetteront
she will throw	elle jettera	*they will throw (f.)*	elles jetteront

PAYER *(TO PAY, TO PAY FOR)* - **PRESENT**			
I pay	je paye/je paie	*we pay*	nous payons
you pay (infml.)	tu payes/tu paies	*you pay (pl./fml.)*	vous payez
he pays	il paye/il paie	*they pay (m.)*	ils payent/ils paient
she pays	elle paye/elle paie	*they pay (f.)*	elles payent/elles paient

PRÉFÉRER (TO PREFER) - **PRESENT**			
I prefer	je préfère	we prefer	nous préférons
you prefer (infml.)	tu préfères	you prefer (pl./fml.)	vous préférez
he prefers	il préfère	they prefer (m.)	ils préfèrent
she prefers	elle préfère	they prefer (f.)	elles préfèrent

PRÉFÉRER (TO PREFER) - **FUTURE**			
I will prefer	je préférerai	we will prefer	nous préférerons
you will prefer (infml.)	tu préféreras	you will prefer (pl./fml.)	vous préférerez
he will prefer	il préférera	they will prefer (m.)	ils préféreront
she will prefer	elle préférera	they will prefer (f.)	elles préféreront

Unit 1 Quiz

Now let's see how you've done so far!

In this section you'll find a short quiz testing what you learned in Unit 1. After you've answered all of the questions, score your quiz and see how you did! If you find that you need to go back and review, please do so before continuing on to Unit 2.

As in *Intermediate French*, there will be a quiz at the end of every unit.

A. Match the clothing and accessories on the left to the correct French translations on the right.

1. *watch*	a. **le manteau**
2. *sweater*	b. **le parapluie**
3. *coat*	c. **la montre**
4. *bag*	d. **le pull**
5. *umbrella*	e. **le sac**

B. Translate the following phrases into French.

1. *How much is it?* _____

2. *Can I try it on?* _____

3. *What size?* _____

4. *It's on sale.* _____

5. *Where is the register?* _____

C. Give the correct present tense form of the verb in parentheses.

1. tu _____ (employer)

2. elles _____ (appeler)

3. nous _____ (jeter)

4. il _____ (acheter)

5. je _____ (payer)

D. Rewrite the following sentences in French by replacing the underlined phrases with direct or indirect object pronouns.

1. **Tu parles <u>à moi</u>.** *(You speak to me.)*

   _____

2. **Je donne le bracelet <u>à toi</u>.** *(I give the bracelet to you.)*

   _____

3. **Elle prend <u>le train</u>.** *(She takes the train.)*

   _____

4. **Il parle <u>à Nathalie et Paul</u>.** *(He speaks to Nathalie and Paul.)*

   _____

5. **Vous allez aider <u>Sophie</u>.** *(You're going to help Sophie.)*

   _____

ANSWER KEY:
A. 1. c; 2. d; 3. a; 4. e; 5. b
B. 1. C'est combien ? 2. Est-ce que je peux l'essayer ? 3. Quelle taille ? 4. Il/Elle est en solde. 5. Où est la caisse ?
C. 1. emploies; 2. appellent; 3. jetons; 4. achète; 5. paie/paye
D. 1. Tu me parles. 2. Je te donne le bracelet. 3. Elle le prend. 4. Il leur parle. 5. Vous allez l'aider.

How Did You Do?

Give yourself a point for every correct answer, then use the following key to determine whether or not you're ready to move on:

0-7 points: It's probably best to go back and study the lessons again to make sure you understood everything completely. Take your time; it's not a race! Make sure you spend time reviewing the vocabulary and reading through each grammar note carefully.

8-16 points: If the questions you missed were in Section A or B, you may want to review the vocabulary again; if you missed answers mostly in Section C or D, check the Unit 1 Essentials to make sure you have your conjugations and other grammar basics down.

17-20 points: Feel free to move on to the next unit! You're doing a great job.

	Points

The Imperfect Tense (*I Was Speaking*)   The Imperfect Tense vs. The Past Tense

Irregular Imperfect Tense   *I Read, I Write, I Say*

Unit 2:
Work and School

In this unit, you'll learn the vocabulary you need to talk about school and jobs. You'll also learn another very important past tense: l'imparfait *(m.)* (*the imperfect*). Knowing the difference between l'imparfait and le passé composé (*the past tense*) is an essential part of learning to speak naturally in French.

By the end of this unit, you should be able to:

☐ Name different professions

☐ Talk about what you *used to have*

☐ Identify the different departments in a company

☐ Say what you *used to eat* and who you *used to be*

☐ Talk about applying for a job

☐ Describe what was going on when something happened

☐ Talk about school

☐ Say *I read*, *I write*, and *I say*

☐ Describe your work environment

☐ Talk about duration

☐ Talk about classes, tests, and activities at school

☐ Say *I leave* and *I sleep*

☐ Tell someone what you *see*

☐ Say what you *know* and whom you *know*

Lesson 5: Words

By the end of this lesson, you will be able to:

☐ Name different professions

☐ Talk about what you *used to have*

☐ Identify the different departments in a company

☐ Say what you *used to eat* and who you *used to be*

Word Builder 1

Let's get started with **les professions** (*f.*) (*professions*). You should already be familiar with some of them.

▶ 5A Lesson 5 Word Builder 1 (CD 7, Track 17)

accountant	**le comptable/la comptable**
bank clerk	**l'employé de banque/l'employée de banque**
civil servant	**le fonctionnaire/la fonctionnaire**
pharmacist	**le pharmacien/la pharmacienne**
homemaker	**l'homme au foyer/la femme au foyer**
construction worker	**l'ouvrier en bâtiment/l'ouvrière en bâtiment**
author	**l'auteur/l'auteure**
writer	**l'écrivain/l'écrivaine***
computer programmer	**l'informaticien/l'informaticienne**

* As you learned in Essential French, écrivain can be and often is used for both men and women; écrivaine exists, but is less common.

The Imperfect Tense (*I Was Speaking*)   The Imperfect Tense vs. The Past Tense

Irregular Imperfect Tense   *I Read, I Write, I Say*

dentist	le dentiste/la dentiste
nurse	l'infirmier/l'infirmière
actor/actress	l'acteur/l'actrice
plumber	le plombier
farmer	le fermier/la fermière
carpenter	le charpentier
policeman/policewoman	le policier/la femme policier, l'agent de police/l'agente de police
businessman/businesswoman	l'homme d'affaires/la femme d'affaires
beautician	l'esthéticien/l'esthéticienne

Take It Further

Remember that some professions have both masculine and feminine forms, while certain professions only have a masculine form that's used for both men and women. For example, *plumber* and *carpenter* usually only have a masculine form, but you can use it to talk about a man or a woman.

Also remember that French does not use an indefinite article between être and professions:

Je suis écrivain.
I am a writer.

✎ Word Practice 1

Match the following professions to the correct French translations on the right.

1. *nurse*	a. le fonctionnaire/la fonctionnaire
2. *plumber*	b. l'écrivain/l'écrivaine
3. *accountant*	c. le comptable/la comptable
4. *carpenter*	d. l'infirmier/l'infirmière
5. *civil servant*	e. le plombier
6. *writer*	f. le charpentier

ANSWER KEY:

1. d; 2. e; 3. c; 4. f; 5. a; 6. b

✎ Word Recall

Now let's review some of the professions you saw in *Essential French*. Translate each sentence into French.

1. *My father is a doctor.* _____

2. *She is a singer.* _____

3. *My son is a lawyer.* _____

4. *He is a cook.* _____

5. *Sandrine is a manager.* _____

ANSWER KEY:

1. **Mon père est médecin. 2. Elle est chanteuse. 3. Mon fils est avocat. 4. Il est cuisinier. 5. Sandrine est gérante. (Sandrine est directrice.)**

The Imperfect Tense (*I Was Speaking*)   The Imperfect Tense vs. The Past Tense

Irregular Imperfect Tense   *I Read, I Write, I Say*

Grammar Builder 1
THE IMPERFECT TENSE (*I WAS SPEAKING*)

▶ 5B Lesson 5 Grammar Builder 1 (CD 7, Track 18)

You've already learned one way to talk about the past in French: le passé composé (*the past tense*). For example: j'ai mangé (*I ate*), je suis allé(e) (*I went*), etc.

However, you can also talk about the past using l'imparfait (*m.*) (*the imperfect tense*). L'imparfait usually corresponds to the following forms in English: *used to +* verb (*used to talk*) and *was/were + -ing* (*was talking, were talking*). In Lesson 6, we'll look more in-depth at when to use l'imparfait, and the difference between le passé composé and l'imparfait. For now, just focus on learning how to form the tense.

Fortunately, it's very easy to form the imperfect tense. All three groups of verbs form the imperfect in the same way:

1. Take the nous form of the verb in the present tense and drop the -ons ending.

2. Next, add one of the following endings:

PRONOUN	ENDING	PRONOUN	ENDING
je	-ais	nous	-ions
tu	-ais	vous	-iez
il	-ait	ils	-aient
elle	-ait	elles	-aient

And that's it!

Let's look at an example of an **-er** verb in the imperfect: **parler** (*to speak*). In the present tense, the **nous** form of **parler** is **parlons**. So just drop the **-ons** from **parlons** (leaving you with **parl-**) and add the endings to form the imperfect.

PARLER *(TO SPEAK)* - **IMPERFECT**			
je parlais	*I was speaking, I used to speak*	**nous parlions**	*we were speaking, we used to speak*
tu parlais	*you were speaking, you used to speak*	**vous parliez**	*you were speaking, you used to speak*
il parlait	*he was speaking, he used to speak*	**ils parlaient**	*they were speaking, they used to speak*
elle parlait	*she was speaking, she used to speak*	**elles parlaient**	*they were speaking, they used to speak*

Notice that the endings for the imperfect tense are the same as the endings for the conditional tense. Of course, the tenses are not identical; the first part is formed differently. For instance, *I would speak* is **je parlerais**, while *I was speaking* is **je parlais**.

Also note that a verb like **étudier** (*to study*) will have two **i**'s in a row in the **nous** and **vous** imperfect forms. It may look a little strange, but it is correct.

nous étudiions	*we were studying (we used to study)*
vous étudiiez	*you were studying (you used to study)*

The Imperfect Tense (*I Was Speaking*)   The Imperfect Tense vs. The Past Tense

Irregular Imperfect Tense

I Read, I Write, I Say

Now let's look at an **-ir** verb in the imperfect: **finir** (*to finish*). In the present tense, the **nous** form of **finir** is **finissons**. By dropping the **-ons** from **finissons**, you get **finiss-**, and then you just add the endings.

FINIR *(TO FINISH)* - **IMPERFECT**			
je finissais	*I was finishing, I used to finish*	**nous finissions**	*we were finishing, we used to finish*
tu finissais	*you were finishing, you used to finish*	**vous finissiez**	*you were finishing, you used to finish*
il finissait	*he was finishing, he used to finish*	**ils finissaient**	*they were finishing, they used to finish*
elle finissait	*she was finishing, she used to finish*	**elles finissaient**	*they were finishing, they used to finish*

Next, let's look at an **-re** verb: **vendre** (*to sell*). In the present tense, the **nous** form of **vendre** is **vendons**. So drop the **-ons** from **vendons** and then add the endings.

VENDRE *(TO SELL)* - **IMPERFECT**			
je vendais	*I was selling, I used to sell*	**nous vendions**	*we were selling, we used to sell*
tu vendais	*you were selling, you used to sell*	**vous vendiez**	*you were selling, you used to sell*
il vendait	*he was selling, he used to sell*	**ils vendaient**	*they were selling, they used to sell*
elle vendait	*she was selling, she used to sell*	**elles vendaient**	*they were selling, they used to sell*

Finally, let's look at the imperfect of avoir (*to have*). Avoir forms the imperfect normally. In the present tense, the **nous** form of avoir is **avons**, so just drop the **-ons** from **avons** and then add the endings.

AVOIR (*TO HAVE*) - **IMPERFECT**			
j'avais	*I had, I was having, I used to have*	nous avions	*we had, we were having, we used to have*
tu avais	*you had, you were having, you used to have*	vous aviez	*you had, you were having, you used to have*
il avait	*he had, he was having, he used to have*	ils avaient	*they had, they were having, they used to have*
elle avait	*she had, she was having, she used to have*	elles avaient	*they had, they were having, they used to have*

Notice that the imperfect of avoir is usually translated as *had, was/were having*, or *used to have*.

As an additional note, remember the expression il y a (*there is, there are*)? Its imperfect form is il y avait (*there was, there were*).

Il y a un concert samedi soir.
There is a concert on Saturday evening.

Il y avait un concert samedi soir.
There was a concert on Saturday evening.

The Imperfect Tense (*I Was Speaking*)   The Imperfect Tense vs. The Past Tense

Irregular Imperfect Tense   *I Read, I Write, I Say*

Also keep in mind that if a verb has an irregular nous form in the present tense, then that irregular form will carry over into the imperfect. For example, the nous form of boire (*to drink*) is buvons, so the imperfect of boire would be je buvais, tu buvais, etc. Same goes for faire, conduire, prendre, etc.

Work Out 1

Fill in the blanks with the correct imperfect tense form of the verbs in parentheses. Note that vouloir (*to want*) and aller (*to go*) form the imperfect normally.

1. il ne _____ (finir) pas

2. elle _____ (vendre)

3. tu _____ (danser)

4. nous ne _____ (marcher) pas

5. il _____ (boire)

6. vous _____ (aller)

7. nous _____ (étudier)

8. je n' _____ (avoir) pas

9. elles _____ (vouloir)

ANSWER KEY:
1. finissait; 2. vendait; 3. dansais; 4. marchions; 5. buvait; 6. alliez; 7. étudiions; 8. avais; 9. voulaient

Word Builder 2

Here is some more useful vocabulary related to work.

▶ 5C Lesson 5 Word Builder 2 (CD 7, Track 19)

job, work	le boulot, le travail
factory	l'usine (*f.*)
company	la société
accounting	la comptabilité
computer science (IT)	l'informatique (*f.*)
computer	l'ordinateur (*m.*)
software	le logiciel
meeting	la réunion
staff	le personnel
colleague	le collègue/la collègue
boss	le patron/la patronne
salary	le salaire

Take It Further

Instead of just la comptabilité or l'informatique, you might also hear le service de comptabilité (*accounting department*) or le service d'informatique (*IT department*). As you can probably tell, le service means *department*.

Here are some other services within a company:

finance department	le service financier
sales department	le service des ventes
legal department	le service juridique

The Imperfect Tense (*I Was Speaking*)   The Imperfect Tense vs. The Past Tense

Irregular Imperfect Tense   *I Read, I Write, I Say*

marketing department	le service de marketing
public relations (PR) department	le service des relations publiques
shipping department, mail room	le service du courrier
customer service department	le service clientèle, le service client

And of course:

| management | la direction |

✎ Word Practice 2

Translate the following phrases into French:

1. *my salary* _____

2. *their computer* _____

3. *her (female) boss* _____

4. *our company* _____

5. *your (plural/polite) job* _____

ANSWER KEY

1. mon salaire; 2. leur ordinateur; 3. sa patronne; 4. notre société; 5. votre boulot/travail

✎ Word Recall

Rewrite the following verbs in the passé composé (*past tense*).

1. je finis _____

2. vous travaillez _____

3. elles vendent _____

4. j'ai _____

5. nous buvons _____

6. elle arrive _____

ANSWER KEY:
1. j'ai fini; 2. vous avez travaillé; 3. elles ont vendu; 4. j'ai eu; 5. nous avons bu; 6. elle est arrivée

Grammar Builder 2
IRREGULAR IMPERFECT TENSE

▶ 5D Lesson 5 Grammar Builder 2 (CD 7, Track 20)

Unfortunately, there are some verbs with irregular forms in the imperfect.

As you know, verbs like manger (*to eat*) and commencer (*to begin, to start*) have a spelling change in the present tense nous form: nous mangeons, nous commençons. You also know that since the imperfect is based on the nous form, this spelling change should carry over into the imperfect.

Well, it does, but, somewhat ironically, that spelling change **does not** carry over for the nous and vous forms. In other words, in the imperfect, verbs like manger and commencer carry over the spelling change for all forms except nous and vous.

Here are the full conjugations of manger and commencer in the imperfect:

MANGER (*TO EAT*) - **IMPERFECT**			
je mangeais	*I was eating, I used to eat*	nous mangions	*we were eating, we used to eat*
tu mangeais	*you were eating, you used to eat*	vous mangiez	*you were eating, you used to eat*

The Imperfect Tense (*I Was Speaking*)   The Imperfect Tense vs. The Past Tense

Irregular Imperfect Tense   *I Read, I Write, I Say*

MANGER *(TO EAT)* - **IMPERFECT**			
il mangeait	*he was eating, he used to eat*	ils mangeaient	*they were eating, they used to eat*
elle mangeait	*she was eating, she used to eat*	elles mangeaient	*they were eating, they used to eat*

COMMENCER *(TO BEGIN, TO START)* - **IMPERFECT**			
je commençais	*I was beginning, I used to begin*	nous commencions	*we were beginning, we used to begin*
tu commençais	*you were beginning, you used to begin*	vous commenciez	*you were beginning, you used to begin*
il commençait	*he was beginning, he used to begin*	ils commençaient	*they were beginning, they used to begin*
elle commençait	*she was beginning, she used to begin*	elles commençaient	*they were beginning, they used to begin*

Finally, it is probably not surprising that the verb être (*to be*) is entirely irregular in the imperfect. Here are its forms:

ÊTRE *(TO BE)* - **IMPERFECT**			
j'étais	*I was, I used to be*	nous étions	*we were, we used to be*
tu étais	*you were, you used to be*	vous étiez	*you were, you used to be*
il était	*he was, he used to be*	ils étaient	*they were, they used to be*
elle était	*she was, she used to be*	elles étaient	*they were, they used to be*

Notice that the imperfect of **être** is usually translated as *was/were* or *used to be*.

✎ Work Out 2

Put the verbs in parentheses in the imperfect tense.

1. je _____ (manger)

2. vous _____ (commencer)

3. j' _____ (être)

4. nous _____ (manger)

5. elle _____ (commencer)

6. vous _____ (être)

ANSWER KEY:

1. mangeais; 2. commenciez; 3. étais; 4. mangions; 5. commençait; 6. étiez

✎ Drive It Home

Fill in the blanks with the imperfect form of each verb.

1. J' _____ (avancer).

2. J' _____ (avoir).

3. Je _____ (danser).

4. J' _____ (être).

5. Je _____ (voyager).

6. J' _____ (étudier).

7. Je _____ (choisir).

The Imperfect Tense (*I Was Speaking*)   The Imperfect Tense vs. The Past Tense

Irregular Imperfect Tense   *I Read, I Write, I Say*

8. Je _____ (répondre).

9. J' _____ (aller).

10. Je _____ (boire).

ANSWER KEY:
1. avançais; 2. avais; 3. dansais; 4. étais; 5. voyageais; 6. étudiais; 7. choisissais; 8. répondais;
9. allais; 10. buvais

How Did You Do?

Let's see how you did! By now, you should be able to:

☐ Name different professions
(Still unsure? Jump back to page 91)

☐ Talk about what you *used to have*
(Still unsure? Jump back to page 94)

☐ Identify the different departments in a company
(Still unsure? Jump back to page 99)

☐ Say what you *used to eat* and who you *used to be*
(Still unsure? Jump back to page 101)

Lesson 6: Phrases

By the end of this lesson, you will be able to:

☐ Talk about applying for a job

☐ Describe what was going on when something happened

☐ Talk about school

☐ Say *I read, I write,* and *I say*

Phrase Builder 1

Ever thought about working abroad? Here is some vocabulary that will come in handy if you're looking for a job or just talking about salary, hours, and other similar issues in French.

▶ 6A Lesson 6 Phrase Builder 1 (CD 7, Track 21)

at work	au travail
at the office	au bureau
to earn money	gagner de l'argent
personnel manager (human resources manager)	le directeur du personnel
to apply for a job	faire une demande d'emploi
to have an interview	avoir une entrevue
full-time	à plein temps
part-time	à temps partiel
retired	à la retraite
unemployment	le chômage
to be unemployed	être sans emploi (être sans travail)

The Imperfect Tense (*I Was Speaking*)   The Imperfect Tense vs. The Past Tense

Irregular Imperfect Tense   *I Read, I Write, I Say*

summer job	l'emploi (*m.*) saisonnier
to work hard	travailler dur
to be busy	être occupé/occupée
to be growing (as in, the company is growing)	être en pleine expansion

---

Take It Further

We're going to take a look at the difference between **l'imparfait** and **le passé composé** in Grammar Builder 1. But first, let's look at **l'imparfait** on its own.

Here's a short paragraph in **l'imparfait** to help give you a better sense of the tense.

Quand j'étais jeune, j'avais un petit chien. Il était brun. Il aimait aller se promener avec mes amis et moi. Nous jouions toujours ensemble.

When I was young, I used to have a little dog. He was brown. He liked to go take a walk with my friends and me. We always used to play together.

✎ Phrase Practice 1

Translate the following dialogue into English:

A: Bonjour mademoiselle. _____

B: Bonjour monsieur. Je voudrais faire une demande d'emploi. _____

_____

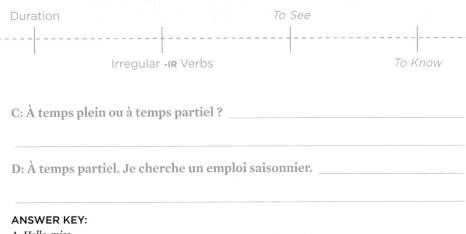

C: À temps plein ou à temps partiel ? _____

_____

D: À temps partiel. Je cherche un emploi saisonnier. _____

_____

ANSWER KEY:
A: Hello, miss.
B: Hello, sir. I would like to apply for a job.
C: Full-time or part-time?
D: Part-time. I'm looking for a summer job.

Word Recall

Fill in the blanks with the most appropriate verb from the word bank below.

chante	écrit
joue	pratique

1. Le médecin _____ la médecine.

2. La chanteuse _____ des chansons.

3. L'actrice _____ des rôles.

4. L'écrivain _____ des livres.

ANSWER KEY:
1. pratique (*The doctor practices medicine.*) 2. chante (*The singer sings songs.*) 3. joue (*The actress plays roles.*) 4. écrit (*The writer writes books.*)

Grammar Builder 1
THE IMPERFECT TENSE VS. THE PAST TENSE

6B Lesson 6 Grammar Builder 1 (CD 7, Track 22)

You saw a paragraph with l'imparfait in Take It Further. Here are a few more examples of l'imparfait in use:

The Imperfect Tense (*I Was Speaking*)   The Imperfect Tense vs. The Past Tense

Irregular Imperfect Tense   *I Read, I Write, I Say*

Je lui parlais tous les jours.
I used to talk to him (her) every day.

Quand j'étais jeune, je dansais bien.
When I was young, I used to dance well.

Quand j'étais jeune, ma mère me chantait une chanson tous les soirs.
When I was young, my mother used to sing a song to me every night.

Hier, j'avais un problème avec ma voiture...
Yesterday, I was having a problem with my car ...

Now let's review some of the sentences you've seen with le passé composé:

J'ai fait des achats.
I ran some errands. (lit., I did some purchases.)

Tu n'as pas mangé à neuf heures.
You didn't eat at 9:00.

Vous avez parlé ?
Did you speak?/Have you spoken?/You spoke?

Quand êtes-vous arrivée, Marie ?
When did you arrive, Marie?

Le petit garçon est tombé.
The little boy fell.

And now let's take a look at a sentence that contains both l'imparfait and le passé composé:

Il faisait froid quand j'ai quitté la maison ce matin.
It was cold when I left the house this morning.

So why do you use the imperfect in the first part of the sentence and the past tense in the second part? Although both tenses describe the past, they're used in different ways.

Here is how they're used:

TENSE	HOW IT'S USED	EXAMPLES
Imperfect	actions that are continuous, habitual, or repetitive; descriptions	set the scene; describe the weather, the time of day, an emotion, a wish, what someone used to do, or what someone was doing when something else happened; express a condition or state without a specified duration
Past	actions that have been completed	express something that happened all of a sudden or a specified number of times; express a completed action

So, when the two tenses are used together, the imperfect often sets the scene for an action expressed in the past tense. An even bigger clue to use the passé composé is if the action happens soudain (*suddenly*) or tout à coup/tout d'un coup (*all of a sudden*).

In the example sentence you saw, il faisait froid (*it was cold*) is in the imperfect because it describes the weather, setting the scene for the completed action: j'ai quitté la maison (*I left the house*).

The Imperfect Tense (*I Was Speaking*)   The Imperfect Tense vs. The Past Tense

Irregular Imperfect Tense   *I Read, I Write, I Say*

Let's look at some more examples:

Elles commençaient à parler quand il est entré dans la salle.
They were beginning to speak when he entered the room.

Il était minuit quand je suis revenu(e).
It was midnight when I returned.

Je prenais un bain quand le téléphone a sonné.
I was taking a bath when the phone rang.

J'ai entendu la chanson que tu chantais.
I heard the song that you were singing.

Tu chantais, for example, is in the imperfect because it expresses what someone was doing (*singing*) when something else happened (*heard the song*).

If you're confused, don't worry. It'll get much easier to identify which tense to use with—what else?—practice, practice, practice.

Ⅱ

✎ Work Out 1

Fill in the blanks with either **l'imparfait** or **le passé composé** of the verb in parentheses. Pay attention to the English translations. Don't forget that the past participle agrees with the subject if the verb uses **être** in the **passé composé**.

1. **Je n'** _____ (être) pas à la maison quand tu

   _____ (téléphoner). (*I was not at home when you called.*)

2. **Tout le monde** _____ (parler) quand l'auteur

   _____ (entrer). (*Everyone was talking when the author entered.*)

3. Il _____ (faire) beau quand ils

_____ (aller) au parc dimanche. *(It was beautiful outside*

when they went to the park on Sunday.)

4. Elle nous _____ (regarder). *(She was watching us.)*

5. Nous _____ (chanter) beaucoup. *(We used to sing a lot.)*

6. Nous _____ (décider) d'aller au restaurant.

(We decided to go to the restaurant.)

7. Je _____ (arriver) au restaurant à neuf heures du soir.

(I arrived at the restaurant at 9:00 in the evening.)

8. Il y _____ (avoir) quatre voitures. *(There were four cars.)*

ANSWER KEY:
1. étais, as téléphoné; 2. parlait, est entré; 3. faisait, sont allés; 4. regardait; 5. chantions; 6. avons décidé; 7. suis arrivé(e); 8. avait

Phrase Builder 2

Now let's move on to vocabulary related to l'école *(f.)* *(school)*.

▶ 6C Lesson 6 Phrase Builder 2 (CD 7, Track 23)

at school	à l'école
in middle school	au collège
in high school	au lycée
in college	à l'université
classroom	la salle de classe
to teach	enseigner

The Imperfect Tense (*I Was Speaking*)   The Imperfect Tense vs. The Past Tense

Irregular Imperfect Tense

I Read, I Write, I Say

diploma	le diplôme
bachelor's degree	la licence
master's degree	la maîtrise (le master)
academic year	l'année (*f.*) scolaire
back-to-school	la rentrée
difficult subjects	les matières (*f.*) difficiles
literature	la littérature
foreign language	la langue étrangère
gym (physical education)*	la gym(nastique)
report card	le bulletin scolaire

* If you want to say *gym* in the sense of the location (a school gymnasium, or a health club) and not *gym* class, then you need to say le gymnase.

Take It Further

In the first Take It Further of this lesson, you saw a short paragraph using just l'imparfait. Now let's look at a paragraph using both l'imparfait and le passé composé. Study it carefully. The more exposure you get to the two tenses, the more comfortable you'll be knowing when to use each one.

Ce week-end, j'étais très occupée. Mon mari et moi, nous avons décidé d'aller au parc parce qu'il faisait beau. Nous sommes arrivés au parc à midi. C'était très joli ! Au parc, il y avait beaucoup de monde. À deux heures, nous avons quitté le parc et nous sommes allés au musée. Je voulais voir les vieux tableaux. Nous regardions les tableaux quand nous avons entendu nos amis Joelle et Robert. Quelle coïncidence ! Après la visite au musée, nous avons mangé dans un bon restaurant en ville avec Joelle et Robert.

This weekend, I was very busy. My husband and I (lit., me), we decided to go to the park because it was beautiful (outside). We arrived at the park at noon. It was very pretty! In the park, there were a lot of people. At 2:00, we left the park and we went to the museum. I wanted to see the old paintings. We were looking at the paintings when we heard our friends Joelle and Robert. What a coincidence! After the visit to the museum, we ate in a good restaurant in town with Joelle and Robert.

✎ Phrase Practice 2

Circle the word that best completes each sentence.

1. Ma sœur a dix-sept ans. Elle est étudiante (au lycée, au collège, à l'université).

2. Mon frère a vingt et un ans. Il est étudiant (au lycée, au collège, à l'université).

3. Pour moi, la littérature n'est pas (une matière difficile, une rentrée, un bulletin scolaire).

4. Le prof et tous les étudiants étaient dans (la salle de classe, la licence, la maîtrise).

5. C'est le premier jour de l'école. C'est (le bulletin scolaire, la rentrée, la maîtrise).

ANSWER KEY:
1. au lycée (*My sister is 17 years old. She's a student in high school.*) 2. à l'université (*My brother is 21 years old. He's a student in college.*) 3. une matière difficile (*For me, literature isn't a difficult subject.*) 4. la salle de classe (*The professor/teacher and all of the students were in the classroom.*) 5. la rentrée (*It's the first day of school. It's back-to-school.*)

The Imperfect Tense (*I Was Speaking*)   The Imperfect Tense vs. The Past Tense

Irregular Imperfect Tense   *I Read, I Write, I Say*

✎ Word Recall

Match the places on the left to the correct English translations on the right.

1. la bibliothèque	a. *store*
2. la librairie	b. *office*
3. le bureau	c. *library*
4. l'usine	d. *factory*
5. le magasin	e. *bookstore*

ANSWER KEY:
1. c; 2. e; 3. b; 4. d; 5. a

Grammar Builder 2
I READ, I WRITE, I SAY

▶ 6D Lesson 6 Grammar Builder 2 (CD 7, Track 24)

If you want to talk about schools and education, then you need to learn how to use the irregular verbs lire (*to read*), écrire (*to write*), and dire (*to say*).

You've seen all of these verbs in some form already, whether in *Essential French* or *Intermediate French*. In fact, you saw the full conjugation of lire in *Essential French*. However, let's review. Here is lire in the present tense:

LIRE *(TO READ)* - **PRESENT**			
je lis	*I read*	nous lisons	*we read*
tu lis	*you read*	vous lisez	*you read*
il lit	*he reads*	ils lisent	*they read*
elle lit	*she reads*	elles lisent	*they read*

Les enfants lisent une bonne histoire.
The children are reading a good story.

The past participle of lire is lu.

Pendant le voyage, nous avons lu beaucoup de livres.
During the trip, we read a lot of books.

Now let's look at écrire.

ÉCRIRE *(TO WRITE)* - **PRESENT**			
j'écris	*I write*	nous écrivons	*we write*
tu écris	*you write*	vous écrivez	*you write*
il écrit	*he writes*	ils écrivent	*they write*
elle écrit	*she writes*	elles écrivent	*they write*

J'écris une lettre à mes amis à l'université.
I'm writing a letter to my friends in college.

The past participle of écrire is écrit.

Le petit garçon a écrit une lettre au Père Noël.
The little boy wrote a letter to Santa Claus (lit., Father Christmas).

Finally, here is the verb dire (*to say, to tell*):

DIRE *(TO SAY, TO TELL)* - **PRESENT**			
je dis	*I say*	nous disons	*we say*
tu dis	*you say*	vous dites	*you say*
il dit	*he says*	ils disent	*they say*
elle dit	*she says*	elles disent	*they say*

Qu'est-ce que vous dites ?
What are you saying?

The Imperfect Tense (*I Was Speaking*)   The Imperfect Tense vs. The Past Tense

Irregular Imperfect Tense   *I Read, I Write, I Say*

The past participle of dire is dit.

J'ai dit qu'elle avait une jolie robe.
I said (that) she had a pretty dress.

The future and conditional of écrire, lire, and dire are formed normally, in the same way as other -re verbs: drop the final e from the infinitive and add the appropriate ending. The imperfect is also formed normally: just drop the -ons from the present tense nous form and add the ending.

Going forward in *Advanced French*, if you don't see a note about a specific tense when discussing an irregular verb, that means the tense is formed normally.

✎ Work Out 2

Fill in the blanks with the correct present tense forms.

1. Qu'est-ce que tu _____ (lire) ? *(What are you reading?)*

2. Nous _____ (écrire) en français. *(We're writing in French.)*

3. Ils _____ (lire) très bien. *(They read very well.)*

4. Elle _____ (dire) bonjour à Sophie. *(She's saying hello to Sophie.)*

5. Vous n'_____ (écrire) pas à votre mère ? *(You're not writing to your mother?)*

ANSWER KEY:
1. lis; 2. écrivons; 3. lisent; 4. dit; 5. écrivez

✎ Drive It Home

A. Conjugate each verb in the imparfait.

1. Il _____ (téléphoner).

2. Il _____ (vendre).

3. Il _____ (être).

4. Il _____ (tomber).

5. Il _____ (finir).

6. Il _____ (regarder).

7. Il _____ (faire).

B. Now conjugate each verb in the passé composé.

1. Il _____ (téléphoner).

2. Il _____ (vendre).

3. Il _____ (être).

4. Il _____ (tomber).

5. Il _____ (finir).

6. Il _____ (regarder).

7. Il _____ (faire).

The Imperfect Tense (*I Was Speaking*)   The Imperfect Tense vs. The Past Tense

Irregular Imperfect Tense   *I Read, I Write, I Say*

C. Finally, decide if you need le passé composé or l'imparfait to complete each of these sentences.

1. Il _____ (être) au bureau quand elle

   _____ (vendre) la maison.

2. Il _____ (regarder) la télé ; tout à coup, elle

   _____ (téléphoner).

3. La nuit dernière, il _____ (faire) froid.

ANSWER KEY:
A. 1. téléphonait; 2. vendait; 3. était; 4. tombait; 5. finissait; 6. regardait; 7. faisait
B. 1. a téléphoné; 2. a vendu; 3. a été; 4. est tombé; 5. a fini; 6. a regardé; 7. a fait
C. 1. était, a vendu (*He was at the office when she sold the house.*) 2. regardait, a téléphoné (*He was watching television; all of a sudden, she called.*) 3. faisait/a fait (*Last night, it was cold.*)

 Tip

Earlier in the lesson, you saw some vocabulary for school matières (*subjects*). Here is a more comprehensive list:

math	les maths (*f.*), les mathématiques (*f.*)
calculus	le calcul
geometry	la géométrie
history	l'histoire (*f.*)*
spelling	l'orthographe (*f.*)
English literature	la littérature anglaise
English	l'anglais (*m.*)
French	le français
foreign language	la langue étrangère
science	la science
chemistry	la chimie

* Remember that histoire can mean *history, story,* or *tale.*

biology	**la biologie**
physics	**la physique**
gym, physical education	**la gym, la gymnastique, l'éducation physique**
art	**l'art** (*m.*)
drawing	**le dessin**
music	**la musique**
computer science	**l'informatique** (*f.*)
extracurricular activities	**les activités** (*f.*) **extra-scolaires/ parascolaires**

If you want to say that you're taking a class in a certain subject, just use **cours** (*class*) + **de** (**d'**). For example, you could say **mon cours de français** (*my French class*), **un cours de maths** (*a math class*), etc.

How Did You Do?

Let's see how you did! By now, you should be able to:

☐ Talk about applying for a job
(Still unsure? Jump back to page 105)

☐ Describe what what was going on when something happened
(Still unsure? Jump back to page 107)

☐ Talk about school
(Still unsure? Jump back to page 111)

☐ Say *I read, I write*, and *I say*
(Still unsure? Jump back to page 114)

The Imperfect Tense (*I Was Speaking*)   The Imperfect Tense vs. The Past Tense

Irregular Imperfect Tense   *I Read, I Write, I Say*

Lesson 7: Sentences

By the end of this lesson, you will be able to:

☐ Describe your work environment

☐ Talk about duration

☐ Talk about classes, tests, and activities at school

☐ Say *I leave* and *I sleep*

Sentence Builder 1

▶ 7A Lesson 7 Sentence Builder 1 (CD 8, Track 1)

I get along well with my boss.	**Je m'entends bien avec mon patron/ ma patronne.**
The people where I work are great.	**Les gens où je travaille sont super.**
Here is my office.	**Voici mon bureau.***
Here is my cubicle.	**Voici mon cubicule.****
I'm a salesman/saleswoman.	**Je suis vendeur/vendeuse.**
I'm on vacation.	**Je suis en vacances.**
(I) can't wait for the end of the day!	**Vivement la fin de la journée !**
I work very hard.	**Je travaille très dur.**
I work forty hours a week (per week).	**Je travaille quarante heures par semaine.**

* Notice that bureau can mean *office* in the sense of the building where you work, but also the room that you are assigned to work in. It can also mean *desk*.
**Colloquially, box is the French word for *cubicle*.

I've been working for this company for two months. (lit., I work for this company for two months.)	Je travaille pour cette société depuis deux mois.
I worked for that company for two years.	J'ai travaillé pour cette société pendant deux ans.

Take It Further

You know that indefinite articles are not used between être and professions in French. However, you should use an indefinite article if the profession is preceded by an adjective.

Je suis vendeur.
I am a salesman.

Je suis un bon vendeur.
I am a good salesman.

In Sentence Builder 1, you saw some good expressions to use in conversation:

to get along with	s'entendre avec
to get along well with	s'entendre bien avec

And you saw the word vivement, which literally means *strongly* (as in, *I strongly feel that ...*), but is often used to mean *can't wait for*:

Vivement vendredi !
Can't wait for Friday!

Vivement les vacances !
Can't wait for vacation!

The Imperfect Tense (*I Was Speaking*) | The Imperfect Tense vs. The Past Tense

Irregular Imperfect Tense | *I Read, I Write, I Say*

Vivement la suite !

Can't wait for what happens next!/Can't wait for the rest!

Note that la suite can mean *the rest, the next part,* or *what happens next.*

✎ Sentence Practice 1

Translate the following sentences into English.

1. **Voici mon bureau.** _____

2. **Voici mon box.** _____

3. **Voici mon patron.** _____

4. **Voici mon comptable.** _____

ANSWER KEY:
1. *Here is my office.* 2. *Here is my cubicle.* 3. *Here is my boss.* 4. *Here is my accountant.*

✎ Word Recall

Fill in the blanks using the following word bank:

une carafe	un verre
une bouteille	une tasse

1. **Elle voulait** _____ **d'eau.** *(She wanted a pitcher of water.)*

2. **Paul m'a donné** _____ **de vin.** *(Paul gave me a bottle of wine.)*

3. **J'ai bu** _____ **d'eau parce que j'avais soif.**

   (I drank a glass of water because I was thirsty.)

4. **Il faisait froid, donc j'ai bu** _____ **de chocolat chaud.**

(It was cold, so I drank a cup of hot chocolate.)

ANSWER KEY:
1. une carafe; 2. une bouteille; 3. un verre; 4. une tasse

Grammar Builder 1
DURATION

▶ 7B Lesson 7 Grammar Builder 1 (CD 8, Track 2)

Depuis *(since, for)*, **pour** *(for)*, and **pendant** *(during, for)* are helpful words to know when talking about lengths of time. You've already seen these words in various sentences, but let's look at them in detail and see when and how they're used.

Pour *(for)* is used to express how long an action will take in the future or near future.

Je vais travailler pour cette société pour un an.
I'm going to work for this company for one year.

If a situation or action began in the past and is still going on, use the present tense + **depuis** *(since, for)* to talk about the time that has elapsed. For example, if someone asks if you are working at a company and you still work there, you might say:

Je travaille pour cette société depuis un an.
I've been working for this company for a year. (lit., I work for this company for a year.)

Use the past tense or the imperfect + **pendant** *(during, for)* to talk about an action that was completed in the past, and is not connected to the present at all. For example, if you no longer work at the company, you could say:

The Imperfect Tense (*I Was Speaking*)   The Imperfect Tense vs. The Past Tense

Irregular Imperfect Tense   *I Read, I Write, I Say*

J'ai travaillé pour cette société pendant un an.
I worked for that company for one year.

Pendant can also be used instead of pour to talk about the future. In this case, you would use the near future/future tense + pendant: Je vais travailler pour cette société pendant un an. (*I'm going to work for this/that company for a year.*)

So, to summarize:

1. To talk about the duration of a completed action in the past, use the past tense or the imperfect + pendant.

2. To talk about the duration of an action that started in the past and continues in the present, use the present tense + depuis.

3. To talk about the duration of an action that will take place in the future or near future, use the near future or future tense + pour or pendant.

Depuis can be used in certain expressions as well. For instance, you can use depuis combien de temps ? with the present tense to ask (*for*) *how long?*

Depuis combien de temps attend-il ?
How long has he been waiting?

Il attend depuis dix minutes.
He's been waiting for ten minutes.

The expression depuis quand ? means *since when?* It is also used with the present tense.

Depuis quand travaillez-vous ici ?
Since when have you been working here?

Je travaille ici depuis janvier.
I've been working here since January.

✎ Work Out 1

Use depuis, pour, or pendant.

1. Nous sommes ici _____ trois heures. *(We've been here since 3:00.)*

2. Mes amis vont aller au Canada _____ trois semaines.

   (My friends are going to go to Canada for three weeks.)

3. J'étais en France _____ un mois. *(I was in France for a month.)*

4. _____ combien de temps est-ce que tu habites à New York ?

   (How long have you been living in New York?)

5. Il travaille en ville _____ deux ans.

   (He's been working in the city for two years.)

6. _____ l'hiver, nous sommes allés en Floride.

   (During the winter, we went to Florida.)

ANSWER KEY:
1. depuis; 2. pour/pendant; 3. pendant; 4. Depuis; 5. depuis; 6. Pendant

Sentence Builder 2

▶ 7C Lesson 7 Sentence Builder 2 (CD 8, Track 3)

I did my homework.	J'ai fait mes devoirs.
I made a spelling mistake.	J'ai fait une faute d'orthographe.

The Imperfect Tense (*I Was Speaking*)   The Imperfect Tense vs. The Past Tense

Irregular Imperfect Tense   *I Read, I Write, I Say*

I'm taking a class. (I'm attending a class.)	J'assiste à un cours.
I'm going to the (school) cafeteria.	Je vais à la cantine.
The children play in the schoolyard (playground).	Les enfants jouent dans la cour de récréation.
She's a member of the French club.	Elle fait partie du cercle français.
It's necessary to learn the poem by heart.	Il faut apprendre le poème par cœur.
I'm taking my calculus test.	Je passe mon examen de calcul.
I did well on my test.	J'ai réussi à mon examen.
I failed my test.	J'ai échoué à mon examen.
I failed.	J'ai raté.

Take It Further

You learned a lot of helpful words, phrases, and verbs for talking about school in the sentences above. Let's review, and look at some related terms:

school cafeteria	la cantine
cafeteria (general term)	la cafétéria
schoolyard, playground	la cour de récréation
recess, break	la récré, la récréation
club	le cercle, le club
member	le membre
to be a member of	faire partie de, être membre de
by heart	par cœur
to learn by heart	apprendre par cœur
poem	le poème
test, exam	l'examen (*m.*)

lesson	la leçon
class, course	le cours
to attend (a class), to take (a class)	assister à (un cours)
to take (a test)	passer (un examen)
to do well, to succeed	réussir
to pass a test/class, to do well on a test/ in a class	réussir à un examen/cours
to fail (a test/class)	échouer à (un examen/cours), rater (un examen/cours)
mistake	la faute, l'erreur (f.)
to make a mistake	faire une faute/erreur

Note that passer is a "false" similar word when talking about school. For example, passer un examen does not mean *to pass a test*, it means *to take a test*.

✎ Sentence Practice 2

Match the following English phrases to the correct French translations.

1. *to take a test*	a. assister à un cours
2. *to fail a test*	b. faire une faute
3. *to do well on a test*	c. réussir à un examen
4. *to attend a class*	d. passer un examen
5. *to be a member of*	e. échouer à un examen
6. *to make a mistake*	f. faire partie de

ANSWER KEY:
1. d; 2. e; 3. c; 4. a; 5. f; 6. b

The Imperfect Tense (*I Was Speaking*)   The Imperfect Tense vs. The Past Tense

Irregular Imperfect Tense   *I Read, I Write, I Say*

Word Recall

Now match the following verbs to the correct French translations.

1. *to pay*	a. employer
2. *to throw*	b. payer
3. *to prefer*	c. acheter
4. *to use*	d. préférer
5. *to buy*	e. jeter

ANSWER KEY:
1. b; 2. e; 3. d; 4. a; 5. c

Grammar Builder 2
IRREGULAR -IR VERBS

 7D Lesson 7 Grammar Builder 2 (CD 8, Track 4)

As you know, there are groups of irregular -er verbs that follow specific patterns.

For example, you've already learned about verbs that are similar to manger, commencer, appeler, acheter, préférer, employer, and payer.

Now let's look at a group of irregular -ir verbs known as the "SST" verbs. They're called SST verbs because their je, tu, and il/elle forms end in -s, -s, and -t.

To create the je, tu, and il/elle forms of SST verbs in the present tense, drop the last **three** letters of the infinitive form and add the endings shown below. To create the nous, vous, and ils/elles forms, drop the last **two** letters of the infinitive form and add the endings.

	DROP THE LAST *THREE* LETTERS OF THE INFINITIVE AND ADD …		DROP THE LAST *TWO* LETTERS OF THE INFINITIVE AND ADD …
je	-s	nous	-ons
tu	-s	vous	-ez
il	-t	ils	-ent
elle	-t	elles	-ent

Dormir (*to sleep*), for example, is an SST verb. So to create its je, tu, and il/elle forms, drop the last three letters of the infinitive (leaving you with dor-) and add the endings. To create its nous, vous, and ils/elles forms, drop the last two letters of the infinitive (leaving you with dorm-) and add the endings.

DORMIR *(TO SLEEP)* - **PRESENT**			
je dors	*I sleep*	nous dormons	*we sleep*
tu dors	*you sleep*	vous dormez	*you sleep*
il dort	*he sleeps*	ils dorment	*they sleep*
elle dort	*she sleeps*	elles dorment	*they sleep*

Partir (*to leave*) is also an SST verb:

PARTIR *(TO LEAVE)* - **PRESENT**			
je pars	*I leave*	nous partons	*we leave*
tu pars	*you leave*	vous partez	*you leave*
il part	*he leaves*	ils partent	*they leave*
elle part	*she leaves*	elles partent	*they leave*

Other common SST verbs include:

sentir	*to feel*
servir	*to serve*
sortir	*to go out, to leave*

You actually saw the full conjugation of sortir already, in *Essential French*.

The Imperfect Tense (*I Was Speaking*)   The Imperfect Tense vs. The Past Tense

Irregular Imperfect Tense   *I Read, I Write, I Say*

Here are some examples of SST verbs in sentences:

Le samedi soir, je sors avec mes amis.
On Saturday night, I go out with my friends.

Quand partez-vous en vacances ?
When are you leaving on vacation?

Mon mari dort toujours devant la télévision.
My husband always sleeps in front of the television.

The past participles of SST verbs are formed normally: cut off the **-ir** from the infinitive form and add -i. For example, the past participle of partir is parti and the past participle of dormir is dormi.

Vous avez bien dormi hier soir ?
Did you sleep well last night?

J'ai servi le dessert avec le café.
I served the dessert with coffee.

Remember that the verbs partir and sortir form the passé composé with the verb être, so their past participles need to agree in gender and number with the subject of the sentence.

Marie est sortie avec Jean.
Marie went out with Jean.

✎ Work Out 2

Conjugate the following verbs in the present tense.

1. Les filles _____ (dormir). *(The girls are sleeping.)*

2. À quelle heure est-ce que nous _____ (partir) ?

   (At what time are we leaving?)

3. _____ -elle (sortir) avec Jean ? *(Is she going out with Jean?)*

4. Vous _____ (servir) le dîner. *(You serve dinner.)*

   ANSWER KEY:
   1. dorment; 2. partons; 3. Sort; 4. servez

✎ Drive It Home

A. Fill in the blanks with depuis or pendant.

1. Nous habiterons à Paris _____ deux ans.

   (We will live in Paris for two years.)

2. Nous habitons à Paris _____ deux ans.

   (We've been living in Paris for two years.)

3. Nous avons habité à Paris _____ deux ans.

   (We lived in Paris for two years.)

4. Nous allons habiter à Paris _____ deux ans.

   (We're going to live in Paris for two years.)

The Imperfect Tense (*I Was Speaking*)   The Imperfect Tense vs. The Past Tense

Irregular Imperfect Tense   *I Read, I Write, I Say*

B. Give the correct present tense of the following verbs.

1. Je _____ (dormir)

2. Tu _____ (servir)

3. Elle _____ (sentir)

4. Il _____ (partir)

5. Nous _____ (sortir)

6. Vous _____ (dormir)

7. Ils _____ (sortir)

8. Elles _____ (partir)

ANSWER KEY:
A. 1. pendant; 2. depuis; 3. pendant; 4. pendant
B. 1. dors; 2. sers; 3. sent; 4. part; 5. sortons; 6. dormez; 7. sortent; 8. partent

⊕ Culture Note

School life in France begins with l'école (*f.*) maternelle, the equivalent of *nursery school* or *preschool*. It continues with l'école (*f.*) primaire (*elementary* or *primary school*). Le collège is the equivalent of the American *middle school* or *junior high school*, followed by le lycée (*high school*).

French children generally attend school on Monday, Tuesday, Thursday, Friday, and only sometimes Saturday morning. Wednesdays and Sundays are days off, although some schools require half days on Wednesdays. The school day begins around 8 or 8:30 a.m. and finishes around 4:30 or 5 p.m. with a two-hour break for lunch.

In the last grade, or la classe terminale, of high school, a student wishing to continue his or her education beyond high school must take a special exam called le baccalauréat (informally known as le bac). Successful completion of this rigorous exam is one of the key components of acceptance to a French university.

How Did You Do?

Let's see how you did! By now, you should be able to:

☐ Describe your work environment
(Still unsure? Jump back to page 120)

☐ Talk about duration
(Still unsure? Jump back to page 123)

☐ Talk about classes, tests, and activities at school
(Still unsure? Jump back to page 125)

☐ Say *I leave* and *I sleep*
(Still unsure? Jump back to page 128)

Lesson 8: Conversations

By the end of this lesson, you will be able to:

☐ Tell someone what you *see*

☐ Say what you *know* and whom you *know*

Conversation 1

Marie is a literature student at a university in Paris and her friend René is visiting her for the weekend. They're eating lunch at a Paris café that was frequented by two of their favorite écrivains: Jean-Paul Sartre and Simone de Beauvoir.

▶ 8A Lesson 8 Conversation 1 (CD 8, Track 5)

Marie :	Tu te souviens ? Ils étaient toujours assis à cette table.
René :	Qui donc ?
Marie :	Sartre et Beauvoir !

The Imperfect Tense (*I Was Speaking*)   The Imperfect Tense vs. The Past Tense

Irregular Imperfect Tense   *I Read, I Write, I Say*

René :	C'est vrai ! Ils buvaient du café toute la journée. Et ils parlaient de politique avec tous leurs amis.
Marie :	Il avait toujours une montagne de livres à côté de lui.
René :	Moi, je me souviens que tu commandais toujours le même sandwich.
Marie :	Un jambon-beurre !

Marie:	*Do you remember? They were always sitting at this table.*
Réné:	*Who? (lit., Who then?)*
Marie:	*Sartre and de Beauvoir!*
Réné:	*That's true! They used to drink coffee all day. And they used to talk about politics with all of their friends.*
Marie:	*He always had a mountain of books next to him.*
Réné:	*Me, I remember that you always used to order the same sandwich.*
Marie:	*A ham and butter (sandwich)!*

Take It Further

You've seen that both le jour and la journée mean *day*, and you know that both l'an *(m.)* and l'année *(f.)* mean *year*. So what's the difference?

Well, it's complicated, and there are many exceptions. However, in general, use the words that end in -ée if you want to emphasize the amount of time that has passed (as in *all day, all year, the whole year,* etc.), use an adjective or a possessive, or use the word in an exclamation.

Here are some examples:

J'ai travaillé toute l'année.
I worked all year.

Je parle de ma journée.
I'm talking about my day.

Bonne journée !
Have a good day!

However, don't use the -ée words if you want to talk about *every*:

tous les jours
every day

Other words like jour/journée and an/année include:

evening, night	le soir, la soirée
morning	le matin, la matinée

Finally, note the two new words in the dialogue:

mountain	la montagne
politics	la politique

✎ Conversation Practice 1

Translate the following phrases into English.

1. **tu te souviens** _____

2. **toute la journée** _____

3. **parler de politique** _____

The Imperfect Tense (*I Was Speaking*)   The Imperfect Tense vs. The Past Tense

Irregular Imperfect Tense   *I Read, I Write, I Say*

4. à côté de lui _____

5. le même sandwich _____

ANSWER KEY:
1. *you remember;* 2. *all day;* 3. *to talk about politics;* 4. *next to him;* 5. *the same sandwich*

✎ Word Recall

Quelle heure est-il ? Rewrite the following times using numbers. For example:
12h10, 4h37, etc.

1. **Il est deux heures et quart.** _____

2. **Il est quatre heures moins vingt.** _____

3. **Il est cinq heures dix.** _____

4. **Il est onze heures vingt-cinq.** _____

5. **Il est dix heures moins dix.** _____

6. **Il est sept heures et demie.** _____

ANSWER KEY:
1. 2h15; 2. 3h40; 3. 5h10; 4. 11h25; 5. 9h50; 6. 7h30

Grammar Builder 1
TO SEE

▶ 8B Lesson 8 Grammar Builder 1 (CD 8, Track 6)

Another good irregular verb to know is **voir** (*to see*). Here are its forms in the
present tense:

VOIR (*TO SEE*) - **PRESENT**			
je vois	*I see*	**nous voyons**	*we see*
tu vois	*you see*	**vous voyez**	*you see*

Irregular **-IR** Verbs

VOIR *(TO SEE)* - **PRESENT**			
il voit	*he sees*	ils voient	*they see*
elle voit	*she sees*	elles voient	*they see*

The past participle of voir is vu. The conditional and future tenses are formed with verr- + the endings.

Here are some examples:

Hier soir, j'ai vu un film extraordinaire.
Last night, I saw an extraordinary film.

Je te verrai demain.
I'll see you tomorrow.

Work Out 1

Fill in the blanks with the correct form of voir in the present tense.

1. Nous _____ le patron. (*We see the boss.*)

2. Ils _____ beaucoup de personnes au bureau.

(*They see a lot of people at the office.*)

3. Vous _____ le directeur du personnel.

(*You see the human resources manager.*)

4. Elle _____ le pharmacien. (*She sees the pharmacist.*)

5. Je _____ une voiture rouge. (*I see a red car.*)

ANSWER KEY:
1. voyons; 2. voient; 3. voyez; 4. voit; 5. vois

The Imperfect Tense (*I Was Speaking*)   The Imperfect Tense vs. The Past Tense

Irregular Imperfect Tense   *I Read, I Write, I Say*

Conversation 2

Patrick is meeting his friend Karine at a party and he shows up very late. He begins to tell her the story of what happened.

▶ 8C Lesson 8 Conversation 2 (CD 8, Track 7)

Karine :	Nous t'attendons depuis deux heures ! Qu'est-ce qui t'est arrivé ?
Patrick :	Quelle histoire ! Je traversais la place de la Victoire quand soudain j'ai vu une foule de gens en blouse blanche.
Karine :	Un accident ?
Patrick :	Non, c'était une manifestation des étudiants en médecine.
Karine :	Pourquoi manifestaient-ils ?
Patrick :	Je ne sais pas vraiment.
Karine :	Qu'est-ce que tu as fait... ?

Karine:	*We've been waiting for you for two hours ! What happened to you?*
Patrick:	*What a story! I was crossing the Place de la Victoire when suddenly I saw a crowd of people in white coats (lit., in white coat).*
Karine:	*An accident?*
Patrick:	*No, it was a demonstration of medical students.*
Karine:	*Why were they demonstrating?*
Patrick:	*I don't really know.*
Karine:	*What did you do ... ?*

⏸

Take It Further

If you spend any time in France, chances are you will encounter une grève (*a strike*) or une manifestation (*a demonstration, a protest*) at some point.

They are pretty common, whether they're formed by des étudiants en médecine (*medical students*), des employés (*workers, employees*), or even des lycéens (*high schoolers, high school students*).

As a result, some good words to know include:

on strike	en grève
to strike	faire (la) grève
to demonstrate, to protest	manifester
demonstrator, protestor	le manifestant/la manifestante
to march	défiler

Finally, you know that arriver can mean *to arrive* or *to manage/be able to do something*. However, it can also mean *to happen*.

Arriver is used this way in the expression Qu'est-ce qui t'arrive ? which means *What's happening to you?* but can also carry the sense of *What's wrong with you?* or *What's up with you?* or *What's going on with you?* Note that the t' in the expression is the indirect object pronoun te (t') since you're talking about something happening *to you*.

You saw the expression in the past tense in Conversation 2:

Qu'est-ce qui t'est arrivé ?
What happened to you?

Of course, keep in mind that te (t') is informal. Use the indirect object pronoun vous instead of te if you want or need to be more formal:

Qu'est-ce qui vous est arrivé ?
What happened to you?

The Imperfect Tense (*I Was Speaking*)   The Imperfect Tense vs. The Past Tense

Irregular Imperfect Tense   *I Read, I Write, I Say*

So why do you use qu'est-ce qui... ? and not qu'est-ce que... ? to mean *what* ... ?
Don't worry about it for now. You'll learn all about it in Unit 3.

Conversation Practice 2

Re-read Conversation 2. Then say whether each sentence below is vrai (*true*) or
faux (*false*). Next to each sentence, write down V for vrai or F for faux.

1. Karine attend depuis plus d'une heure. _____

2. Il y avait beaucoup de gens sur la place de la Victoire. _____

3. C'était un accident. _____

4. Les gens avaient des blouses blanches. _____

ANSWER KEY:
1. V (*She's been waiting for two hours, so she has been waiting for more than an hour.*) 2. V (*Yes, there were a lot of people in the place de la Victoire. He says there was a crowd.*) 3. F (*No, it wasn't an accident; it was a demonstration.*) 4. V (*Yes, they had white coats.*)

Word Recall

Give the feminine form of the following adjectives.

1. cher _____

2. vieux _____

3. nouveau _____

4. inquiet _____

5. fier _____

6. heureux _____

7. gentil _____

8. national _____

ANSWER KEY:
1. chère (*dear, expensive*); 2. vieille (*old*); 3. nouvelle (*new*); 4. inquiète (*worried, anxious*); 5. fière (*proud*); 6. heureuse (*happy*); 7. gentille (*nice, kind*); 8. nationale (*national*)

Grammar Builder 2
TO KNOW

▶ 8D Lesson 8 Grammar Builder 2 (CD 8, Track 8)

The phrases je sais (*I know*) and je ne sais pas (*I don't know*) are very useful expressions to know. They're forms of the irregular verb savoir (*to know*).

Here is the full conjugation of savoir in the present tense:

SAVOIR (*TO KNOW*) - **PRESENT**			
je sais	*I know*	nous savons	*we know*
tu sais	*you know*	vous savez	*you know*
il sait	*he knows*	ils savent	*they know*
elle sait	*she knows*	elles savent	*they know*

The past participle of savoir is su.

Comment a-t-il su ?
How did he know?

Note that savoir is irregular in the conditional and future tenses. The conditional and future tenses of savoir are both formed with saur- + the endings.

The Imperfect Tense (*I Was Speaking*)   The Imperfect Tense vs. The Past Tense

Irregular Imperfect Tense   *I Read, I Write, I Say*

The irregular verb connaître also means *to know*. Here is its full conjugation in the present tense. Notice the î in the infinitive form and the il/elle form.

CONNAÎTRE *(TO KNOW)* - **PRESENT**			
je connais	*I know*	nous connaissons	*we know*
tu connais	*you know*	vous connaissez	*you know*
il connaît	*he knows*	ils connaissent	*they know*
elle connaît	*she knows*	elles connaissent	*they know*

The past participle of connaître is connu.

Est-ce que tu as connu cet homme ?
Did you know this man?

Although they both mean to know, savoir and connaître are actually *not* interchangeable. They are used in different ways.

Savoir refers to the possession of knowledge. It can also be translated as *to know how* and is placed in front of a verb, an adverb, or a question word.

Il sait nager.
He knows how to swim.

Je sais où il est.
I know where he is.

Je sais pourquoi j'ai raté.
I know why I failed.

On the other hand, connaître refers to familiarity with someone or something. It is sometimes translated as *to be familiar with* and is placed in front of a noun.

Je connais les chansons d'Édith Piaf.
I know the songs of Edith Piaf. (I am familiar with the songs of Edith Piaf.)

Je connais bien Denise.
I know Denise well.

Elle connaît très bien ce nouveau restaurant.
She knows this new restaurant very well.

✎ Work Out 2

Fill in the blanks with either connaître or savoir in the present tense.

1. Je ne _____ pas la sœur de Marie. *(I don't know Marie's sister.)*

2. Est-ce que tu _____ pourquoi il est en retard ? *(Do you know why he's late?)*

3. Ils _____ jouer au foot. *(They know how to play soccer.)*

4. Vous _____ l'histoire de Cendrillon ?

(Do you know the story of Cinderella?)

ANSWER KEY:
1. connais; 2. sais; 3. savent; 4. connaissez

✎ Drive It Home

A. Fill in the blanks with the present tense form of savoir.

1. Quelle heure est-il ? Je ne _____ pas. *(What time is it? I don't know.)*

2. Quelle heure est-il ? Il ne _____ pas. *(What time is it? He doesn't know.)*

3. Quelle heure est-il ? Nous ne _____ pas. *(What time is it? We don't know.)*

The Imperfect Tense (*I Was Speaking*)   The Imperfect Tense vs. The Past Tense

Irregular Imperfect Tense   *I Read, I Write, I Say*

4. Quelle heure est-il ? Elles ne_____ pas. (*What time is it? They don't know.*)

5. Quelle heure est-il ? Elle ne _____ pas. (*What time is it? She doesn't know.*)

6. Quelle heure est-il ? Ils ne _____ pas. (*What time is it? They don't know.*)

B. Now fill in the blanks with the present tense form of connaître.

1. Sophie ? Je ne la _____ pas. (*Sophie? I don't know her.*)

2. Sophie ? Elles ne la _____ pas. (*Sophie? They don't know her.*)

3. Sophie ? Ils ne la _____ pas. (*Sophie? They don't know her.*)

4. Sophie ? Vous ne la _____ pas. (*Sophie? You don't know her.*)

5. Sophie ? Nous ne la _____ pas. (*Sophie? We don't know her.*)

6. Sophie ? Il ne la _____ pas. (*Sophie? He doesn't know her.*)

ANSWER KEY:

A. 1. sais; 2. sait; 3. savons; 4. savent; 5. sait; 6. savent

B. 1. connais; 2. connaissent; 3. connaissent; 4. connaissez; 5. connaissons; 6. connaît

 Tip

Now that you know how to talk about what you *know*, you should also know how to say what you *believe*. The irregular verb croire means *to believe* in French, and it's a good verb to know.

CROIRE *(TO BELIEVE)* - **PRESENT**			
je crois	*I believe*	nous croyons	*we believe*
tu crois	*you believe*	vous croyez	*you believe*
il croit	*he believes*	ils croient	*they believe*
elle croit	*she believes*	elles croient	*they believe*

Elle travaille dans un restaurant, je crois.

She works in a restaurant, I believe.

The past participle of croire is cru.

How Did You Do?

Let's see how you did! By now, you should be able to:

- ☐ Tell someone what you *see*
  (Still unsure? Jump back to page 136)

- ☐ Say what you *know* and who you *know*
  (Still unsure? Jump back to page 141)

Unit 2 Essentials

Remember that if the word has more than one translation, or different masculine and feminine forms, make sure to write them all down.

Don't forget to go to **www.livinglanguage.com/languagelab** to access your free online tools for this lesson: audiovisual flashcards, and interactive games and quizzes.

Vocabulary Essentials

PROFESSIONS

accountant		dentist	
bank clerk		nurse	
civil servant		actor/actress	
pharmacist		plumber	
homemaker		farmer	
construction worker		carpenter	
author		beautician	
writer		policeman/ policewoman	
computer programmer		businessman/ businesswoman	

[Pg. 91] (If you're stuck, visit this page to review!)

AT THE OFFICE

job, work		meeting	
factory		staff	
company		colleague	
computer		boss	
software		salary	

[Pg. 99]

DEPARTMENTS WITHIN A COMPANY

department	
accounting department	
computer science/IT department	
finance department	
sales department	
legal department	
marketing department	
public relations (PR) department	
shipping department, mail room	
customer service department	
management	

[Pg. 99]

APPLYING FOR A JOB

at the office		retired	
to earn money		unemployment	
human resources manager, personnel manager		to be unemployed	
to apply for a job		summer job	
to have an interview		to work hard	
full-time		to be busy	
part-time			

[Pg. 105]

AT SCHOOL

school		to teach	
middle school		diploma	
high school		academic year	
college		back-to-school	
classroom		report card	

[Pg. 111]

WORK EXPRESSIONS

I get along well with my boss.	
I'm on vacation.	
(I) can't wait for the end of the day!	
I work forty hours a week/per week.	

[Pg. 120]

SCHOOL EXPRESSIONS

I did my homework.	
I'm taking a class.	
I'm taking my calculus test.	
I did well on my test.	
I failed my test.	
I failed.	

[Pg. 125]

DURATION EXPRESSIONS

how long?/ *for how long?*		*since when?*	

[Pg. 124]

Grammar Essentials

THE IMPERFECT (L'IMPARFAIT)

To form the imperfect tense:

1. Take the **nous** form of the verb in the present tense and drop the **-ons** ending.

2. Next, add one of the following endings:

PRONOUN	ENDING	PRONOUN	ENDING
je	-ais	nous	-ions
tu	-ais	vous	-iez
il	-ait	ils	-aient
elle	-ait	elles	-aient

AVOIR (TO HAVE) - IMPERFECT

I had	j'avais	we had	nous avions
you had (infml.)	tu avais	you had (pl./fml.)	vous aviez
he had	il avait	they had (m.)	ils avaient
she had	elle avait	they had (f.)	elles avaient

COMMENCER (TO BEGIN, TO START) - IMPERFECT

I was beginning	je commençais	we were beginning	nous commencions
you were beginning (infml.)	tu commençais	you were beginning (pl./fml.)	vous commenciez
he was beginning	il commençait	they were beginning (m.)	ils commençaient
she was beginning	elle commençait	they were beginning (f.)	elles commençaient

ÊTRE (TO BE) - IMPERFECT

I was	j'étais	we were	nous étions
you were (infml.)	tu étais	you were (pl./fml.)	vous étiez
he was	il était	they were (m.)	ils étaient
she was	elle était	they were (f.)	elles étaient

MANGER (TO EAT) - IMPERFECT

I was eating	je mangeais	we were eating	nous mangions
you were eating (infml.)	tu mangeais	you were eating (pl./fml.)	vous mangiez

MANGER *(TO EAT)* - **IMPERFECT**			
he was eating	il mangeait	*they were eating (m.)*	ils mangeaient
she was eating	elle mangeait	*they were eating (f.)*	elles mangeaient

PARLER *(TO SPEAK, TO TALK)* - **IMPERFECT**			
I was speaking	je parlais	*we were speaking*	nous parlions
you were speaking (infml.)	tu parlais	*you were speaking (pl./fml.)*	vous parliez
he was speaking	il parlait	*they were speaking (m.)*	ils parlaient
she was speaking	elle parlait	*they were speaking (f.)*	elles parlaient

THE IMPERFECT VS THE PAST TENSE

TENSE	HOW IT'S USED
Imperfect (l'imparfait)	actions that are continuous, habitual, or repetitive; descriptions
Past Tense (le passé composé)	actions that have been completed

DURATION

1. To talk about the duration of a completed action in the past, use the past tense or the imperfect + pendant.

2. To talk about the duration of an action that started in the past and continues in the present, use the present tense + depuis.

3. To talk about the duration of an action that will take place in the future or near future, use the near future or future tense + pour or pendant.

SST VERBS

	DROP THE LAST *THREE* LETTERS OF THE INFINITIVE AND ADD ...		DROP THE LAST *TWO* LETTERS OF THE INFINITIVE AND ADD ...
je	-s	nous	-ons
tu	-s	vous	-ez
il	-t	ils	-ent
elle	-t	elles	-ent

PARTIR (*TO LEAVE*) - **PRESENT**			
I leave	je pars	*we leave*	nous partons
you leave (infml.)	tu pars	*you leave (pl./fml.)*	vous partez
he leaves	il part	*they leave (m.)*	ils partent
she leaves	elle part	*they leave (f.)*	elles partent
Past Participle: parti			

SAVOIR **VS** CONNAÎTRE

Savoir refers to the possession of knowledge. It can also be translated as *to know how.*

SAVOIR (*TO KNOW, TO KNOW HOW*) - **PRESENT**			
I know	je sais	*we know*	nous savons
you know (infml.)	tu sais	*you know (pl./fml.)*	vous savez
he knows	il sait	*they know (m.)*	ils savent
she knows	elle sait	*they know (f.)*	elles savent
Past Participle: su; Future and Conditional stem: saur-			

Connaître refers to familiarity with someone or something. It is sometimes translated as *to be familiar with.*

CONNAÎTRE *(TO KNOW, TO BE FAMILIAR WITH)* - **PRESENT**			
I know	je connais	*we know*	nous connaissons
you know (infml.)	tu connais	*you know (pl./ fml.)*	vous connaissez
he knows	il connaît	*they know (m.)*	ils connaissent
she knows	elle connaît	*they know (f.)*	elles connaissent
Past Participle: connu			

OTHER VERBS

ÉCRIRE *(TO WRITE)* - **PRESENT**			
I write	j'écris	*we write*	nous écrivons
you write (infml.)	tu écris	*you write (pl./ fml.)*	vous écrivez
he writes	il écrit	*they write (m.)*	ils écrivent
she writes	elle écrit	*they write (f.)*	elles écrivent
Past Participle: écrit			

LIRE *(TO READ)* - **PRESENT**			
I read	je lis	*we read*	nous lisons
you read (infml.)	tu lis	*you read (pl./fml.)*	vous lisez
he reads	il lit	*they read (m.)*	ils lisent
she reads	elle lit	*they read (f.)*	elles lisent
Past Participle: lu			

DIRE *(TO SAY, TO TELL)* - **PRESENT**			
I say	je dis	*we say*	nous disons
you say (infml.)	tu dis	*you say (pl./fml.)*	vous dites
he says	il dit	*they say (m.)*	ils disent
she says	elle dit	*they say (f.)*	elles disent
Past Participle: dit			

VOIR *(TO SEE)* - **PRESENT**			
I see	je vois	*we see*	nous voyons
you see (infml.)	tu vois	*you see (pl./fml.)*	vous voyez
he sees	il voit	*they see (m.)*	ils voient
she sees	elle voit	*they see (f.)*	elles voient
Past Participle: vu; Future and Conditional stem: verr-			

Unit 2 Quiz

Now let's see how you did in Unit 2!

In this section you'll find a short quiz testing what you learned in Unit 2. After you've answered all of the questions, don't forget to score your quiz to see how you did. If you find that you need to go back and review, please do so before continuing on to Unit 3.

A. Can you find the English equivalent for these professions?

1. **le pharmacien/la pharmacienne**   a. *nurse*

2. **le fonctionnaire/la fonctionnaire**   b. *bank clerk*

3. **l'infirmier/l'infirmière**   c. *civil servant*

4. **l'employé de banque/ l'employée de banque**   d. *businessman/businesswoman*

5. **l'homme d'affaires/ la femme d'affaires**   e. *pharmacist*

B. Translate the following expressions.

1. *I'm taking a class.* _____

2. *I did well on my test.* _____

3. *I failed my test.* _____

4. *I work forty hours a week.* _____

5. *I'm on vacation.* _____

C. Fill in the blanks with depuis or pendant.

1. **Je connais Sophie** _____ **dix ans.** (*I've known Sophie for ten years.*)

2. **Il va travailler en France** _____ **un an.** (*He's going to work in France for a year.*)

3. **Elle a joué au tennis** _____ **six mois.** (*She played tennis for six months.*)

4. **J'étudie le français** _____ **trois semaines.** (*I've been studying French for three weeks.*)

5. **Elle sera à l'école** _____ **sept ans.** (*She will be in school for seven years.*)

D. Give the imperfect form of each verb.

1. Il y _____ (avoir) beaucoup de gens à la fête. *(There were a lot of people at the party.)*

2. Nous _____ (être) en retard. *(We were late.)*

3. Elle _____ (manger) toujours une salade pour le déjeuner. *(She always used to eat a salad for lunch.)*

4. Je _____ (parler) au prof. *(I was speaking to the professor.)*

5. Tu _____ (finir) tes devoirs. *(You were finishing your homework.)*

ANSWER KEY:
A. 1. e; 2. c; 3. a; 4. b; 5. d
B. 1. J'assiste à un cours. 2. J'ai réussi à mon examen. 3. J'ai échoué à mon examen. (J'ai raté mon examen.) 4. Je travaille quarante heures par semaine. 5. Je suis en vacances.
C. 1. depuis; 2. pendant; 3. pendant; 4. depuis; 5. pendant
D. 1. avait; 2. étions; 3. mangeait; 4. parlais; 5. finissais

How Did You Do?

Give yourself a point for every correct answer, then use the following key to determine whether or not you're ready to move on:

0-7 points: It's probably best to go back and study the lessons again to make sure you understood everything completely. Take your time; it's not a race! Make sure you spend time reviewing the vocabulary and reading through each grammar note carefully.

8-16 points: If the questions you missed were in Section A or B, you may want to review the vocabulary again; if you missed answers mostly in Section C or D, check the Unit 2 Essentials to make sure you have your conjugations and other grammar basics down.

17-20 points: Feel free to move on to Unit 3! Great job!

 **Points**

Unit 3:
Sports and Leisure

In this unit, we're going to talk about les sports *(m.)* (*sports*) and les loisirs *(m.)* (*leisure activities, recreation*). We're also going to look at a few advanced tenses and how to form more complex sentences using *who, that, what,* and *which.*

By the end of this unit, you should be able to:

☐ Name different sports

☐ Say *I will have spoken* or *I will have finished*

☐ Talk about hobbies and other leisure activities

☐ Say *I had spoken* or *I had finished*

☐ Discuss games and matches

☐ Say *I would have spoken* or *I would have finished*

☐ Discuss outdoor activities

☐ Explain where you *put* something

☐ Connect two sentences using *who* or *that*

☐ Tell someone that you understand *what* they are saying

☐ Say *with which* or *in which*

☐ Order someone to *Hurry up!*

☐ Say you *had a good time*

Lesson 9: Words

By the end of this lesson, you will be able to:

☐ Name different sports

☐ Say *I will have spoken* or *I will have finished*

☐ Talk about hobbies and other leisure activities

☐ Say *I had spoken* or *I had finished*

Word Builder 1

Let's get started with **les sports** *(m.)* *(sports)*.

▶ 9A Lesson 9 Word Builder 1 (CD 8, Track 9)

soccer	**le foot(ball)**
(American) football	**le football américain**
ice hockey (lit., hockey on ice)	**le hockey sur glace**
ice skating (lit., skating on ice)	**le patinage sur glace (le patin à glace)**
swimming	**la natation**
gymnastics	**la gymnastique**
track (and field)	**l'athlétisme** *(m.)*
horseback riding	**l'équitation** *(f.)*
(mountain) climbing	**l'alpinisme** *(m.)*
fishing	**la pêche**
bodybuilding, strength training (weight lifting)	**la musculation**
golf	**le golf**
cycling	**le cyclisme**

hunting	la chasse
skiing	le ski
water-skiing	le ski nautique
surfing	le surf
snowboarding (lit., surfing on snow)	le surf sur neige

Take It Further

You've seen **jouer** (*to play*) used many times before. However, let's look at how to use **jouer** when it's followed by the preposition **à** or the partitive.

Jouer à is used with sports and games:

Mon mari joue au golf.
My husband plays golf.

Jouer + partitive (**du, de la,** etc.), on the other hand, is used with musical instruments.

Elle joue du piano.
She plays the piano.

Following that thought, here are a few more sports, games, and musical instruments.

SPORTS AND GAMES	
baseball	le baseball
basketball	le basket(-ball)
volleyball	le volley(-ball)
tennis	le tennis

SPORTS AND GAMES	
wrestling	la lutte
boxing	la boxe
auto racing, car racing	la course automobile
card game	le jeu de cartes
(playing) cards	les cartes (f.) (à jouer)

MUSICAL INSTRUMENTS	
guitar	la guitare
violin	le violon
cello	le violoncelle
flute	la flûte
clarinet	la clarinette
drums	la batterie
saxophone	le saxophone

Tu joues au baseball.
You play baseball.

Je joue au tennis.
I play tennis.

Nous jouons aux cartes.
We're playing cards.

Jouez-vous de la guitare ?
Do you play the guitar?

Ma mère jouait du violon.
My mother used to play the violin.

✎ Word Practice 1

Translate the following words into English.

1. le patinage sur glace _____

2. la natation _____

3. la pêche_____

4. le surf sur neige _____

5. l'athlétisme_____

ANSWER KEY:
1. *ice skating*; 2. *swimming*; 3. *fishing*; 4. *snowboarding*; 5. *track (and field)*

✎ Word Recall

Now let's practice some of the activities you learned in *Essential French*. Match the French to the English below.

1. la moto	a. *sailing*
2. la voile	b. *weight lifting*
3. la course à pied	c. *running*
4. l'haltérophilie	d. *motorcycling*

ANSWER KEY:
1. d; 2. a; 3. c; 4. b

Grammar Builder 1
THE FUTURE PERFECT (*I WILL HAVE SPOKEN*)

Now that we're halfway through *Advanced French*, we're going to begin looking at some more advanced tenses.

To start, let's take a look at a tense known as the "future perfect." It's equivalent to *will have* + past participle in English, as in *I **will have sold** the house by then.*

The future perfect tense is formed in the following way:

future tense of avoir or être + past participle of the verb

The same verbs that use avoir in the past tense use avoir in the future perfect, and the same verbs that use être in the past tense use être in the future perfect.

Remember that être and avoir are irregular in the future tense. Let's review the future tense conjugation of avoir:

AVOIR *(TO HAVE)* - **FUTURE**	
j'aurai	nous aurons
tu auras	vous aurez
il aura	ils auront
elle aura	elles auront

And here is the future tense conjugation of être:

ÊTRE *(TO BE)* - **FUTURE**	
je serai	nous serons
tu seras	vous serez
il sera	ils seront
elle sera	elles seront

▶   9B Lesson 9 Grammar Builder 1 (CD 8, Track 10)

Okay, now let's look at full conjugations of verbs in the future perfect. We'll first look at examples of verbs that use avoir.

Parler (*to speak, to talk*) is an example of a regular **-er** verb that uses **avoir**. So to form the future perfect of **parler**, take the future tense of **avoir** and add the past participle of **parler**, which is **parlé**.

PARLER (*TO SPEAK, TO TALK*) - **FUTURE PERFECT**			
j'aurai parlé	*I will have spoken*	nous aurons parlé	*we will have spoken*
tu auras parlé	*you will have spoken*	vous aurez parlé	*you will have spoken*
il aura parlé	*he will have spoken*	ils auront parlé	*they will have spoken*
elle aura parlé	*she will have spoken*	elles auront parlé	*they will have spoken*

Now here is an example of a regular **-ir** verb that uses **avoir**: **finir** (*to finish*).

FINIR (*TO FINISH*) - **FUTURE PERFECT**			
j'aurai fini	*I will have finished*	nous aurons fini	*we will have finished*
tu auras fini	*you will have finished*	vous aurez fini	*you will have finished*
il aura fini	*he will have finished*	ils auront fini	*they will have finished*
elle aura fini	*she will have finished*	elles auront fini	*they will have finished*

Here is an example of a regular -re verb that uses avoir: vendre (*to sell*).

VENDRE (*TO SELL*) - **FUTURE PERFECT**			
j'aurai vendu	*I will have sold*	nous aurons vendu	*we will have sold*
tu auras vendu	*you will have sold*	vous aurez vendu	*you will have sold*
il aura vendu	*he will have sold*	ils auront vendu	*they will have sold*
elle aura vendu	*she will have sold*	elles auront vendu	*they will have sold*

And here is an example of an irregular verb that uses avoir: faire (*to do, to make*). Notice that faire forms the future perfect normally.

FAIRE (*TO DO, TO MAKE*) - **FUTURE PERFECT**			
j'aurai fait	*I will have made*	nous aurons fait	*we will have made*
tu auras fait	*you will have made*	vous aurez fait	*you will have made*
il aura fait	*he will have made*	ils auront fait	*they will have made*
elle aura fait	*she will have made*	elles auront fait	*they will have made*

Now that you've seen examples of verbs that use avoir, let's look at an example of a verb that uses être. Keep in mind that the past participle of a verb that uses être must agree in gender and number with the subject.

Here is the full conjugation of **aller** (*to go*) in the future perfect:

ALLER *(TO GO)* - **FUTURE PERFECT**			
je serai allé(e)	*I will have gone*	**nous serons allé(e)s**	*we will have gone*
tu seras allé(e)	*you will have gone*	**vous serez allé(e)(s)**	*you will have gone*
il sera allé	*he will have gone*	**ils seront allés**	*they will have gone*
elle sera allée	*she will have gone*	**elles seront allées**	*they will have gone*

Remember that **être** itself actually uses **avoir**, so: **j'aurai été** (*I will have been*), etc.

In English, the future perfect is often followed by the present tense: *He **will have eaten** all of the food when I **arrive***. However, in French, the future perfect is usually followed by the future tense in that type of sentence:

Tu auras mangé toute la nourriture quand j'arriverai.
You will have eaten all of the food when I arrive. (lit., You will have eaten all the food when I will arrive.)

Tu auras commencé la leçon quand j'entrerai dans la classe.
You will have begun the lesson when I enter the classroom. (lit., You will have begun the lesson when I will enter the class.)

Il sera parti quand la police sera là.
He will have left when the police get there. (lit., He will have left when the police will be there.)

When the future perfect is used with **avant de** (*before*), the verb that follows will be in the infinitive:

Nous aurons pris le livre avant de rentrer à la maison.
We will have taken the book before coming home.

Elles auront fini leurs devoirs avant de regarder la télévision.
They will have finished their homework before they watch television (before watching television).

The negative version of that sentence would be: **Elles n'auront pas fini leurs devoirs avant de regarder la télévision.** (*They will not have finished their homework before watching television.*) Notice that **pas** comes in between **avoir** and the past participle. The same is true for verbs that use **être**.

Finally, a good phrase to know when using the future perfect is **d'ici**. It literally means *from here,* but it can also mean *by* or *until* when combined with a time word or phrase:

d'ici demain	by tomorrow, until tomorrow
d'ici juin	by June, until June
d'ici la fin de la semaine	by the end of the week, until the end of the week

You can also say:

d'ici là	by then, from now on, from now until, until then (lit., from here there)

D'ici là, j'aurai vendu la maison.
By then, I will have sold the house.

(II)

✎ Work Out 1

Fill in the blanks with the correct future perfect form of the verbs in parentheses.

1. **Mes amis** _____ **(finir) avant six heures.**

   (My friends will have finished before 6:00.)

2. **D'ici demain, j'**_____ **(regarder) le film.**

   (By tomorrow, I will have watched the movie.)

3. **Nous n'** _____ **pas** _____ **(attendre) trois jours.**

   (We will not have waited three days.)

4. **Elle** _____ **(partir) quand mon père arrivera.**

   (She will have left when my father arrives.)

   ANSWER KEY:
   1. **auront fini**; 2. **aurai regardé**; 3. **aurons, attendu**; 4. **sera partie**

Word Builder 2

Here are some hobbies and other activities that you might do in your spare time.

▶ 9C Lesson 9 Word Builder 2 (CD 8, Track 11)

hobbies (pastimes)	**les passe-temps** *(m.)*
chess	**les échecs** *(m.)*
checkers	**les dames** *(f.)*
entertainment	**le divertissement**
play	**la pièce**
theater	**le théâtre**
ballet	**le ballet**

movies	**le cinéma***
sewing	**la couture**
knitting	**le tricot**
vacation	**les vacances** (*f.*)
camping	**le camping**
yoga	**le yoga**
dance class	**le cours de danse**
reading	**la lecture**
painting	**la peinture**

* Remember that **le cinéma** also means *movie theater*.

Take It Further

When you're on vacation, you may want to visit some sites in the area. Use the verb **visiter** (*to visit*) when you want to talk about visiting places, cities, monuments, etc.

Je visite la Tour Eiffel.
I'm visiting the Eiffel Tower.

However, use **rendre visite à** (*to visit, to pay a visit*) when you want to talk about visiting a person.

Je rends visite à ma tante Nancy.
I'm visiting my aunt Nancy.

Word Practice 2

Let's talk about your **passe-temps favori** (*favorite hobby*). Fill in the blanks with the correct French translations.

1. **Mon passe-temps favori est** _____ *(knitting)*.

2. **Mon passe-temps favori est** _____ *(reading)*.

3. **Mon passe-temps favori est** _____ *(chess)*.

4. **Mon passe-temps favori est** _____ *(yoga)*.

5. **Mon passe-temps favori est** _____ *(painting)*.

ANSWER KEY:
1. le tricot; 2. la lecture; 3. les échecs; 4. le yoga; 5. la peinture

✎ Word Recall

Fill in the blanks with the correct question word.

1. _____ **de sœurs avez-vous ?** *(How many sisters do you have?)*

2. _____ **est-elle toujours en retard ?** *(Why is she always late?)*

3. _____ **habitent-elles ?** *(Where do they live?)*

4. _____ **partez-vous?** *(When are you leaving?)*

5. _____ **vas-tu ?** *(How are you?)*

ANSWER KEY:
1. Combien; 2. Pourquoi; 3. Où; 4. Quand; 5. Comment

Grammar Builder 2
THE PAST PERFECT *(I HAD SPOKEN)*

If you want to talk about the past, another good tense to know is the "past perfect," also known as the "pluperfect." It's equivalent to *had* + past participle in English, as in *the train **had left** when we arrived.*

Forming the past perfect is similar to forming the future perfect. Here's what you do:

imperfect tense of avoir or être + past participle of the verb

Again, if a verb uses avoir in the past tense then it uses avoir in the past perfect. The same goes for être.

Before we look at verbs in the past perfect, let's review the imperfect tense of avoir:

AVOIR (TO HAVE) - IMPERFECT	
j'avais	nous avions
tu avais	vous aviez
il avait	ils avaient
elle avait	elles avaient

And être:

ÊTRE (TO BE) - IMPERFECT	
j'étais	nous étions
tu étais	vous étiez
il était	ils étaient
elle était	elles étaient

▶ 9D Lesson 9 Grammar Builder 2 (CD 8, Track 12)

Now let's look at some verbs in the past perfect. As we did with the future perfect, let's start with verbs that use avoir.

Parler (to speak, to talk) uses avoir, so to form the past perfect of parler, take the imperfect form of avoir and add the past participle of parler: parlé.

PARLER *(TO SPEAK, TO TALK)* - **PAST PERFECT**			
j'avais parlé	*I had spoken*	**nous avions parlé**	*we had spoken*
tu avais parlé	*you had spoken*	**vous aviez parlé**	*you had spoken*
il avait parlé	*he had spoken*	**ils avaient parlé**	*they had spoken*
elle avait parlé	*she had spoken*	**elles avaient parlé**	*they had spoken*

Now let's look at **finir** (*to finish*):

FINIR *(TO FINISH)* - **PAST PERFECT**			
j'avais fini	*I had finished*	**nous avions fini**	*we had finished*
tu avais fini	*you had finished*	**vous aviez fini**	*you had finished*
il avait fini	*he had finished*	**ils avaient fini**	*they had finished*
elle avait fini	*she had finished*	**elles avaient fini**	*they had finished*

Here is **vendre** (*to sell*):

VENDRE *(TO SELL)* - **PAST PERFECT**			
j'avais vendu	*I had sold*	**nous avions vendu**	*we had sold*
tu avais vendu	*you had sold*	**vous aviez vendu**	*you had sold*
il avait vendu	*he had sold*	**ils avaient vendu**	*they had sold*
elle avait vendu	*she had sold*	**elles avaient vendu**	*they had sold*

And **faire** (*to do, to make*):

FAIRE *(TO DO, TO MAKE)* - **PAST PERFECT**			
j'avais fait	*I had done*	**nous avions fait**	*we had done*
tu avais fait	*you had done*	**vous aviez fait**	*you had done*
il avait fait	*he had done*	**ils avaient fait**	*they had done*
elle avait fait	*she had done*	**elles avaient fait**	*they had done*

Now that we've looked at several examples of verbs that use **avoir**, let's look at an example of a verb that uses **être**. Don't forget that the past participle of a verb that uses **être** must agree in gender and number with the subject.

Here is **aller** *(to go)* in the past perfect:

ALLER *(TO GO)* - **PAST PERFECT**			
j'étais allé(e)	*I had gone*	nous étions allé(e)s	*we had gone*
tu étais allé(e)	*you had gone*	vous étiez allé(e)(s)	*you had gone*
il était allé	*he had gone*	ils étaient allés	*they had gone*
elle était allée	*she had gone*	elles étaient allées	*they had gone*

As in English, the past perfect in French is often followed by the past tense:

Le train était parti quand nous sommes arrivés à la gare.
The train had left when we arrived at the station.

Here are some more examples of sentences with the past perfect:

Elle était partie à midi.
She had left at noon.

Nous avions eu un rendez-vous.
We had had an appointment.

Aviez-vous pu le faire...
Had you been able to do it ...

Ⅱ

✎ Work Out 2

Fill in the blanks with the correct form of avoir or être to create the past perfect.

1. j' _____ pris *(I had taken)*

2. il _____ sorti *(he had gone out)*

3. vous _____ été *(you had been)*

4. ils _____ partis *(they had left)*

5. elle _____ bu *(she had drunk)*

ANSWER KEY:
1. avais; 2. était; 3. aviez; 4. étaient; 5. avait

✎ Drive It Home

A. Conjugate each verb in the future perfect.

1. Je/J' _____ (choisir). *(I will have chosen.)*

2. Je/J' _____ (aller). *(I will have gone.)*

3. Je/J' _____ (répondre). *(I will have responded.)*

4. Je/J' _____ (avoir). *(I will have had.)*

5. Je/J' _____ (danser). *(I will have danced.)*

6. Je/J' _____ (tomber). *(I will have fallen.)*

7. Je/J' _____ (lire). *(I will have read.)*

8. Je/J' _____ (savoir). *(I will have known.)*

B. Great! Now give each verb in the past perfect.

1. J' _____ (choisir). (*I had chosen.*)

2. J' _____ (aller). (*I had gone.*)

3. J' _____ (répondre). (*I had responded.*)

4. J' _____ (avoir). (*I had had.*)

5. J' _____ (danser). (*I had danced.*)

6. J' _____ (tomber). (*I had fallen.*)

7. J' _____ (lire). (*I had read.*)

8. J' _____ (savoir). (*I had known.*)

ANSWER KEY:

A. 1. aurai choisi; 2. serai allé(e); 3. aurai répondu; 4. aurai eu; 5. aurai dansé; 6. serai tombé(e); 7. aurai lu; 8. aurai su

B. 1. avais choisi; 2. étais allé(e); 3. avais répondu; 4. avais eu; 5. avais dansé; 6. étais tombé(e); 7. avais lu; 8. avais su

⊕ Culture Note

Speaking of **visiter** and **vacances**, here is some background information on Paris and the surrounding area with a few highlights of places to see.

Paris, known as **Lutèce** (*Lutetia*) around Roman times, gets its current name from an ancient Gaelic tribe called the **Parisii** who were early settlers of the area. They first settled on the **Île de la Cité** (lit., *city island*) around 2,000 years ago. **L'Île de la Cité** is a small island in the Seine that is now at the heart of the modern city of Paris (and home to **Notre Dame** cathedral).

Here's a sampling of some of the most popular tourist sites in modern Paris:

La Tour Eiffel (*Eiffel Tower*) was built out of steel by Alexandre Gustave Eiffel for the World's Fair of 1889. It is approximately 1,100 feet high and serves as a radio

and television transmitter. It is also a world-famous tourist site open to visitors
all year round. You can climb the stairs or take the elevator to the top. There are
three levels open to visitors and a high-end restaurant on the second level.

L'Arc de Triomphe (lit., *Arch of Triumph*), built to commemorate the victories of
Napoléon, is located in the center of a busy traffic circle called **la Place Charles
de Gaulle**. The circle used to be called **la Place de l'Étoile** (lit., *Place of the Star*)
because twelve avenues converge there. The Arch stands around 160 feet tall. The
Tomb of the Unknown Soldier lies beneath the Arch, with a flame that burns in
honor of all departed soldiers.

Le Musée du Louvre (*Louvre Museum*) started out as a fortress and was built up
and expanded over the centuries into a residence of the French kings. Today it is
one of the largest museums in the world, with masterpieces such as **La Joconde**
(*Mona Lisa*), **La Vénus de Milo**, and **La Victoire de Samothrace** (*Winged Victory
of Samothrace*). In 1989, glass pyramids designed by the architect Ieoh Ming Pei
were added in front of the museum. The largest one was built to serve as a new
entrance to the always crowded museum.

Across the Seine river from the **Louvre**, **Le Musée d'Orsay** (*Orsay Museum*) is a
former train station that was transformed into a museum in the 1980s. It houses
many realist and impressionist works of famous artists, such as Manet, Degas, Van
Gogh, and Monet.

Le Centre National d'Art et de Culture Georges-Pompidou (lit., *the National
Center of Art and Culture Georges-Pompidou*) is a futuristic, industrial-style
structure housing a museum of modern art, a large library, a center for industrial
creation, and an institute for musical experimentation. It opened its doors in 1977
and is also known as **Le Centre Pompidou** or **Beaubourg**, after the district of
Paris in which it is located.

When visiting Paris, don't miss la Cathédrale Notre-Dame (*Notre Dame Cathedral*) on L'Île de la Cité in the center of Paris. Construction of the cathedral began in the 12th century and took more than 100 years to complete. The cathedral is famous for its stained-glass rose windows and beautiful gothic architecture.

There are also numerous parks and gardens throughout Paris, including the two massive ones at the edges of Paris: Le Bois de Boulogne and Le Bois de Vincennes.

If you care to venture beyond Paris, you can take a short trip to Versailles, Louis XIV's extravagant palace and its grounds, or take a longer excursion to the Loire Valley, where you will find more than one hundred châteaux (*castles*) with beautiful views and gardens.

How Did You Do?

Let's see how you did! By now, you should be able to:

☐ Name different sports
(Still unsure? Jump back to page 160)

☐ Say *I will have spoken* or *I will have finished*
(Still unsure? Jump back to page 165)

☐ Talk about hobbies and other leisure activities
(Still unsure? Jump back to page 169)

☐ Say *I had spoken* or *I had finished*
(Still unsure? Jump back to page 173)

Lesson 10: Phrases

By the end of this lesson, you will be able to:

☐ Discuss games and matches

☐ Say *I would have spoken* or *I would have finished*

☐ Discuss outdoor activities

☐ Explain where you *put* something

Phrase Builder 1

▶ 10A Lesson 10 Phrase Builder 1 (CD 8, Track 13)

to play a sport (to do a sport)	**faire du sport**
to play a game (to play a match)	**jouer un match**
to win a game (to win a match)	**gagner un match**
to lose a game (to lose a match)	**perdre un match**
spectator	**le spectateur/la spectatrice**
end of the game (end of the match)	**la fin du match**
final score	**le score final**
to kick (lit., to give a kick)	**donner un coup de pied**
first/second/third base	**la première/deuxième/troisième base**
rugby team	**l'équipe *(f.)* de rugby**
to dive in(to) the pool	**plonger dans la piscine**
to run the marathon	**courir le marathon**
to jump a hurdle	**sauter une haie**
to go horseback riding (to ride a horse)	**monter à cheval**
skateboard	**la planche à roulettes, le skateboard**

Take It Further

Like jouer (to play), faire (to do, to make) is often used when talking about sports and other activities. It can mean *to do* or *to play* or *to go (do)* a sport or activity. Note that, when talking about activities, faire is frequently followed by the partitive (du, de la, etc.).

You should already be familiar with some of these examples:

to play a sport, to do a sport, to play sports, to do sports	faire du sport
to play soccer, to do soccer	faire du foot(ball)
to do horseback riding, to go horseback riding	faire de l'équitation
to swim, to go swimming	faire de la natation
to ski, to go skiing	faire du ski
to water-ski, to go water-skiing	faire du ski nautique
to camp, to go camping	faire du camping
to do yoga	faire du yoga

✎ Phrase Practice 1

Unscramble the sentences below based on Phrase Builder 1.

1. plonge / la / Elle / dans / piscine / . _____

2. allez / monter / à / Vous / cheval / . _____

3. j'ai / pied / coup / donné / de / un / . _____

4. marathon / Nous / courir / le / allons / . _____

ANSWER KEY:
1. **Elle plonge dans la piscine.** (*She dives in/into the pool.*) 2. **Vous allez monter à cheval.** (*You're going to go horseback riding./You're going to ride a horse.*) 3. **J'ai donné un coup de pied.** (*I kicked.*) 4. **Nous allons courir le marathon.** (*We're going to run the marathon.*)

✎ Word Recall

Identify the following weather conditions by filling in the correct sentence
in French.

1. _____

2. _____

3. _____

4. _____

5. _____

6. _____

ANSWER KEY:
1. **Il fait soleil./Il fait du soleil.** 2. **Il fait du vent.** 3. **Il pleut.** 4. **Il neige.** 5. **Il fait chaud.** 6. **Il fait froid.**

Grammar Builder 1
THE PAST CONDITIONAL (*I WOULD HAVE SPOKEN*)

If you want to talk about what you *would have* done in French, then you need to
use the "past conditional."

Fortunately, forming the past conditional is similar to forming both the future
perfect and the past perfect. Here's what you do:

conditional of **avoir** or **être** + past participle of the verb

Once again, if a verb uses avoir in the past tense then it uses avoir in the past conditional. The same goes for être.

Before we look at verbs in the past conditional, let's review the conditional of avoir:

AVOIR *(TO HAVE)* - CONDITIONAL	
j'aurais	nous aurions
tu aurais	vous auriez
il aurait	ils auraient
elle aurait	elles auraient

And être:

ÊTRE *(TO BE)* - CONDITIONAL	
je serais	nous serions
tu serais	vous seriez
il serait	ils seraient
elle serait	elles seraient

▶ 10B Lesson 10 Grammar Builder 1 (CD 8, Track 14)

Now let's look at some examples of verbs in the past conditional. As we did with the future perfect and past perfect, let's start with verbs that use avoir.

Parler *(to speak)* uses avoir, so to form the past conditional, take the conditional form of avoir and add the past participle of parler: parlé.

PARLER *(TO SPEAK)* - PAST CONDITIONAL			
j'aurais parlé	*I would have spoken*	nous aurions parlé	*we would have spoken*
tu aurais parlé	*you would have spoken*	vous auriez parlé	*you would have spoken*

PARLER *(TO SPEAK)* - **PAST CONDITIONAL**			
il aurait parlé	*he would have spoken*	ils auraient parlé	*they would have spoken*
elle aurait parlé	*she would have spoken*	elles auraient parlé	*they would have spoken*

Now let's look at finir *(to finish)*:

FINIR *(TO FINISH)* - **PAST CONDITIONAL**			
j'aurais fini	*I would have finished*	nous aurions fini	*we would have finished*
tu aurais fini	*you would have finished*	vous auriez fini	*you would have finished*
il aurait fini	*he would have finished*	ils auraient fini	*they would have finished*
elle aurait fini	*she would have finished*	elles auraient fini	*they would have finished*

Here is vendre *(to sell)*:

VENDRE *(TO SELL)* - **PAST CONDITIONAL**			
j'aurais vendu	*I would have sold*	nous aurions vendu	*we would have sold*
tu aurais vendu	*you would have sold*	vous auriez vendu	*you would have sold*
il aurait vendu	*he would have sold*	ils auraient vendu	*they would have sold*
elle aurait vendu	*she would have sold*	elles auraient vendu	*they would have sold*

And here is faire (*to do, to make*):

FAIRE *(TO DO, TO MAKE)* - **PAST CONDITIONAL**			
j'aurais fait	*I would have done*	nous aurions fait	*we would have done*
tu aurais fait	*you would have done*	vous auriez fait	*you would have done*
il aurait fait	*he would have done*	ils auraient fait	*they would have done*
elle aurait fait	*she would have done*	elles auraient fait	*they would have done*

Also, it's important to mention that the past conditional of devoir (*to have to, must, should*) is usually translated as *should have*: tu aurais dû attendre (*you should have waited*). Notice that the verb following dû is in its infinitive form in French, even though it's in the past tense in English.

Similarly, the past conditional of pouvoir (*can, to be able to*) is usually translated as *could have*: Tu aurais pu attendre. (*You could have waited.*)

Now that we've looked at some examples of verbs that use avoir, let's look at an example of a verb that uses être. Again, remember that the past participle of a verb that uses être must agree in gender and number with the subject.

Here is aller (*to go*) in the past conditional:

ALLER *(TO GO)* - **PAST CONDITIONAL**			
je serais allé(e)	*I would have gone*	nous serions allé(e)s	*we would have gone*
tu serais allé(e)	*you would have gone*	vous seriez allé(e)(s)	*you would have gone*

ALLER *(TO GO)* - **PAST CONDITIONAL**			
il serait allé	*he would have gone*	ils seraient allés	*they would have gone*
elle serait allée	*she would have gone*	elles seraient allées	*they would have gone*

In both French and English, the past conditional is often used with the word si (*if*) plus the past perfect (which you already know how to form!).

J'aurais fait un gâteau pour son anniversaire si j'avais été à la maison.
I would have made a cake for his birthday if I had been (at) home.

Vous seriez resté à la maison si elle avait été là.
You would have stayed (at) home if she had been there.

✎ Work Out 1

Translate the following sentences into French.

1. *She would have gone* _____.

2. *We would have finished* _____.

3. *I should have studied* _____.

4. *You (infml.) would have waited* _____.

5. *They (m.) could have finished* _____.

ANSWER KEY:
1. **Elle serait allée.** 2. **Nous aurions fini./On aurait fini.** 3. **J'aurais dû étudier.** 4. **Tu aurais attendu.**
5. **Ils auraient pu finir.**

Phrase Builder 2

10C Lesson 10 Phrase Builder 2 (CD 8, Track 15)

outdoor activities	les activités (f.) de plein air
to go to the beach	aller à la plage
to sunbathe (lit., to take a bath of sun)	prendre un bain de soleil
to make a sandcastle	faire un château de sable
to go scuba diving	faire de la plongée sous-marine
to go jogging	faire du jogging
to ride a stationary bike (lit., to do stationary bike)	faire du vélo d'appartement
to stay in shape	rester en forme
to go on a picnic (lit., to do a picnic)	faire un pique-nique
to play hide and seek (lit., to play hide-hide)	jouer à cache-cache
to roll the dice	lancer les dés
TV series	le feuilleton (télévisé)
sitcom	la comédie de situation
to spend time with friends	passer du temps avec des amis

Take It Further

If you want to talk about hobbies and leisure activities, a good word to know is temps (time, weather).

Temps is used in a variety of French phrases and expressions dealing with time. Here are some examples:

to spend time	passer du temps
hobby, pastime (lit., the spend-time)	le passe-temps

free time	le temps libre
halftime (of a game)	la mi-temps
long time	longtemps
full-time	à plein temps
part-time	à temps partiel
for how long? (lit., since how much time?)	depuis combien de temps ?
from time to time	de temps en temps
to have (the) time	avoir le temps
to waste time (lit., to lose time)	perdre du temps
to waste your time	perdre votre/ton temps
It is time to .../Now is the time to ...	Il est temps de...

il y a longtemps
a long time ago

Avez-vous le temps d'aller avec moi ?
Do you have time to go with me?

J'ai le temps. Je n'ai pas le temps.
I have time. I don't have time.

Nous aurions joué au tennis si nous avions eu le temps.
We would have played tennis if we had had the time.

Il perd son temps.
He's wasting his time.

Il est temps de te reposer.
It's time for you to relax.

✎ Phrase Practice 2

Choose the correct translation of the following English words.

1. *beach*
   a. la plage
   b. le château de sable
   c. la plongée sous-marine
   d. le pique-nique

2. *scuba diving*
   a. le vélo d'appartement
   b. la plongée sous-marine
   c. le cache-cache
   d. le feuilleton

3. *TV series*
   a. les dés
   b. le feuilleton
   c. la comédie de situation
   d. le vélo d'appartement

4. *hide and seek*
   a. la comédie de situation
   b. les dés
   c. le cache-cache
   d. le vélo d'appartement

ANSWER KEY:
1. a; 2. b; 3. b; 4. c

✎ Word Recall

Replace each word with its opposite. For example, if one of the words was **jour**, you would write **nuit**.

1. droite _____

2. près _____

3. ici _____

4. toujours _____

ANSWER KEY:
1. **gauche** (*right and left*); 2. **loin** (*near and far*); 3. **là** (*here and there*); 4. **jamais** (**ne... jamais**) (*always and never*)

Grammar Builder 2
TO PUT

▶ 10D Lesson 10 Grammar Builder 2 (CD 8, Track 16)

Mettre (*to put, to put on*) is an irregular verb. Its conjugation in the present tense is actually very similar to the SST verbs:

METTRE (*TO PUT, TO PUT ON*) - **PRESENT**			
je mets	*I put*	nous mettons	*we put*
tu mets	*you put*	vous mettez	*you put*
il met	*he puts*	ils mettent	*they put*
elle met	*she puts*	elles mettent	*they put*

The past participle of **mettre** is **mis**.

Hier soir il faisait froid, alors j'ai mis mon manteau.
Last night it was cold, so I put on my coat.

The verb **permettre** (*to allow, to permit*) is conjugated in the same way as **mettre**.

✎ Work Out 2
Fill in the blanks with the correct present tense form of **mettre**.

1. **Où** _____ **-vous vos livres ?** (*Where are you putting your books?*)

2. **Tu ne** _____ **pas ton pull.** (*You're not putting on your sweater.*)

3. **Est-ce qu'elle** _____ **l'écharpe ?** (*Is she putting on the scarf?*)

4. Les enfants _____ leurs devoirs sur la table.

   (The children put their homework on the table.)

5. Je _____ mon violon dans ma chambre.

   (I'm putting my violin in my bedroom.)

   ANSWER KEY:
   1. mettez; 2. mets; 3. met; 4. mettent; 5. mets

✎ Drive It Home

Change each verb from the conditional to the past conditional.

1. elle finirait _____

2. elle irait _____

3. elle jouerait _____

4. elle arriverait _____

5. elle vendrait _____

6. elle serait _____

7. elle aurait _____

8. elle ferait _____

9. elle devrait _____

10. elle pourrait _____

   ANSWER KEY:
   1. elle aurait fini; 2. elle serait allée; 3. elle aurait joué; 4. elle serait arrivée; 5. elle aurait vendu;
   6. elle aurait été; 7. elle aurait eu; 8. elle aurait fait; 9. elle aurait dû; 10. elle aurait pu

How Did You Do?

Let's see how you did! By now, you should be able to:

☐ Discuss games and matches
  (Still unsure? Jump back to page 179)

☐ Say *I would have spoken* or *I would have finished*
  (Still unsure? Jump back to page 181)

☐ Discuss outdoor activities
  (Still unsure? Jump back to page 186)

☐ Explain where you *put* something
  (Still unsure? Jump back to page 189)

Lesson 11: Sentences

By the end of this lesson, you will be able to:

☐ Connect two sentences using *who* or *that*

☐ Tell someone that you understand *what* they are saying

Sentence Builder 1

▶ 11A Lesson 11 Sentence Builder 1 (CD 8, Track 17)

We're going to a ski resort (lit., winter sports resort).	**Nous allons à une station de sports d'hiver.**
I'm wearing my ice skates.	**Je porte mes patins à glace.**
I'm going to the bunny slope (lit., beginners' slope).	**Je vais à la piste pour débutants.**

The kids are making a snowman.	**Les enfants font un bonhomme de neige.**
I'm a fan. (sports)	**Je suis un supporteur./Je suis une supportrice.**
I like the commercials at halftime (lit., of halftime).	**J'aime les publicités de la mi-temps.**
This golf course is difficult.	**Ce parcours de golf est difficile.**
I'm looking for a partner.	**Je cherche un partenaire.**
I'm showing my horse in a competition. (lit., I'm presenting my horse at a competition.)	**Je présente mon cheval à un concours.**
Children must wear a helmet to go bike riding (to ride a bike).	**Les enfants doivent porter un casque pour monter à bicyclette.**
I'm having a good time. (I'm having fun.)	**Je m'amuse.**
You shouldn't cheat. (One shouldn't cheat.)	**On ne doit pas tricher.**

Take It Further

If you want to talk about sports in French, then you're going to need to know the word for *ball*. There are actually two words in French for *ball*: **le ballon** and **la balle**. Here's the difference:

la balle	*smaller ball (tennis, table tennis, juggling, etc.)*
le ballon	*larger ball (basketball, volleyball, soccer, etc.)*

You also saw a lot of new words in Sentence Builder 1. Let's take a look at some of them, along with some related words and phrases:

ski resort (lit., a resort of winter sports)	la station de sports d'hiver
ice skate	le patin à glace
trail, slope, track	la piste
beginner	le débutant/la débutante
bunny slope/hill, beginners' slope/hill	la piste pour débutants
snowman	le bonhomme de neige
fan (sports)	le supporteur/la supportrice
commercials	les publicités (f.), les pubs (f.)
golf course	le parcours de golf, le terrain de golf
partner	le partenaire/la partenaire
horse	le cheval
competition, contest	le concours, la compétition
helmet	le casque
to go bike riding, to ride a bike	monter à bicyclette
to cheat	tricher

Also remember that *halftime* is la mi-temps.

✎ Sentence Practice 1

Match the French translations on the left to the correct English phrases on the right.

1. un bonhomme de neige	a. *a fan*
2. un supporteur	b. *a competition*
3. un patin à glace	c. *a helmet*
4. un concours	d. *a snowman*
5. un casque	e. *an ice skate*

ANSWER KEY:
1. d; 2. a; 3. e; 4. b; 5. c

✎ Word Recall

Now match the food terms on the left to the correct French translations on the right.

1. *vegetable*	a. le citron
2. *lemon*	b. le repas
3. *apple*	c. le maïs
4. *corn*	d. le légume
5. *meal*	e. la pomme

ANSWER KEY:
1. d; 2. a; 3. e; 4. c; 5. b

Grammar Builder 1
WHO AND THAT

▶ 11B Lesson 11 Grammar Builder 1 (CD 8, Track 18)

English uses words like *who* and *that* to connect two sentences. For example:

There's the book. I read the book.

You can connect these two sentences with *that* to get:

There's the book **that** *I read.*

As you can see, *that* replaced *the book* from the second sentence: *I read* **the book** became **that** *I read.* In other words, when *that* connects two sentences, it replaces a person or thing from the second sentence. The same is true for *who.*

When they are used to connect two sentences, *who* and *that* are known as "relative pronouns."

The main relative pronouns in French are **qui** and **que**. They connect two sentences, just like in English. Here's how they're used:

1. **Qui** can mean *who* or *that*. It functions as the **subject** of the second sentence. It is usually followed by a verb **without** a subject (so it would be followed by **aime, ai lu, a parlé, s'amuse, lui parlent**, etc.).

2. **Que** (or **qu'**) can mean *whom* or *that*. It functions as the **object** of the second sentence. It is usually followed by a verb **with** a subject (so it would be followed by **Christine aime, j'ai lu, quelqu'un a parlé, elle s'amuse, ils lui parlent**, etc.).

Keep in mind that both **qui** and **que** can refer to either people or things.

Let's first look at an example using **que**:

Voilà le livre. J'ai lu le livre.
There's the book. I read the book.

Voilà le livre que j'ai lu.
There's the book that I read.

In the sentence *I read the book*, *I* is the subject and *the book* is the object. *I* is the subject because it is doing the action of the verb *read*: *I read*. *The book* is the object because it is receiving the action, it is being read. So **que** is used here because it replaces the object of the second sentence: *the book*.

Also notice that **que** is followed by a verb with a subject pronoun (**j'ai lu**). This is true in English as well.

Now here's an example using **qui**:

Je vois le pain. Le pain est sur la table.
I see the bread. The bread is on the table.

Je vois le pain qui est sur la table.
I see the bread that is on the table.

Qui is used here because it replaces the subject of the second sentence: *the bread*. You can also see that in both French and English, **qui** (*who*) is followed by a verb without a subject: **est** (*is*).

This can definitely be a bit confusing at first, but it will get easier with practice. Keeping that in mind, here are some more examples:

C'est la voiture que je conduis.
That's the car that I drive.

Natalie est la fille qui chante bien.
Natalie is the girl who sings well.

In English, you don't always have to use relative pronouns in sentences like this. However, you ***must*** use them in French.

Tu manges le dessert que j'ai fait.
You're eating the dessert that I made.
(You're eating the dessert I made.)

Marie est la fille qu'il aime.
Marie is the girl that he loves.
(Marie is the girl he loves.)

Finally, qui can be preceded by a preposition when it refers to a person or people. In this case, it translates as *whom* or *whose*.

à qui	to whom
avec qui	with whom
chez qui	at whose house
de qui	from whom, of whom, about whom
pour qui	for whom

Note that a preposition + qui is usually followed by a verb **with** a subject, in both French and English.

C'est la femme pour qui je travaille.
She's (lit., It's) the woman for whom I work.

La dame à qui vous parlez s'appelle Sophie.
The woman (lit., lady) to whom you are speaking is named Sophie.

C'est le jeune homme avec qui elle sort.
It's the young man she goes out with.
(lit., It's the young man with whom she goes out.)

You can also use a preposition + qui as a question: Avec qui ? (*With whom?*), Chez qui ? (*At whose house?*), etc.

✎ Work Out 1

Fill in the blanks with **qui** or **que**.

1. Voici le garçon_____ est tombé. (*Here is the boy that fell.*)

2. Voilà la jeune fille avec _____ Jean joue au tennis.

   (*There is the young girl with whom Jean plays tennis.*)

3. Je n'ai pas vu le livre _____ Christine cherche.

   (*I didn't see the book that Christine is looking for.*)

4. Donnez-moi le verre_____ est sur la table, s'il vous plaît.

   (*Give me the glass that is on the table, please.*)

5. Voici les cartes _____ j'ai. (*Here are the cards that I have.*)

   ANSWER KEY:
   1. qui; 2. qui; 3. que; 4. qui; 5. que

Sentence Builder 2

▶ 11C Lesson 11 Sentence Builder 2 (CD 8, Track 19)

We go to the opera from time to time.	Nous allons à l'opéra de temps en temps.
My nephew is a ballet dancer.	Mon neveu est danseur classique. (Mon neveu est danseur de ballet.)
I'm a lifeguard.	Je suis maître-nageur.
They like bus tours.	Ils aiment les excursions en autocar.
We visited the castles of the Loire (Valley).	Nous avons visité les châteaux de la Loire.
I (really) like to spend time with friends.	J'aime bien passer du temps avec des amis.

I (really) like to tinker. (I really like to fix things/fiddle with things.)	J'aime bien bricoler.
I collect butterflies.	Je collectionne les papillons.
I (really) like to relax.	J'aime bien me reposer.

Take It Further

Okay, now that you've been introduced to the relative pronouns qui and que, let's talk more about the question qu'est-ce que ? (*what?*).

The relative pronoun que is actually in qu'est-ce que? That question is composed of qu'est-ce, which literally means *what is this* or *what is it* and is simply a way of forming a question in French, plus que.

So qu'est-ce que literally translates as *what is this that* or *what is it that*:

Qu'est-ce que tu dis ?
What are you saying? (lit., What is this that you're saying?)

However, now you know that que is usually followed by a verb with a subject. So what do you do if you want to ask *what?* followed by a verb without a subject? In that case, you have to use qu'est-ce qui... ? For example, remember the phrase from Unit 2:

Qu'est-ce qui t'est arrivé ?
What happened to you?

Here's another common expression that uses qu'est-ce qui:

Qu'est-ce qui se passe ?
What's going on?/What's happening?

Finally, you saw a lot of new words for talking about hobbies and leisure activities in Sentence Builder 2. Let's review:

opera	l'opéra (*m.*)
ballet dancer	le danseur/la danseuse de ballet, le danseur/la danseuse classique, la ballerine
lifeguard	la maître-nageur, le sauveteur
bus tour	l'excursion (*f.*) en autocar
to tinker, to fiddle with things, to fix/repair things	bricoler
to collect	collectionner
butterfly	le papillon

✎ Sentence Practice 2

Translate the following sentences into French.

1. *I like to go to the opera.* _____

2. *I like bus tours.* _____

3. *I like to visit the castles.* _____

4. *I like to go to a ski resort.* _____

5. *I like to go to the bunny slope.* _____

ANSWER KEY:

1. J'aime aller à l'opéra. 2. J'aime les excursions en autocar. 3. J'aime visiter les châteaux. 4. J'aime aller à une station de sports d'hiver. 5. J'aime aller à la piste pour débutants.

✎ Word Recall

Translate the following menu into English.

le potage _____

les coquilles Saint-Jacques _____

la purée de pommes de terre _____

la glace à la fraise _____

la tisane _____

ANSWER KEY:
soup
scallops
mashed potatoes
strawberry ice cream
herbal tea

Grammar Builder 2
WHAT AS RELATIVE PRONOUN

▶ 11D Lesson 11 Grammar Builder 2 (CD 8, Track 20)

In English, the word *what* can also be used as a relative pronoun, but in a different way from *who* and *that*. Here is an example:

I see what is on the table.

Notice that *what* is used as a way of referring to something without explicitly identifying or naming it. You don't know *what* is on the table—as opposed to a sentence like *I see the bread that is on the table,* where you know *bread* is on the table.

In French, the relative pronouns **ce qui** and **ce que** are the equivalent of *what* as a relative pronoun in English. Here's how they're used:

1. **Ce qui** acts as a subject (***what** is on the table*). As a result, it is usually followed by a verb without a subject (such as *is*).

2. **Ce que** (or **ce qu'**) acts as a direct object (***what** you are saying*, or, in other words, *you are saying **what***). As a result, it is usually followed by a verb with a subject (such as *you are saying*).

Je vois ce qui est sur la table.
I see what is on the table.

Je comprends ce que tu dis.
I understand what you are saying.

Marc dit toujours ce qu'il pense.
Marc always says what he's thinking.

✎ Work Out 2

Insert **ce qui** or **ce que** in the sentences below.

1. **Il n'aime pas** _____ **est arrivé à Paul.** (*He doesn't like what happened to Paul.*)

2. **Je ne sais pas** _____ **vous faites.** (*I don't know what you're doing.*)

3. **J'adore** _____ **Sophie chante.** (*I love what Sophie is singing.*)

4. **Apportez-moi** _____ **est dans la cuisine.** (*Bring me what is in the kitchen.*)

ANSWER KEY:
1. ce qui; 2. ce que; 3. ce que; 4. ce qui

✎ Drive It Home

Although this may seem repetitive and easy, make sure to read through each
sentence carefully and then say it out loud.

A. Fill in the blanks with qui.

1. **Nous lisons un livre** _____ **est très intéressant.** (*We're reading a book that is very interesting.*)

2. **Denise a une jupe** _____ **est très longue.** (*Denise has a skirt that is very long.*)

3. **Voici un homme** _____ **est très fier.** (*Here is a man who is very proud.*)

4. **Elle aime le restaurant** _____ **est très loin.** (*She likes the restaurant that is very far.*)

5. **Nous allons à la piste** _____ **est très difficile.** (*We're going to the slope that is very difficult.*)

B. Now fill in the blanks with que.

1. **Nous lisons un livre** _____ **tu aimes.** (*We're reading a book that you like.*)

2. **Denise a une jupe** _____ **tu aimes.** (*Denise has a skirt that you like.*)

3. **Voici un homme** _____ **tu aimes.** (*Here is a man that you like.*)

4. **Elle aime le restaurant** _____ **tu aimes.** (*She likes the restaurant that you like.*)

5. **Nous allons à la piste** _____ **tu aimes.** (*We're going to the slope that you like.*)

   ANSWER KEY:
   A. all qui
   B. all que

How Did You Do?

Let's see how you did! By now, you should be able to:

☐ Connect two sentences using *who* and *that*
(Still unsure? Jump back to page 194)

☐ Tell someone that you understand *what* they are saying
(Still unsure? Jump back to page 201)

Lesson 12: Conversations

By the end of this lesson, you will be able to:

☐ Say *with which* or *in which*

☐ Order someone to *Hurry up!*

☐ Say you had a good time

🔊 Conversation 1

Marc recently had a Super Bowl party at his house and he's upset that his friend Paul didn't come.

▶ 12A Lesson 12 Conversation 1 (CD 9, Track 1)

Marc :	Tu n'es pas venu regarder le match de football (américain), le plus important de l'année, le « Super Bowl ». Qu'est-ce qui est arrivé ?
Paul :	Je suis désolé. J'aurais voulu venir si j'avais eu le temps, mais j'ai dû finir du travail chez moi.
Marc :	Tu aurais dû voir le match. C'était extraordinaire, surtout quand ils ont marqué le premier but.
Paul :	J'ai vu seulement une moitié du match.

Marc :	Laquelle ?
Paul :	La deuxième moitié, quand le joueur a envoyé le ballon très loin et notre équipe a gagné !
Marc :	Est-ce que tu avais regardé les publicités à la mi-temps ? Elles étaient si drôles!
Paul :	Pendant que je travaillais, j'ai vu la publicité qui montrait tous les grands chevaux qui parlaient.
Marc :	De toute façon, il y a toujours le match de basket-ball dimanche prochain et cette fois, tout le monde vient chez toi !

Marc:	You didn't come watch the football game, the most important (one) of the year, the "Super Bowl." What happened?
Paul:	I'm sorry. I would have wanted to come if I had had the time, but I had to finish some work at home.
Marc:	You should have seen the game. It was extraordinary, especially when they scored the first goal.
Paul:	I only saw one half of the game.
Marc:	Which one?
Paul:	The second half, when the player threw the ball very far and our team won!
Marc:	Had you watched the commercials at halftime? They were so funny!
Paul:	While I was working, I saw the commercial that showed all the big horses who were talking.
Marc:	At any rate, there's always the basketball game next Sunday and this time, everybody's coming to your house!

(II)

Take It Further

Le but is a general term that means *goal* or *target*. Perhaps since American football isn't really a big sport in France, the word for *touchdown* is simply le touchdown.

And of course, since we're talking about goals, we have to mention another new word that you saw in the dialogue: **marquer** (*to score*).

Finally, note that **si** can mean both *if* and *so*, as in **si drôle** (*so funny*), and the phrase **pendant que** means *while*.

✎ Conversation Practice 1

Unscramble the following phrases from Conversation 1 and then translate them into English.

1. **aurais / voir / dû / tu / match / le** _____

   _____

2. **les / avais / publicités / regardé / tu** _____

   _____

3. **avais / le / eu / temps / j'** _____

   _____

4. **j' / venir / voulu / aurais** _____

   _____

5. **qui / arrivé / qu'est-ce / est / ?** _____

   _____

ANSWER KEY:
1. **tu aurais dû voir le match** (*you should have seen the game/match*); 2. **tu avais regardé les publicités** (*you had watched the commercials*); 3. **j'avais eu le temps** (*I had had the time*); 4. **j'aurais voulu venir** (*I would have wanted to come*); 5. **Qu'est-ce qui est arrivé ?** (*What happened?*)

✎ Word Recall

Translate the following daily routine into French.

1. *I get up.* _____

2. *I wash up.* _____

3. *I get dressed.* _____

4. *I go to bed.* _____

ANSWER KEY:
1. Je me lève. 2. Je me lave. 3. Je m'habille. 4. Je me couche.

Grammar Builder 1
WHICH

▶ 12B Lesson 12 Grammar Builder 1 (CD 9, Track 2)

Another relative pronoun in French is **lequel** (*which*).

Lequel is used after a preposition (**dans**, **avec**, etc.) and acts as the *which* in the phrases *with which, for which, in which*, etc. in English.

Lequel must agree in gender and number with the noun it is referring to. Here are its forms:

	SINGULAR	PLURAL
Masculine	lequel	lesquels
Feminine	laquelle	lesquelles

Let's look at an example using **le crayon** (*pencil*) and the preposition **avec** (*with*):

Où est le crayon avec lequel j'écrivais ?
Where's the pencil with which I was writing?

In this case, *which* refers to the masculine noun **crayon** (the item *with which* you were writing), so you need to use the masculine singular form **lequel**.

Here is another example, this time using **la maison** (*the house*) and the preposition **dans** (*in*):

Voici la maison dans laquelle nous habitions.
Here's the house in which we used to live.

In this case, *which* refers to **la maison** (the place *in which* you used to live), so you need to use the feminine singular form **laquelle**.

Also note that sometimes **où** (*where*) can be used instead of **dans lequel**. The same is true in English.

Voici la maison dans laquelle nous habitions.
Here's the house in which we used to live.

Voici la maison où nous habitions.
Here's the house where we used to live.

Finally, as you saw in the dialogue, **lequel** can be used as a question. When used as a question, it can appear without a preposition. For instance, if someone says **J'ai lu le livre.** (*I read the book.*), you could ask **Lequel ?** (*Which one?*). Of course, it can also be used **with** a preposition in a question. If someone says **J'écris avec le crayon.** (*I'm writing with the pencil.*), you could ask **Avec lequel ?** (*With which one?*).

Another relative pronoun in French is **dont**. **Dont** is typically used to replace de (*of*) or the partitive (**du**, **de la**, etc.) + noun (person or thing). As a result, it literally translates as *of which* or *of whom*, although it doesn't always translate that way when used.

For example, instead of saying **Voici le stylo. J'ai besoin du stylo.** (*Here is the pen. I need the pen.*) you can say:

Voici le stylo dont j'ai besoin.
Here's the pen I need. (lit., Here's the pen of which I have need.)

In this case, **dont** replaced **du stylo** in the second sentence.

Note that **dont** can also be used to indicate possession, in which case it means *whose*. Instead of saying, for example, **C'est le mari. Sa femme est actrice.** (*That's the husband. His wife is an actress.*) you could say:

C'est le mari dont la femme est actrice.
That's the husband whose wife is an actress.

Work Out 1

Choose the correct relative pronoun to complete the sentence. Pay close attention to the English translations.

1. **Marie est la petite fille** _____ **j'ai parlé.**

   (*Marie is the little girl of whom I spoke.*)

2. **Voici le papier sur** _____ **j'ai écrit.** (*Here is the paper on which I wrote.*)

3. C'est le film _____ j'ai peur.

   (This is the movie of which I'm afraid.)

4. Où est la salle dans _____ j'ai dansé ?

   (Where is the room in which I danced?)

   ANSWER KEY:
   1. dont; 2. lequel; 3. dont; 4. laquelle

❝ Conversation 2

Martine and Donna are discussing what they did during summer vacation.

▶ 12C Lesson 12 Conversation 2 (CD 9, Track 3)

Martine :	Dis-moi ce que tu as fait pendant les vacances cet été. Je sais bien que tu as fait quelque chose d'extraordinaire, comme toujours !
Donna :	Tu sais que j'adore voyager avec mes amis, mais ils avaient décidé d'aller faire du camping dans les montagnes. Je serais allée avec eux, mais franchement, je voulais aller à la plage.
Martine :	Alors, qu'est-ce que tu as fait ?
Donna :	J'ai fait ce qui me plaît. Je suis allée au Mexique.
Martine :	Avec qui as-tu voyagé ?
Donna :	J'y suis allée avec Claire et Dominique, les deux sœurs dont le père est le meilleur ami de mon père.
Martine :	Ah, oui, les filles qui sont dans tes photos de l'année dernière.
Donna :	Il y avait beaucoup à faire ; nous avons nagé et nous étions à la plage tous les jours, en train de jouer au volley-ball.
Martine :	Tu es toute bronzée, ma chère !
Donna :	Eh bien, qu'est-ce que tu as fait l'été dernier ?
Martine :	Mon mari et moi, nous avons préparé un beau séjour en France. Ce qui me rend heureuse, c'est d'être à Paris ! C'est la ville que j'adore.

Martine:	Tell me what you did during vacation this summer. I definitely know that you did something extraordinary, as always!
Donna:	You know that I love to travel with my friends, but they had decided to go camping in the mountains. I would have gone with them, but frankly, I wanted to go to the beach.
Martine:	So, what did you do?
Donna:	I did what I want (lit., I did what pleases me). I went to Mexico.
Martine:	With whom did you travel?
Donna:	I went there with Claire and Dominique, the two sisters whose father is my father's best friend.
Martine:	Oh, yes, the girls who are in your photos from last year.
Donna:	There was a lot to do; we went swimming and we were at the beach every day, playing volleyball.
Martine:	You're all tan, my dear!
Donna:	Well, what did you do last summer?
Martine:	My husband and I prepared a beautiful trip to France. What makes me happy, it's to be in Paris! It's the city that I love.

Take It Further

Être en train de is a very useful expression to know. It basically means *to be in the middle of* or *to be in the process of*. It can also be translated as *to be* + the *-ing* form of a verb (*to be playing, to be doing*, etc.).

To use it, simply say:

form of **être** + **en train de** + verb in the infinitive

For example:

Je suis en train de jouer au volley-ball.
I'm in the middle of playing volleyball.

Je ne peux pas venir, je suis en train de faire mes devoirs.
I can't come, I'm doing my homework.

Elle était en train de tricher.
She was cheating.

Note that **en train de** doesn't have to immediately follow **être**:

Nous étions à la plage tous les jours, en train de jouer au volley-ball.
We were at the beach every day, playing volleyball.

Il est là-bas, en train de faire du yoga.
He's over there, doing yoga.

In the dialogue, you also saw the reflexive verb **se rendre**. It means *to surrender*, but it can mean a variety of other things as well, depending on what follows the verb.

to make oneself happy	se rendre heureux/heureuse
to make oneself sick	se rendre malade
to realize, to notice (to make oneself aware)	se rendre compte (de)
to go to, to take oneself to (a place)	se rendre à (+ location)
to give in to, to yield to	se rendre à (+ evidence, an argument, etc.)

Finally, you saw some other new vocabulary in the dialogue:

frankly, honestly	franchement
trip, stay, sojourn	le séjour
tan, tanned (adjective)	bronzé/bronzée

A related verb is **bronzer**, which means *to tan* or *to get a tan.*

✎ Conversation Practice 2

Fill in the blanks in the following sentences based on Conversation 2.

1. les filles _____ sont dans tes photos. (*the girls who are in your photos*)

2. Dis-moi_____ tu as fait. (*Tell me what you did.*)

3. J'ai fait _____ me plaît. (*I did what I want.*)

4. Tu sais_____ j'adore voyager. (*You know that I love to travel.*)

5. Les deux sœurs_____ le père est le meilleur ami de mon père.

(*The two sisters whose father is my father's best friend.*)

ANSWER KEY:
1. qui; 2. ce que; 3. ce qui; 4. que; 5. dont

✎ Word Recall

Find the correct match for each French word.

1. le magasin	a. *shoe*
2. le chapeau	b. *hat*
3. la chemise	c. *sock*
4. la chaussure	d. *shirt*
5. la chaussette	e. *store*

ANSWER KEY:
1. e; 2. b; 3. d; 4. a; 5. c

Grammar Builder 2
THE IMPERATIVE AND PAST TENSE OF REFLEXIVE VERBS

▶ 12D Lesson 12 Grammar Builder 2 (CD 9, Track 4)

You first learned about reflexive verbs in *Essential French* and studied them more in-depth in Unit 2 of *Intermediate French*.

As a review, here is the full conjugation of the reflexive verb se laver (*to wash oneself, to wash up*) in the present tense:

SE LAVER (*TO WASH ONESELF, TO WASH UP*) - **PRESENT**			
je me lave	*I wash myself*	nous nous lavons	*we wash ourselves*
tu te laves	*you wash yourself*	vous vous lavez	*you wash yourselves (or you wash yourself, fml.)*
il se lave	*he washes himself (or it washes itself)*	ils se lavent	*they wash themselves*
elle se lave	*she washes herself (or it washes itself)*	elles se lavent	*they wash themselves*

And here are some example sentences with reflexive verbs in the present tense:

Je m'amuse.
I'm having a good time. (I'm having fun.)

Je ne me dépêche pas.
I do not hurry.

If you want to use a reflexive verb in the imperative—in other words, if you want
to use the verb in a command or strong request—do the following:

verb in the imperative + hyphen (-) + reflexive pronoun

To review the imperative, see Lesson 17 in Unit 5 of *Intermediate French*.

Here are some examples:

Amusez-vous bien !
Have a (very) good time! (Have a lot of fun!)

Dépêchons-nous !
Let's hurry!

Note that, in the imperative, the te reflexive pronoun becomes toi.

Amuse-toi bien!
Have a (very) good time! (Have a lot of fun!)

Dépêche-toi !
Hurry up!

If you want to use a reflexive verb in the past tense, do the following:

reflexive pronoun + present tense of être + past participle of the verb

Note that **all** reflexive verbs form the past tense with être.

Let's look at an example.

Here's the full conjugation of se laver in the past tense. Remember that the past participles of verbs that use être must agree in gender and number with the subject.

SE LAVER *(TO WASH ONESELF, TO WASH UP)* - **PAST**			
je me suis lavé(e)	*I washed myself*	nous nous sommes lavé(e)s	*we washed ourselves*
tu t'es lavé(e)	*you washed yourself*	vous vous êtes lavé(e)(s)	*you washed yourselves (or you washed yourself, fml.)*
il s'est lavé	*he washed himself (or it washed itself)*	ils se sont lavés	*they washed themselves*
elle s'est lavée	*she washed herself (or it washed itself)*	elles se sont lavées	*they washed themselves*

Elle s'est lavée.
She washed herself.

Mes amis se sont amusés.
My friends had a good time. (My friends had fun.)

However, there are certain times when the past participle of a reflexive verb does **not** agree with the subject. If a reflexive verb's past participle is followed by a direct object, then the past participle does not agree with the subject:

Elle s'est lavé la figure.
She washed her face. (lit., She washed the face herself.)

Ils se sont brossé les dents.
They brushed their teeth. (lit., They brushed the teeth themselves.)

In these sentences, la figure (*the face*) and les dents (*f.*) (*the teeth*) are direct objects that follow the past participles lavé and brossé. As a result, lavé and brossé retain their original form and do not agree with the subject (elle or ils) in gender or number.

Also note that French uses le, la, or les instead of a possessive (ma, mes, ta, tes, etc.) when expressing an action with a part of the body: Elle s'est lavé la figure. Saying Elle s'est lavé sa figure would be incorrect. This applies to all verbs, not just reflexive ones: Je lève la main. (*I raise my hand.*)

Finally, keep in mind that since reflexive verbs use être in the past tense, they also use être in the future perfect, past perfect, and past conditional. (Note that the direct object exception regarding past participles applies to those tenses as well.)

For instance, here is se laver in the future perfect:

SE LAVER *(TO WASH ONESELF, TO WASH UP)* - **FUTURE PERFECT**			
je me serai lavé(e)	*I will have washed myself*	nous nous serons lavé(e)s	*we will have washed ourselves*
tu te seras lavé(e)	*you will have washed yourself*	vous vous serez lavé(e)(s)	*you will have washed yourselves* (or *you will have washed yourself, fml.*)
il se sera lavé	*he will have washed himself* (or *it will have washed itself*)	ils se seront lavés	*they will have washed themselves*
elle se sera lavée	*she will have washed herself* (or *it will have washed itself*)	elles se seront lavées	*they will have washed themselves*

To review the future perfect and past perfect, see Lesson 9 of Unit 3 in this book. To review the past conditional, see Lesson 10 of Unit 3.

✎ Work Out 2

Translate the following sentences into English.

1. **Elle s'était levée.** _____

2. **Tu t'es habillé.** _____

3. **Ils se seraient couchés.** _____

4. **Levez-vous !** _____

ANSWER KEY:
1. *She had gotten up. (She had risen.)* 2. *You got dressed. (You dressed yourself.)* 3. *They would have gone to bed. (They would have lain down.)* 4. *Get up! (Rise!)*

✎ Drive It Home

A. Fill in the blanks with the correct form of lequel.

1. **Où est la table sur** _____ **j'écrivais ?**

   (Where is the table on which I was writing?)

2. **Où est le stylo avec** _____ **j'écrivais ?**

   (Where is the pen with which I was writing?)

3. *3.* **Où sont les cahiers** *(m.)* **dans** _____ **j'écrivais ?**

   (Where are the notebooks in which I was writing?)

4. **Où sont les choses** *(f.)* **avec** _____ **j'écrivais ?**

   (Where are the things with which I was writing?)

B. Now fill in the blanks with dont.

1. Voici l'ordinateur _____ j'ai besoin. (*Here is the computer I need.*)

2. Voici le footballeur _____ j'ai peur. (*Here is the soccer player I'm afraid of.*)

3. Voici la prof _____ le mari est mon cousin. (*Here is the professor whose husband is my cousin.*)

4. Voici le livre _____ vous avez parlé. (*Here is the book of which you spoke.*)

C. Finally, change the following reflexive verbs to the past tense.

1. Elle s'amuse. _____

2. Elle se couche. _____

3. Elle s'habille. _____

4. Elle se lève. _____

5. Elle se lave les mains. _____

ANSWER KEY:
A. 1. laquelle; 2. lequel; 3. lesquels; 4. lesquelles
B. all dont
C. 1. Elle s'est amusée. 2. Elle s'est couchée. 3. Elle s'est habillée. 4. Elle s'est levée. 5. Elle s'est lavé les mains.

Tip

In one of the Tips in Unit 1, you saw how to use more than one pronoun in a sentence. Now let's look at how to use more than one pronoun in the imperative.

In the positive imperative, use the following order of pronouns:

ORDER OF PRONOUNS IN THE POSITIVE IMPERATIVE				
positive imperative form of verb	le la les	me (moi) te (toi) lui nous vous leur	y	en

Donnez-le-lui.
Give it to him.

Donnez-leur-en.
Give them some.

Remember that the direct and indirect object pronoun me becomes moi in the positive imperative. Also, the direct object, indirect object, and reflexive pronoun te becomes toi in the positive imperative.

Montrez-moi.
Show me.

However, when moi and toi are followed by en or y, they become m' and t'.

Montrez-m'en.
Show me some.

In the negative imperative, just use the same order for sentences that you learned in the Unit 1 Tip, bracketed by ne and pas.

Ne le lui donnez pas.
Don't give it to him.

Ne m'en montrez pas.
Don't show me any.

How Did You Do?

Let's see how you did! By now, you should be able to:

☐ Say *with which* or *in which*
(Still unsure? Jump back to page 207)

☐ Order someone to *Hurry up!*
(Still unsure? Jump back to page 214)

☐ Say you *had a good time*
(Still unsure? Jump back to page 214)

Unit 3 Essentials

Don't forget to go to **www.livinglanguage.com/languagelab** to access your free online tools for this lesson: audiovisual flashcards, and interactive games and quizzes.

Vocabulary Essentials

SPORTS

sports		horseback riding	
soccer		fishing	
(American) football		golf	
swimming		skiing	
gymnastics		snowboarding	
track, track and field			

[Pg. 160] (If you're stuck, visit this page to review!)

HOBBIES AND OTHER LEISURE ACTIVITIES

hobbies, pastimes		movies	
chess		vacation	
entertainment		dance class	
play (at a theater)		reading	
theater		painting	

[Pg. 169]

Advanced French

SPORTS PHRASES

to play a sport, to do a sport	
to play a game/match	
to win a game/match	
to lose a game/match	
spectator	
end of the game/match	
final score	
to kick (lit., to give a kick)	
rugby team	
to run the marathon	
to ride a horse, to go horseback riding	

[Pg. 179]

MORE LEISURE ACTIVITIES

outdoor activities	
to go to the beach	
to sunbathe	
to go scuba diving	
to go jogging	
to stay in shape	
to go on a picnic	
to play hide and seek	
to roll the dice	
TV series	
to spend time with friends	

[Pg. 186]

SPORTS EXPRESSIONS

We're going to a ski resort (lit., winter sports resort).	
I'm a fan. (sports)	
I like the commercials at halftime.	
I'm having a good time./I'm having fun.	
You shouldn't cheat./One shouldn't cheat.	

[Pg. 191]

ACTIVITIES EXPRESSIONS

I'm a lifeguard.	
They like bus tours.	
I really like to spend time with my friends.	
I really like to relax.	

[Pg. 198]

Grammar Essentials

FUTURE PERFECT

1. To form the future perfect, use the future tense of **avoir** or **être** + past participle of the verb.

2. The future perfect is equivalent to *will have* + past participle in English.

PARLER *(TO SPEAK, TO TALK)* - **FUTURE PERFECT**			
I will have spoken	j'aurai parlé	*we will have spoken*	nous aurons parlé
you will have spoken (infml.)	tu auras parlé	*you will have spoken (pl./fml.)*	vous aurez parlé
he will have spoken	il aura parlé	*they will have spoken (m.)*	ils auront parlé
she will have spoken	elle aura parlé	*they will have spoken (f.)*	elles auront parlé

PAST PERFECT

1. To form the past perfect, use the imperfect tense of avoir or être + past participle of the verb.

2. The past perfect is equivalent to *had* + past participle in English.

FINIR *(TO FINISH)* - **PAST PERFECT**			
I had finished	j'avais fini	*we had finished*	nous avions fini
you had finished (infml.)	tu avais fini	*you had finished (pl./fml.)*	vous aviez fini
he had finished	il avait fini	*they had finished (m.)*	ils avaient fini
she had finished	elle avait fini	*they had finished (f.)*	elles avaient fini

PAST CONDITIONAL

1. To form the past conditional, use the conditional of avoir or être + past participle of the verb.

2. The future perfect is equivalent to *would have* + verb in English.

3. The past conditional of devoir is usually translated as *should have*. The past conditional of pouvoir is usually translated as *could have*.

VENDRE *(TO SELL)* - **PAST CONDITIONAL**			
I would have sold	j'aurais vendu	*we would have sold*	nous aurions vendu
you would have sold (infml.)	tu aurais vendu	*you would have sold (pl./fml.)*	vous auriez vendu
he would have sold	il aurait vendu	*they would have sold (m.)*	ils auraient vendu
she would have sold	elle aurait vendu	*they would have sold (f.)*	elles auraient vendu

ALLER *(TO GO)* - **PAST CONDITIONAL**			
I would have gone	je serais allé(e)	*we would have gone*	nous serions allé(e)s
you would have gone (infml.)	tu serais allé(e)	*you would have gone (pl./fml.)*	vous seriez allé(e)(s)
he would have gone	il serait allé	*they would have gone (m.)*	ils seraient allés
she would have gone	elle serait allée	*they would have gone (f.)*	elles seraient allées

RELATIVE PRONOUN QUI

1. **Qui** can mean *who* or *that*.
2. **Qui** replaces the ***subject*** in the second sentence.
3. It is usually followed directly by a verb (**qui** is the subject).
4. **Qui** can be preceded by a preposition when it refers to a person or people. In this case, it translates as *whom* or *whose*. These phrases are usually followed by a verb **with** a subject.

to whom	à qui
with whom	avec qui
at whose house	chez qui
from whom, of whom, about whom	de qui
for whom	pour qui

RELATIVE PRONOUN QUE/QU'

1. **Que** (or **qu'**) can mean *whom* or *that*.
2. **Que** (or **qu'**) replaces the ***object*** of the second sentence.
3. It is usually followed by a verb **with** a subject.

RELATIVE PRONOUN CE QUI

1. **Ce qui** is the equivalent of *what* as a relative pronoun in English.
2. **Ce qui** acts as a subject.
3. It is usually followed by a verb without a subject.

RELATIVE PRONOUN CE QUE/CE QU'

1. **Ce que/Ce qu'** is the equivalent of *what* as a relative pronoun in English.
2. **Ce que/Ce qu'** acts as a direct object.
3. It is usually followed by a verb with a subject.

RELATIVE PRONOUN LEQUEL

1. Lequel means *which*.
2. It is used after a preposition.

Here are its forms:

	SINGULAR	PLURAL
Masculine	lequel	lesquels
Feminine	laquelle	lesquelles

RELATIVE PRONOUN DONT

1. Dont is typically used to replace de (*of*) or the partitive (du, de la, etc.) + noun (person or thing).
2. It literally translates as *of which* or *of whom*.
3. It can also be used to indicate possession, in which case it means *whose*.

IMPERATIVE OF REFLEXIVE VERBS

1. To form the imperative of reflexive verbs, use the verb in the imperative + hyphen (-) + reflexive pronoun
2. In the imperative, the reflexive pronoun te becomes toi.

PAST TENSE OF REFLEXIVE VERBS

1. To form a reflexive verb in the past tense, use reflexive pronoun + present tense of être + past participle of the verb.
2. All reflexive verbs use être in the past tense.

3. If the reflexive verb's past participle is followed by a direct object, then the past participle does not agree with the subject.

SE LAVER (TO WASH ONESELF, TO WASH UP) - PAST			
I washed myself	je me suis lavé(e)	we washed ourselves	nous nous sommes lavé(e)s
you washed yourself	tu t'es lavé(e)	you washed yourselves (or you washed yourself, fml.)	vous vous êtes lavé(e)(s)
he washed himself (or it washed itself)	il s'est lavé	they washed themselves	ils se sont lavés
she washed herself (or it washed itself)	elle s'est lavée	they washed themselves	elles se sont lavées

OTHER VERBS

METTRE (TO PUT, TO PUT ON) - PRESENT			
I put	je mets	we put	nous mettons
you put (infml.)	tu mets	you put (pl./fml.)	vous mettez
he puts	il met	they put (m.)	ils mettent
she puts	elle met	they put (f.)	elles mettent
Past Participle: mis			

Unit 3 Quiz

Now let's see how you did in Unit 3!

After you've answered all of the questions, don't forget to score your quiz to see how you did. If you find that you need to go back and review, please do so before continuing on to Unit 4.

A. Translate these sports into English.

1. **la natation** _____

2. **l'athlétisme** _____

3. **l'équitation** _____

4. **le surf sur neige** _____

5. **la pêche** _____

B. Now fill in the blanks with qui, que, or dont.

1. **C'est la fille** _____ **est partie.** (*It's the girl who left.*)

2. **C'est la fille** _____ **tu as aimée.** (*It's the girl that you loved.*)

3. **C'est la fille** _____ **tu as parlé.** (*It's the girl of whom you spoke.*)

4. **C'est la fille avec** _____ **tu as parlé.** (*It's the girl with whom you spoke.*)

5. **C'est la fille** _____ **le père est acteur.** (*It's the girl whose father is an actor.*)

C. Now translate these sentences into English.

1. Nous avons gagné le match.

   _____

2. C'est la fin du match.

   _____

3. Je voudrais monter à cheval.

   _____

4. Elle sera allée à la plage.

   _____

5. Tu serais resté en forme.

   _____

D. Fill in the blanks with the past perfect tense of the verbs in parentheses.

1. Nous _____ (parler) avec nos amis.
   (We had spoken with our friends.)

2. Il _____ (aller) à l'université. (He had gone to college.)

3. Tu _____ (lire) le livre. (You had read the book.)

4. Mon professeur _____ (écrire) ce livre.
   (My professor had written that book.)

5. Elles _____ (se réveiller) tôt.
   (They had woken up early.)

How Did You Do?

Give yourself a point for every correct answer, then use the following key to determine whether or not you're ready to move on:

0-7 points: It's probably best to go back and study the lessons again to make sure you understood everything completely. Take your time; it's not a race! Make sure you spend time reviewing the vocabulary and reading through each grammar note carefully.

8-16 points: If the questions you missed were in Section A or B, you may want to review the vocabulary again; if you missed answers mostly in Section C or D, check the Unit 3 Essentials to make sure you have your conjugations and other grammar basics down.

17-20 points: Feel free to move on to the next unit! You're doing a great job.

 **Points**

Unit 4:
Doctors and Health

You've made it to the very last unit of *Advanced French*. Congratulations!

In this last unit, we're going to look at vocabulary dealing with la santé (*health*) and le corps humain (*the human body*). We'll also tackle a final verb tense that deals with wishes, doubts, and necessities: the subjunctive.

By the end of this unit, you should be able to:

☐ Name different parts of the body

☐ Tell someone that you're hurt or in pain

☐ Say whether you have a *cold* or the *flu*

☐ Talk about *each other*

☐ Name different injuries and disabilities

☐ Tell someone to *follow* the instructions

☐ Talk about exercise

☐ Say *I saw her*

☐ Explain what's wrong to a doctor

☐ Understand what you hear in an emergency situation

☐ Express wishes, desires, doubts, and needs

☐ Talk about what you need to *buy*, *take*, or *see*

☐ Say what you have to *be* or what you doubt someone *can* do

Lesson 13: Words

By the end of this lesson, you will be able to:

☐ Name different parts of the body

☐ Tell someone that you're hurt or in pain

☐ Say whether you have a *cold* or the *flu*

☐ Talk about *each other*

Word Builder 1

Let's get started with **les parties** *(f.)* **du corps** *(parts of the body)*.

▶ 13A Lesson 13 Word Builder 1 (CD 9, Track 5)

head	**la tête**
eye	**l'œil** *(m.)*
eyes	**les yeux** *(m.)*
nose	**le nez**
mouth	**la bouche**
ear	**l'oreille** *(f.)*
tooth	**la dent**
neck	**le cou**
shoulder	**l'épaule** *(f.)*
back	**le dos**
arm	**le bras**
hand	**la main**
leg	**la jambe**

knee	**le genou**
foot	**le pied**

Take It Further

Les parties du corps provide a good review of irregular plurals:

SINGULAR	PLURAL
l'œil *(eye)*	**les yeux** *(eyes)*
le nez *(nose)*	**les nez** *(noses)*
le dos *(back)*	**les dos** *(backs)*
le bras *(arm)*	**les bras** *(arms)*
le genou *(knee)*	**les genoux** *(knees)*

Note that **cou** *(neck)* becomes **cous** *(necks)* in the plural, not **coux**. **Genoux** vs. **cous** is a good example of the fact that only *some* words that end in -ou add -x in the plural.

To review the patterns of irregular plurals, see Lesson 5 of *Essential French* and Lesson 2 of *Intermediate French*. Of course, **œil/yeux** doesn't follow any particular rule, it's just entirely irregular.

Also don't forget that French uses **le**, **la**, or **les** instead of a possessive (**ma**, **mes**, **ta**, **tes**, etc.) when expressing an action with a part of the body:

Je me lave les mains.
I'm washing my hands. (lit., I'm washing up the hands.)

✎ Word Practice 1

Identify the following body parts in French. Make sure to include the appropriate definite article (**le**, **la**, **l'**, **les**).

1. _____

2. _____

3. _____

4. _____

ANSWER KEY:
1. l'œil; 2. le nez; 3. l'oreille; 4. la bouche

✎ Word Recall

Now conjugate the verbs below in the present tense.

1. je _____ (mettre)

2. tu _____ (sortir)

3. il _____ (employer)

4. nous _____ (commencer)

5. vous _____ (savoir)

6. elles _____ (acheter)

ANSWER KEY:
1. mets; 2. sors; 3. emploie; 4. commençons; 5. savez; 6. achètent

Grammar Builder 1
TO HAVE PAIN OR *TO HURT*

▶ 13B Lesson 13 Grammar Builder 1 (CD 9, Track 6)

Hopefully you won't have to use these expressions very often, but just in case, it's good to know how to explain that you're hurt or in pain.

To express a hurt or pain in a certain part of your body, use avoir mal à (*to have pain in, to ache, to have an ache, to have a sore something*) + part of the body.

Il a mal aux pieds.
He has sore feet.

J'ai mal aux dents.
I have a toothache.

Note that avoir du mal à is very different from avoir mal à. Avoir du mal à means *to have trouble (doing something)*. For example: j'ai du mal à choisir (*I'm having trouble choosing*).

If your pain is caused by someone or something, use an indirect object pronoun (me, te, lui, etc.) + faire mal (*to hurt*).

Tu me fais mal.
You're hurting me.

Mes chaussures me font mal.
My shoes hurt me.

Son dentiste ne lui fait jamais mal.
His dentist never hurts him.

You can also use **faire mal à** + indirect object: **Les chaussures font mal à Marie.** (_The shoes are hurting Marie._)

✎ Work Out 1

Translate the following sentences into French.

1. _He has a backache._ _____

2. _I have a headache._ _____

3. _My earring is hurting me._ _____

4. _I have a tooth that is hurting me._ _____

ANSWER KEY:
1. **Il a mal au dos.** 2. **J'ai mal à la tête.** 3. **Ma boucle d'oreille me fait mal.**
4. **J'ai une dent qui me fait mal.**

Word Builder 2

Now let's look at **les maladies** (_f._) (_illnesses, diseases_) and other words you might need to know at the doctor's office.

▶ 13C Lesson 13 Word Builder 2 (CD 9, Track 7)

medical checkup	**l'examen** (_m._) **médical**
doctor's office	**le cabinet médical**
doctor	**le docteur/la doctoresse***
patient	**le patient/la patiente**
laboratory	**le laboratoire**
x-ray	**la radiographie, la radio**

* **Docteur/doctoresse** and **médecin** are synonyms. Remember, however, that **médecin** only has a masculine form.

diagnosis	le diagnostic
(common) cold	le rhume
fever	la fièvre
flu	la grippe
virus	le virus
allergy	l'allergie (*f.*)
infection	l'infection (*f.*)
care	le soin

Take It Further

Let's look at some more words related to la santé (*health*) that are good to know:

LE CORPS (BODY)	
finger	le doigt
fingernail	l'ongle (*m.*)
toe	l'orteil (*m.*), le doigt de pied
toenail	l'ongle (*m.*) de pied
ankle	la cheville
wrist	le poignet
elbow	le coude
skin	la peau
mole	le grain de beauté
heart	le cœur
heart attack	la crise cardiaque
brain	le cerveau
stroke	l'attaque (*f.*) cérébrale
throat	la gorge
lung	le poumon

LE CORPS (BODY)	
belly, stomach (general term)	le ventre
stomach	l'estomac (m.)
abdomen	l'abdomen (m.)

J'ai mal au ventre.
I have a bellyache.

LE MÉDECIN (DOCTOR)	
sick	malade
to be sick	être malade
to get sick	tomber malade
to cure, to get better	guérir
to examine	examiner
results	les résultats (m.)
instructions	les instructions (f.)
prescription	l'ordonnance (f.)
pill	la pilule, le comprimé
antibiotics	les antibiotiques (m.)
needle	l'aiguille (f.)
vaccine	le vaccin
shot, injection	la piqûre, l'injection (f.)
to get a shot	recevoir une piqûre
allergic	allergique

J'ai peur des aiguilles.
I'm afraid of needles.

Je suis allergique à la pénicilline.
I'm allergic to penicillin.

 ## Word Practice 2

Choose the correct translation of each French word.

1. le rhume

   a. *flu*
   b. *fever*
   c. *common cold*
   d. *virus*

2. la grippe

   a. *fever*
   b. *flu*
   c. *care*
   d. *infection*

3. le soin

   a. *allergy*
   b. *diagnosis*
   c. *x-ray*
   d. *care*

4. le cabinet médical

   a. *doctor's office*
   b. *medical checkup*
   c. *laboratory*
   d. *diagnosis*

ANSWER KEY:
1. c; 2. b; 3. d; 4. a

 ## Word Recall

Give the feminine form of the following words.

1. le docteur (*doctor*) _____

2. l'infirmier (*nurse*) _____

3. le dentiste (*dentist*) _____

4. le patient *(patient)* _____

5. l'esthéticien *(beautician)* _____

ANSWER KEY:
1. la doctoresse; 2. l'infirmière; 3. la dentiste; 4. la patiente; 5. l'esthéticienne

Grammar Builder 2
EACH OTHER

▶ 13D Lesson 13 Grammar Builder 2 (CD 9, Track 8)

You know that you use reflexive pronouns to talk about something that is happening to the *self*: **je me lave** *(I wash myself)*, **tu te blesses** *(you hurt yourself)*, etc.

However, you can also use reflexive pronouns to talk about *each other*. To do so, just use one of the plural reflexive pronouns—**nous, vous,** or **se (s')**—the same way you would normally use it.

Here are some examples using **se:**

Ils se regardent.
They look at each other. (They watch each other.)

Jennifer et Carol se voient de temps en temps.
Jennifer and Carol see each other from time to time.

Thomas et Nicole se marient dimanche.
Thomas and Nicole are getting married on Sunday. (Thomas and Nicole are marrying each other on Sunday.)

When a verb uses a plural reflexive pronoun to mean *each other*, it is known as a "reciprocal verb." As with reflexive verbs, there are some common reciprocal verbs, such as s'aimer (*to like/love each other*) and se dire (*to tell each other, to say to each other*). You will find a list of common reciprocal verbs in the Tip at the end of this lesson.

Of course, some verbs can have both reflexive and reciprocal meanings. Whether the reflexive pronoun means *self* or *each other* often depends simply on context. For example, se regarder could mean *to look at oneself* or *to look at each other*. You could say nous nous regardons and mean *we look at each other* or *we look at ourselves* depending on what you're talking about.

Also remember that only ***plural*** reflexive pronouns can mean *each other*. If it's a singular reflexive pronoun, it will never mean *each other*. For instance, you would never translate je me vois (*I see myself*) as *I see each other*. That wouldn't make sense in French or in English.

⏸

✎ Work Out 2
Change the verbs in the following sentences to reciprocal verbs.

1. **Ils parlent de temps en temps.** (*They speak from time to time.*)

   _____

2. **Nous téléphonons tous les jours.** (*We call every day.*)

   _____

3. **Mes parents comprennent.** (*My parents understand.*)

   _____

4. **Est-ce que vous parlez souvent ?** (*Do you speak often?*)

   _____

ANSWER KEY:
1. **Ils se parlent de temps en temps.** (*They speak to each other from time to time.*) 2. **Nous nous téléphonons tous les jours.** (*We call each other every day.*) 3. **Mes parents se comprennent.** (*My parents understand each other.*) 4. **Est-ce que vous vous parlez souvent ?** (*Do you speak to each other often?*)

✎ Drive It Home

You've learned a lot in *Advanced French* so far, so let's go back a bit and review what you saw in *Intermediate French*. Change the following verbs to the past tense.

1. je bois _____

2. j'ai _____

3. je parle _____

4. je finis _____

5. je prends _____

6. je vois _____

7. je fais _____

8. je réponds _____

9. je suis _____

10. je dois _____

ANSWER KEY:
1. j'ai bu; 2. j'ai eu; 3. j'ai parlé; 4. j'ai fini; 5. j'ai pris; 6. j'ai vu; 7. j'ai fait; 8. j'ai répondu; 9. j'ai été; 10. j'ai dû

Tip

Here are some common reciprocal verbs. Notice that, as with the *self* in reflexive verbs, sometimes the *each other* in reciprocal verbs isn't translated into English.

se parler	*to speak to each other*
se téléphoner	*to call each other*
se comprendre	*to understand each other*
se regarder	*to look at each other, to watch each other*
se voir	*to see each other*
se marier	*to get married (to each other)*
se fiancer	*to get engaged (to each other)*
s'aimer	*to like/love each other*
s'embrasser	*to hug (each other), to kiss (each other)*
se dire	*to tell each other, to say to each other*
se disputer	*to argue (with each other)*
se connaître	*to know each other*

Nous nous aimons.
We love each other.

Vous vous connaissez ?
You know each other?

How Did You Do?

Let's see how you did! By now, you should be able to:

☐ Name different parts of the body
(Still unsure? Jump back to page 234)

☐ Tell someone that you're hurt or in pain
(Still unsure? Jump back to page 237)

☐ Say whether you have a *cold* or the *flu*
(Still unsure? Jump back to page 238)

☐ Talk about *each other*
(Still unsure? Jump back to page 242)

Lesson 14: Phrases

By the end of this lesson, you will be able to:

☐ Name different injuries and disabilities

☐ Tell someone to *follow* the instructions

☐ Talk about exercise

☐ Say *I saw her*

Phrase Builder 1

▶ 14A Lesson 14 Phrase Builder 1 (CD 9, Track 9)

to break one's arm	se casser le bras
to sprain one's ankle	se fouler la cheville
to walk with a cane	marcher avec une canne
to walk with crutches	marcher avec des béquilles

wheelchair	la chaise roulante
to be disabled	être handicapé/handicapée
to have Alzheimer's disease	avoir la maladie d'Alzheimer
to have Parkinson's disease	avoir la maladie de Parkinson
to be deaf	être sourd/sourde
to use sign language	utiliser le langage des signes
to be paralyzed	être paralysé/paralysée
to wear contact lenses	porter des verres de contact (porter des lentilles de contact)
to be blind	être aveugle
to need a seeing-eye dog	avoir besoin d'un chien d'aveugle

Take It Further

You know that la langue means *language*, so why do you say le langage des signes (*sign language*)?

Well, la langue, which can also mean *tongue*, is generally only used to refer to the language of a country or a language that is spoken:

Marc parle trois langues.
Marc speaks three languages.

L'anglais est la langue des États-Unis.
English is the language of the United States.

By contrast, le langage (*language*) is commonly used to describe a way of talking or writing, such as using "formal language" or "inappropriate language," or the terminology of a specific field (computer language, legal language, etc.). It is also used to refer to a non-spoken language system, or, more abstractly, to the idea of language in general.

Here are some examples using le langage:

informal language, familiar language	le langage familier
formal language	le langage soutenu
everyday language	le langage courant
bad language	le langage grossier
body language	le langage du corps
baby talk (baby language)	le langage enfantin
sign language	le langage des signes
programming language	le langage informatique
legal language, legal terminology	le langage juridique

✎ Phrase Practice 1

Translate the following sentences into English.

1. Je me suis cassé le bras. _____

2. Il s'est foulé la cheville. _____

3. Elle marchait avec des béquilles. _____

_____

4. **Est-ce que tu portes des verres de contact ?** _____

_____

5. **Mon père est aveugle.** _____

ANSWER KEY:
1. *I broke my arm.* 2. *He sprained his ankle.* 3. *She was walking with crutches./She used to walk with crutches.* 4. *Do you wear contact lenses?* 5. *My father is blind.*

✎ Word Recall

Match the French phrases on the left to the correct English translations on the right.

1. avoir peur de	a. *to be sleepy*
2. avoir besoin de	b. *to be afraid*
3. avoir honte	c. *to feel like*
4. avoir sommeil	d. *to be ashamed*
5. avoir envie de	e. *to need*

ANSWER KEY:
1. b; 2. e; 3. d; 4. a; 5. c

Grammar Builder 1
TO FOLLOW

▶ 14B Lesson 14 Grammar Builder 1 (CD 9, Track 10)

You already know how to conjugate a lot of verbs that are irregular in the present tense: avoir, être, aller, faire, vouloir, pouvoir, conduire, voir, savoir, connaître, etc.

Well, here's one more to add to your list. The verb suivre (*to follow*) is irregular in the present tense. Here are its forms:

SUIVRE *(TO FOLLOW)* - **PRESENT**			
je suis	*I follow*	**nous suivons**	*we follow*
tu suis	*you follow*	**vous suivez**	*you follow*
il suit	*he follows*	**ils suivent**	*they follow*
elle suit	*she follows*	**elles suivent**	*they follow*

Nous suivons la route vers la ville.
We follow the road to town.

Suivez les instructions.
Follow the instructions.

Suivez-moi au café du quartier.
Follow me to the neighborhood café.

Pour être en bonne santé, il faut suivre un bon régime.
To be in good health, you must follow a good diet.

S'il vous plaît, faites suivre mon courrier à la nouvelle adresse.
Please forward my mail to the new address.

Note that **faire suivre** means *to forward* or *to redirect*. Also note that **suivre** is used in education to mean *to take*: **suivre un cours** (*to take a class*).

The past participle of **suivre** is **suivi**: **J'ai suivi les instructions.** (*I followed the instructions.*)

(❚❚)

✎ Work Out 1

Fill in the blanks with the correct form of **suivre**. Pay attention to the tense in the English translations.

1. Marc _____ la route de l'école. (*Marc followed the road to school.*)

2. _____-ils les instructions du médecin ?

   (*Are they following the doctor's instructions?*)

3. Nous _____ un régime pour maigrir.

   (*We're following a diet to lose weight.*)

4. Est-ce que vous _____ mes instructions ?

   (*Did you follow my instructions?*)

5. Tu ne _____ pas la route. (*You're not following the road.*)

ANSWER KEY:
1. a suivi; 2. Suivent; 3. suivons; 4. avez suivi; 5. suis

Phrase Builder 2

Now we're going to look at **l'exercice** (*m.*) (*exercise, exercising*). Remember from Unit 2 that *gym* is **le gymnase**.

▶ 14C Lesson 14 Phrase Builder 2 (CD 9, Track 11)

health club	le club de remise en forme (le club de forme/gym)
to train	s'entraîner
to do strength training, to lift weights (to do bodybuilding)	faire de la musculation
treadmill	le tapis de course, le tapis de jogging

sit-ups	les abdominaux (*m.*)
push-ups	les pompes (*f.*)
pull-ups	les tractions (*f.*)
to lift a dumbbell	soulever un haltère
stationary bike	le vélo d'appartement
workout	l'entraînement (*m.*)*
to be sweating	être en sueur (être en nage)
heartbeat	le battement de cœur
to pull a muscle	se faire une élongation
to be fit, to be in shape	être en forme

* **Entraînement** can also mean *training*.

Take It Further

Speaking of irregular verbs like **suivre** (*to follow*), let's review some of the other irregular verbs that you've seen in this program, focusing on verbs that deal with wishes, desires, and needs.

To start, here is the present tense conjugation of **vouloir** (*to want*):

VOULOIR (*TO WANT*) - **PRESENT**			
je veux	*I want*	nous voulons	*we want*
tu veux	*you want*	vous voulez	*you want*
il veut	*he wants*	ils veulent	*they want*
elle veut	*she wants*	elles veulent	*they want*

The past participle of **vouloir** is **voulu**. The future and conditional are formed with **voudr-**.

Here is the present tense of préférer (*to prefer*):

PRÉFÉRER (*TO PREFER*) - **PRESENT**			
je préfère	*I want*	nous préférons	*we want*
tu préfères	*you want*	vous préférez	*you want*
il préfère	*he wants*	ils préfèrent	*they want*
elle préfère	*she wants*	elles préfèrent	*they want*

The past participle of préférer is simply préféré. The future and conditional are formed with préférer-.

Don't forget that verbs like suggérer (*to suggest*) are conjugated in the same way as préférer.

Now let's look at permettre (*to allow, to permit*). Remember that permettre is formed in the same way as mettre (*to put, to put on*).

PERMETTRE (*TO ALLOW, TO PERMIT*) - **PRESENT**			
je permets	*I allow*	nous permettons	*we allow*
tu permets	*you allow*	vous permettez	*you allow*
il permet	*he allows*	ils permettent	*they allow*
elle permet	*she allows*	elles permettent	*they allow*

The past tense of permettre is permis. The future and conditional are formed with permettr-.

Finally, let's look at the important irregular verb falloir (*to be necessary*), which only has an il form. Here is its il form in a variety of tenses, some of which you've already seen and some you haven't:

FALLOIR (*TO BE NECESSARY*)		
Present Tense	il faut	*it is necessary to*
Past Tense	il a fallu	*it was necessary to*

FALLOIR *(TO BE NECESSARY)*		
Imperfect Tense	il fallait	*it was necessary to, it used to be necessary to*
Future Tense	il faudra	*it will be necessary to*
Conditional	il faudrait	*it would be necessary to*

Remember that il faut can also mean *you need to, one needs to, you have to, one has to, you must,* and *one must*. The same is true for the other tenses: il faudra can mean *you will need to, you will have to,* and so on.

✎ Phrase Practice 2

Translate this short conversation into English.

A: **J'adore ce club de remise en forme !**

_____

B: **Moi aussi ! Qu'est-ce que tu veux faire ?**

_____

A: **Je veux faire de la musculation.**

_____

B: **Moi, je veux faire du vélo d'appartement.**

_____

A: **Nous serons en forme !**

_____

ANSWER KEY:
A: I love this health club!
B: Me too! What do you want to do?

A: I want to do strength training./I want to lift weights./I want to do bodybuilding.
B: Me, I want to ride a stationary bike.
A: We'll be in shape!

✎ Word Recall

Let's review direct object pronouns. Fill in the blanks with the correct direct object pronouns in French.

me _____	*us* _____
you _____	*you* _____
him, it (m.) _____	*them (m.)* _____
her, it (f.) _____	*them (f.)* _____

ANSWER KEY:
me/m'; te/t'; le/l'; la/l'; nous; vous; les; les

Grammar Builder 2
DIRECT OBJECTS AND AVOIR

▶ 14D Lesson 14 Grammar Builder 2 (CD 9, Track 12)

You know that the past participles of verbs that use avoir do not need to agree in gender and number with the subject. For instance, you would say elle a parlé, not elle a parlée.

However, there is one case where the past participles of verbs that use avoir *do* need to agree in gender and number with a noun.

If a verb that uses avoir is *preceded* by a direct object noun or pronoun, then that verb's past participle must agree in gender and number with the direct object noun or pronoun. Keep in mind that this does not apply when the direct object noun or pronoun follows the verb.

As a review, here are the direct object pronouns in French:

DIRECT OBJECT PRONOUNS			
me (m')	*me*	nous	*us*
te (t')	*you*	vous	*you*
le (l')	*him, it (m.)*	les	*them (or plural it) (m.)*
la (l')	*her, it (f.)*	les	*them (or plural it) (f.)*

Remember that direct objects are nouns that receive the action of a verb. For example, in the phrase *I took a pill, a pill* is the direct object noun. Direct object pronouns replace direct object nouns: *I took **it**.*

Now take a look at the following sentence:

J'ai vu Christine.
I saw Christine.

In this sentence, Christine is the direct object noun. Notice that the past participle vu does not agree with Christine because Christine follows the verb; it does not precede it.

However:

Je l'ai vue.
I saw her.

In this case, **vu** must be changed to the feminine singular **vue** because the feminine singular pronoun **la (l')** (*her*) precedes it.

Now let's look at some examples of a direct object noun preceding the verb. Remember that **exercice** is a masculine noun.

Il a fait des exercices.
He did some exercises.

Voici les exercices qu'il a faits.
Here are the exercises that he did.

J'ai pris une pilule.
I took a pill.

Voici la pilule que j'ai prise.
Here's the pill that I took.

Note that this rule applies to any tense that uses **avoir**. For example, you would say: **J'aurais pris une pilule. Voici la pilule que j'aurais prise.** (*I would have taken a pill. Here is the pill I would have taken.*)

Also note that it does not apply to verbs that use **être**. Verbs that use **être** always agree with the subject, not the direct object or direct object pronoun.

✎ Work Out 2

Decide whether the past participles in the following sentences are in the correct form. If they aren't, rewrite the past participles in the correct form.

1. **Où sont les voitures que tu as acheté ?** *(Where are the cars that you bought?)*

   _____

2. **Il a acheté trois voitures.** *(He bought three cars.)* _____

3. **Voici les livres que Sophie a donné à Paul.** *(Here are the books that Sophie gave*

   to Paul.) _____

4. **Sophie a donné ces livres à Paul.** *(Sophie gave these books to Paul.)*

   _____

ANSWER KEY:
1. achetées; 2. no change; 3. donnés; 4. no change

✎ Drive It Home

Fill in the blanks with the past tense of the verbs in parentheses.

1. **C'est la doctoresse que j'**_____ (voir).

   (That's the doctor that I saw.)

2. **C'est le docteur que j'**_____ (voir).

   (That's the doctor that I saw.)

3. **Voici les doctoresses que j'**_____ (voir).

   (Here are the doctors that I saw.)

4. **Voici les docteurs que j'**_____ (voir).

   (Here are the doctors that I saw.)

ANSWER KEY:
1. ai vue; 2. ai vu; 3. ai vues; 4. ai vus

How Did You Do?

Let's see how you did! By now, you should be able to:

☐ Name different injuries and disabilities
(Still unsure? Jump back to page 246)

☐ Tell someone to *follow* the instructions
(Still unsure? Jump back to page 249)

☐ Talk about exercise
(Still unsure? Jump back to page 251)

☐ Say *I saw her*
(Still unsure? Jump back to page 255)

Lesson 15: Sentences

By the end of this lesson, you will be able to:

☐ Explain what's wrong to a doctor

☐ Understand what you hear in an emergency situation

☐ Express wishes, desires, doubts, and needs

Sentence Builder 1

▶ 15A Lesson 15 Sentence Builder 1 (CD 9, Track 13)

I would like to make an appointment.	**Je voudrais prendre rendez-vous.**
What's the matter? (lit., What is there?)	**Qu'est-ce qu'il y a ?**
What happened to you? (pl./fml.)	**Qu'est-ce qui vous est arrivé ?**

Ouch!	Aïe !
What should I do?	Qu'est-ce que je dois faire ?
The doctor gives a prescription. (lit., The doctor makes a prescription.)	Le médecin fait une ordonnance.
I have trouble swallowing.	J'ai du mal à avaler.
I have a sore throat.	J'ai mal à la gorge.
You have a frog in your throat. (lit., You have a cat in your throat.)	Tu as un chat dans la gorge.
He has a headache.	Il a mal à la tête.
The child is going to catch a cold.	L'enfant va attraper un rhume.
My nose is stuffed up. (I have a stuffy nose.)	J'ai le nez bouché.
Because of his allergies, he coughs.	À cause de ses allergies, il tousse.
I'm not myself./I'm not feeling well. (lit., I'm not in my plate.)	Je ne suis pas dans mon assiette.

Take It Further

If you're talking about why something happened, two good phrases to know are:

thanks to …	grâce à…
because of … , as a result of … , due to … (in a negative way)	à cause de…

Grâce au médecin, je suis en bonne santé.
Thanks to the doctor, I'm in good health.

Il a mal à la gorge à cause de la grippe.
He has a sore throat because of the flu.

Earlier in this unit we looked at how to conjugate *falloir* in different tenses. However, it's also important to keep in mind how to use the verb in sentences. There are several different ways:

1. *il* + form of *falloir* + noun or verb in the infinitive

Use this construction to say *it is necessary*, or to make a general statement about what *people in general, one, they, we*, or *you* must or need to do.

Il faut prendre votre température.
It is necessary to take your temperature.

Pour être en bonne santé, il faut suivre un bon régime.
To be in good health, you must follow a good diet.

Il faudra un manteau pour aller dehors.
You will need a coat to go outside.

Il faut de la nourriture !
We need food!

2. *il* + indirect object pronoun + form of *falloir* + noun or verb in the infinitive

Use this construction to talk specifically about what *he must do, they must do, it needs, she needs*, etc.

Il nous faut dormir.
We must sleep.

Il lui fallait un plâtre.
He needed a cast.

3. il + form of **falloir** + que

You can use this construction to talk generally or specifically.

Il faut qu'on...
It is necessary that one ... /It is necessary that we ...

Il faut que Marie...
Marie needs to ... /Marie must ...

Il faut que must be followed by what's known as the "subjunctive" tense. You'll learn about the subjunctive in Grammar Builder 1.

Finally, note that **falloir** is also used in certain expressions, such as **s'il le faut** (*if necessary, if needed*).

Elle sera là, s'il le faut.
She'll be there, if necessary.

✎ Sentence Practice 1

Translate the following phrases into French.

1. *I have trouble swallowing.* _____

2. *I have a sore throat.* _____

3. *I have a stuffy nose.* _____

4. *I have a headache.* _____

5. *I'm not feeling well.* _____

   ANSWER KEY:
   1. J'ai du mal à avaler. 2. J'ai mal à la gorge. 3. J'ai le nez bouché. 4. J'ai mal à la tête. 5. Je ne suis pas dans mon assiette.

✎ Word Recall

Let's review indirect object pronouns. Fill in the blanks with the correct indirect object pronouns in French.

to me _____   *to us* _____

to you (infml.) _____   *to you (pl./fml.)* _____

to him/her/it _____   *to them* _____

ANSWER KEY:
me/m'; te/t'; lui; nous; vous; leur

Grammar Builder 1
FORMING THE SUBJUNCTIVE

▶ 15B Lesson 15 Grammar Builder 1 (CD 9, Track 14)

The subjunctive is the final tense that you'll learn in this course. It is used when expressing wishes, necessities, doubts, and other emotions.

We'll go into depth about when and how to use the subjunctive, and what it means, in Grammar Builder 2, but for now, let's just focus on forming it.

Here's how to form the subjunctive:

1. Drop the **-ent** from the **ils/elles** form of the verb in the present tense.

2. Add the following endings:

PRONOUN	ENDING	PRONOUN	ENDING
je	-e	nous	-ions
tu	-es	vous	-iez
il	-e	ils	-ent
elle	-e	elles	-ent

Notice that the ils/elles form drops and then adds -ent. In other words, it often doesn't change at all from the present tense into the subjunctive.

Let's look at an example from each verb group. The subjunctive usually follows the conjunction que (*that*)—not to be confused with the relative pronoun que— so all of the examples will follow that word.

PARLER *(TO SPEAK)*	FINIR *(TO FINISH)*	RÉPONDRE *(TO ANSWER)*
que je parle	que je finisse	que je réponde
que tu parles	que tu finisses	que tu répondes
qu'il parle	qu'il finisse	qu'il réponde
qu'elle parle	qu'elle finisse	qu'elle réponde
que nous parlions	que nous finissions	que nous répondions
que vous parliez	que vous finissiez	que vous répondiez
qu'ils parlent	qu'ils finissent	qu'ils répondent
qu'elles parlent	qu'elles finissent	qu'elles répondent

Note that all of these verbs are in the "present subjunctive." This form of the subjunctive is used for both the present tense and the future tense. For example, qu'elle parle can mean *that she speak* or *that she will speak*.

The subjunctive has four tenses: the present, imperfect, past, and past perfect. However, we will only be covering the present subjunctive in this course.

✎ Work Out 1

Conjugate the following verbs in the present subjunctive.

1. **que tu** _____ (danser)

2. **qu'elle** _____ (répondre)

3. **que je** _____ (vendre)

4. **qu'ils** _____ (choisir)

5. **que nous** _____ (parler)

6. **que vous** _____ (finir)

ANSWER KEY:
1. **danses**; 2. **réponde**; 3. **vende**; 4. **choisissent**; 5. **parlions**; 6. **finissiez**

Sentence Builder 2

If there is ever an emergency, it could be very helpful to know or be able to understand the following sentences.

▶ 15C Lesson 15 Sentence Builder 2 (CD 9, Track 15)

emergency situations	les cas *(m.)* d'urgence
It's necessary to have a first-aid kit.	Il faut avoir une trousse de secours.
to have an accident	avoir un accident
Call the emergency medical service.	Appelez le service d'assistance médicale d'urgence.
The ambulance is arriving.	L'ambulance arrive.
He needs a blood transfusion.	Il lui faut une transfusion de sang.
It's a superficial injury.	C'est une blessure superficielle.
It's not serious.	Ce n'est pas grave.

Do you have insurance?	**Est-ce que vous avez une assurance ?**
Take a pill (a tablet/a capsule).	**Prenez une pilule (un cachet/une capsule).***
Sometimes there are side effects.	**Quelquefois il y a des effets secondaires.**
It's a burn.	**C'est une brûlure.**
It's a cut.	**C'est une coupure.**
The dentist is going to replace the filling.	**Le dentiste va remplacer le plombage.**
It's necessary to have a tooth pulled. (We need to pull a tooth.)	**Il faut arracher une dent.**

* Remember that **le comprimé** is another term for *pill*. It can also mean *tablet*.

Take It Further

Speaking of **quelquefois** (*sometimes*), let's review what are known as the "adverbs of frequency":

sometimes	**quelquefois, parfois**
never	**jamais**
always, still	**toujours**
rarely	**rarement**
usually	**normalement, d'habitude**
occasionally	**de temps en temps**
frequently	**fréquemment**
often	**souvent**

However, if you want to say *how often?* (or *how many times?*), say **combien de fois ?** Note that **fois** (*f.*) means *time*:

once, one time	**une fois**
twice, two times	**deux fois**
last time, final time	**la dernière fois**

Finally, **ce n'est pas grave** (*it's not serious*) is a good expression to know. You can also use this expression casually to mean *It's not a problem, It's not a big deal,* or *Don't worry about it.*

✎ Sentence Practice 2

Match the French words on the left to the correct English translations on the right.

1. la trousse de secours	a. *pill*
2. le cas d'urgence	b. *burn*
3. la pilule	c. *emergency situation*
4. la brûlure	d. *cut*
5. la coupure	e. *first-aid kit*

ANSWER KEY:
1. e; 2. c; 3. a; 4. b; 5. d

✎ Word Recall

Now match the following verbs to their correct French translations.

1. vouloir	a. *to suggest*
2. préférer	b. *to want*
3. permettre	c. *to believe*
4. suggérer	d. *to prefer*
5. croire	e. *to allow*

ANSWER KEY:
1. b; 2. d; 3. e; 4. a; 5. c

Grammar Builder 2
USING THE SUBJUNCTIVE

▶ 15D Lesson 15 Grammar Builder 2 (CD 9, Track 16)

The subjunctive is a tense that conveys specific moods. It expresses requests, commands, doubt, uncertainty, possibility, approval and disapproval, preference, wishing, want, desire, necessity, need, urgency, importance, and emotions like joy and fear.

If a verb or phrase expressing any of these moods is followed by the conjunction que (*that*), then the verb *after* que is usually in the subjunctive. Also, certain specific expressions are always followed by the subjunctive.

Let's look more in detail at when and how the subjunctive is used.

1. The subjunctive is used after verbs of command, request, permission, or other expressions imposing your will on someone else + que.

For example, the subjunctive would be used after these phrases:

demander que	to request that, to ask that
empêcher que	to prevent from, to keep from
exiger que	to demand that, to require that
ordonner que	to order that
permettre que	to allow that
suggérer que	to suggest that

Let's look at some examples:

Il exige que tu partes.
He demands that you leave.

Le professeur suggère que vous parliez français.
The teacher suggests that you speak French.

As you can see, **tu partes** and **vous parliez** are in the subjunctive because they follow the phrases **exige que** and **suggère que**.

Note that it doesn't matter what tense **exiger que**, **suggérer que**, etc. are in. They could be in the future, conditional, past, and so on, and they would still be followed by the subjunctive: **il a exigé que tu partes** (*he demanded that you leave*). This is true of all verbs and phrases that are followed by the subjunctive.

2. The subjunctive is used after verbs or expressions of doubt, denial, uncertainty, or possibility + **que**.

For example, you would use the subjunctive after **douter que** (*to doubt that*):

Je doute que vous m'écoutiez.
I doubt that you're listening to me.

You would also use the subjunctive after the expressions **il semble que** (*it seems that*) and **il est possible que** (*it is possible that*):

Il est possible que nous travaillions samedi.
It's possible that we will work on Saturday.

Remember that the present subjunctive is used to express both the present tense and the future tense, so **nous travaillions** can mean *we work* or *we will work*.

Note that you would ***not*** use the subjunctive after the expression **il est probable que** (*it is probable that*). You also wouldn't use it after expressions of certainty like **il est vrai que** (*it is true that*) or **il est certain que** (*it is certain that*).

3. After verbs or expressions of approval, disapproval, or preference + **que**.

For example, the subjunctive would be used after these phrases:

aimer mieux que	*to prefer that (lit., to like better that)*
préférer que	*to prefer that*
recommander que	*to recommend that*

Aimez-vous mieux que je vous attende ?
Do you prefer that I wait for you?

You would also use the subjunctive after the expression **il est préférable que** (*it is preferable that*): **Il est préférable que vous attendiez.** (*It is preferable that you wait.*)

4. After verbs or expressions of wishing, want, or desire + **que**.

désirer que	to desire that, to want that, to wish that
souhaiter que	to wish that
vouloir que	to want that, to wish that

Je veux qu'elle parte.
I want her to leave. (lit., I want that she leave.)

Sa femme désire qu'il finisse le travail autour de la maison.
His wife wants him to finish the work around the house. (lit., His wife wants that he finish the work around the house.)

Notice that the subjunctive is sometimes translated as the infinitive in English: *I want her **to leave**, His wife wants him **to finish**,* etc.

Also don't forget that **vouloir que, souhaiter que**, etc. don't have to be in the present tense. They could be in any other tense and they would still need to be followed by the subjunctive. So **je voudrais que** (*I would like that*), for instance, would be followed by the subjunctive because it's a conditional form of **vouloir que: Je voudrais que tu partes.** (*I would like you to leave.*)

5. After verbs of thinking or believing when they are negative or in the form of a question + **que**.

For instance, the phrases **penser que** (*to think that*), **croire que** (*to believe that*), and **trouver que** (*to find that, to think that*) are usually followed by the subjunctive when they are negative (such as **je ne pense pas que**) or in the form of a question (**pensez-vous que... ?**) and you want to emphasize a feeling of doubt.

Here is an example:

Je ne pense pas que vous m'écoutiez.
I don't think (that) you're listening to me.

However, make sure to keep in mind that you only use the subjunctive if penser que, croire que, and trouver que are negative or in the form of a question. If they aren't, don't use the subjunctive: Je pense que vous m'écoutez. (*I think that you're listening to me.*)

6. After verbs or expressions of necessity or need + que.

For example, you would use the subjunctive after the expressions il faut que (*it is necessary that, one has to, one needs to, one must*) and il est nécessaire que (*it is necessary that, one has to, one needs to, one must*).

Il faut que ma nièce vende sa maison.
My niece must sell her house. (It is necessary that my niece sell her house.)

Il est nécessaire que je finisse la lettre.
I have to finish the letter. (It is necessary that I finish the letter.)

You would also use the subjunctive after:

avoir besoin que	*to need for*

For instance: j'ai besoin que vous finissiez (*I need for you to finish*).

7. After expressions of urgency or importance + que.

Il est urgent que je finisse la lettre.
It is urgent that I finish the letter.

Il est important que tu arrives à l'heure.
It is important that you arrive on time.

Il est essentiel que vous arriviez à l'heure.
It is essential that you arrive on time.

8. After expressions of emotion, such as joy, fear, sorrow, or regret + que.

Je suis content que vous m'aidiez.
I'm happy that you are helping me.

Je regrette que tu partes si tôt.
I am sorry that you're leaving so soon. (I regret that you're leaving so soon/early.)

Nous avons peur qu'il ne parte.
We are afraid (that) he may leave. (lit., We're afraid that he leaves.)

Notice the ne in that last sentence? In French, expressions of fear often have ne before the verb in the subjunctive, even though the verb isn't negative. This doesn't translate into English; it's just something you have to remember to do in French. Of course, if there is also a pas after the verb, then the verb is negative: **Nous avons peur qu'il ne parte pas.** (*We're afraid that he may not leave.*)

9. After specific conjunctions with que.

afin que, pour que	in order that, so that
avant que	before
à moins que... ne	unless
bien que, quoique	although
sans que	without
jusqu'à ce que	until

Il travaille dur pour que sa famille réussisse.
He works hard so that his family succeeds.

10. The subjunctive is *only* used when the subject of the verb before que is different from the subject of the verb after que.

For example:

Je veux qu'il parte.
I want him to leave. (lit., I want that he leave.)

In this case, the subjunctive can be used because the subject of the verb before que is je, while the subject of the verb after que is il.

However, you couldn't say je veux que je parte (*I want that I leave/I want me to leave*). That is incorrect because the two subjects are the same; they are both je. Instead, you would say:

Je veux partir.
I want to leave.

Notice that the infinitive is used instead of the subjunctive, and the que is removed.

Here is another example:

Ils désirent que nous restions.
They want us to stay. (lit., They want that we stay.)

Ils désirent rester.
They want to stay.

And that's it on the subjunctive for this lesson! Got all that? The subjunctive can definitely be a lot to take in, so don't be afraid to review this section as many times as you need to.

✎ Work Out 2

Conjugate the following verbs in the correct tense: either the present tense or the subjunctive.

1. **Il est important que nous** _____ (arriver) tôt.

   (It is important that we arrive early.)

2. **Il faut que vous** _____ (fermer) la porte. *(You need to close the door.)*

3. **Il est vrai que nous** _____ (vendre) la maison.

   (It's true that we're selling the house.)

4. **Il est possible que vous** _____ (parler) cinq langues.

   (It's possible that you speak five languages.)

5. **Je crois qu'elle** _____ (finir) la lettre. *(I believe she's finishing the letter.)*

   ANSWER KEY:
   1. **arrivions**; 2. **fermiez**; 3. **vendons**; 4. **parliez**; 5. **finit**

✎ Drive It Home

A. Fill in the blanks with the subjunctive form of the regular -er verbs in parentheses.

1. **Il faut que tu** _____ (écouter). *(You need to listen.)*

2. **Il faut que tu** _____ (parler). *(You need to talk.)*

3. Il faut que tu _____ (danser). *(You need to dance.)*

4. Il faut que tu _____ (étudier). *(You need to study.)*

5. Il faut que tu _____ (rester). *(You need to stay.)*

B. Now fill in the blanks with the subjunctive form of the -ir verbs in parentheses. Note that SST verbs form the subjunctive normally.

1. Je suis content qu'elle _____ (partir). *(I'm happy that she's leaving.)*

2. Je suis content qu'elle _____ (dormir). *(I'm happy that she's sleeping.)*

3. Je suis content qu'elle _____ (choisir). *(I'm happy that she's choosing.)*

4. Je suis content qu'elle _____ (finir). *(I'm happy that she's finishing.)*

5. Je suis content qu'elle _____ (réussir). *(I'm happy that she's doing well.)*

C. Finally, fill in the blanks with the subjunctive form of the regular -re verbs in parentheses.

1. Il voudrait que vous _____ (répondre). *(He would like you to respond.)*

2. Il voudrait que vous _____ (attendre). *(He would like you to wait.)*

3. Il voudrait que vous _____ (descendre). *(He would like you to come down.)*

4. Il voudrait que vous _____ (perdre). *(He would like you to lose.)*

5. Il voudrait que vous _____ (entendre). *(He would like you to hear.)*

ANSWER KEY:
A. 1. écoutes; 2. parles; 3. danses; 4. étudies; 5. restes
B. 1. parte; 2. dorme; 3. choisisse; 4. finisse; 5. réussisse
C. 1. répondiez; 2. attendiez; 3. descendiez; 4. perdiez; 5. entendiez

Tip

It can be a challenge to remember when to use the subjunctive. To help yourself remember, think of the word *wedding*. Each letter in *wedding* stands for a kind of verb or expression that is followed by the subjunctive.

W	Wishing and Wanting
E	Emotion
D	Doubt and Denial
D	Disapproval (and approval)
I	Imposing your will
N	Necessity, Need, and Negation (of verbs of thinking or believing)
G	Great importance (a bit of stretch, sure, but that's why you'll remember it!)

Obviously, this doesn't cover everything, but it will help you get started!

How Did You Do?

Let's see how you did! By now, you should be able to:

☐ Explain what's wrong to a doctor
(Still unsure? Jump back to page 259)

☐ Understand what you hear in an emergency situation
(Still unsure? Jump back to page 265)

☐ Express wishes, desires, doubts, and needs
(Still unsure? Jump back to page 268)

Lesson 16: Conversations

By the end of this lesson, you will be able to:

☐ Talk about what you need to *buy, take,* or *see*

☐ Say what you have to *be* or what you doubt someone *can* do

🔊 Conversation 1

Mme Laurent is chez le médecin/docteur (*at the doctor's*) to ask him about her leg.

▶ 16A Lesson 16 Conversation 1 (CD 9, Track 17)

Le docteur :	Qu'est-ce qui ne va pas ? Vous avez du mal à marcher.
Mme Laurent :	J'ai très mal à la jambe.
Le docteur :	Qu'est-ce qui vous est arrivé ? Vous êtes tombée ?
Mme Laurent :	Non, je ne suis pas tombée. Hier, j'étais au club de forme où j'ai fait beaucoup d'exercice. J'ai suivi un cours de danse moderne, j'ai couru, et j'ai nagé un peu.
Le docteur :	Allongez-vous. Je vais vous examiner.
Mme Laurent :	Aïe !!!
Le docteur :	Vous n'avez rien de cassé, mais vous avez une inflammation musculaire.
Mme Laurent :	Qu'est-ce que je dois faire ? C'est grave ?
Le docteur :	Non, mais il vaut mieux cesser toute forme d'exercice et prendre des comprimés anti-inflammatoires trois fois par jour. Voilà votre ordonnance.
Mme Laurent :	Merci, docteur.
Le docteur :	Revenez me voir dans une semaine si vous avez toujours des douleurs.

The doctor:	What's wrong? (lit., What isn't going?) You're having trouble walking.
Mrs. Laurent:	I have a lot of pain in my leg.
The doctor:	What happened to you? Did you fall?
Mrs. Laurent:	No, I didn't fall. Yesterday, I was at the health club where I did a lot of exercising. I took a modern dance class, I ran, and I swam a little.
The doctor:	Lie down. I'm going to examine you.
Mrs. Laurent:	Ouch!!!
The doctor:	You don't have anything broken, but you have a muscular inflammation.
Mrs. Laurent:	What should I do? Is it serious?
The doctor:	No, but it would be better to stop all forms of exercise and to take some anti-inflammatory pills three times per day. There is your prescription.
Mrs. Laurent:	Thank you, doctor.
The doctor:	Come back to see me in one week if you still have pain.

Take It Further

You saw some useful irregular verbs in that dialogue: courir (*to run*) and valoir (*to be worth*).

Here is the full conjugation of courir in the present tense:

COURIR (*TO RUN*) - **PRESENT**			
je cours	*I run*	**nous courons**	*we run*
tu cours	*you run*	**vous courez**	*you run*
il court	*he runs*	**ils courent**	*they run*
elle court	*she runs*	**elles courent**	*they run*

As you saw in the dialogue, the past participle of courir is couru.

J'ai couru le marathon.
I ran the marathon.

The future and conditional are formed with **courr-**. The subjunctive is formed the same way as any other verb (drop the **-ent** from **courent** and add the subjunctive endings).

Now here is the full conjugation of **valoir** (*to be worth*) in the present tense:

VALOIR *(TO BE WORTH)* - **PRESENT**			
je vaux	*I am worth*	**nous valons**	*we are worth*
tu vaux	*you are worth*	**vous valez**	*you are worth*
il vaut	*he is worth*	**ils valent**	*they are worth*
elle vaut	*she is worth*	**elles valent**	*they are worth*

Vous valez combien ?
How much are you worth?

When **il vaut** (*he is worth, it is worth*) is followed by **mieux** (*better*), it becomes a fixed expression that means *it is better* or *it would be better*.

Il vaut mieux cesser toute forme d'exercice.
It would be better to stop all forms of exercise.

Il vaut mieux le faire.
It is better to do it.

Note that **il vaut mieux que** (*it is better that, it would be better that*) is followed by the subjunctive:

Il vaut mieux que vous finissiez.
It would be better for you to finish. (lit., It would be better that you finish.)

Valoir is also used in expressions like **valoir la peine** (*to be worth the trouble*):

Ça ne vaut pas la peine.
It's not worth the trouble./This is not worth the trouble.

The past participle of **valoir** is **valu**. The future and conditional are formed with **vaudr-**. In fact, sometimes the conditional form is used instead of the present tense form:

Il vaudrait mieux...
It would be better ...

Valoir is actually irregular in the subjunctive as well, but you'll learn more about that later on in this lesson.

Regarding the other verbs you saw in the dialogue, remember that **allonger** (*to lay down, to lie down*) and **nager** (*to swim*) conjugate like **manger** (*to eat*) in the present tense. You also saw the verb **cesser** (*to stop, to cease*), which is a regular **-er** verb.

Finally, let's look at some of the new words you saw in the dialogue:

inflammation	l'inflammation (*f.*)
anti-inflammatory	anti-inflammatoire
muscular	musculaire (*medical*), musclé/ musclée (*person*)
form, shape, figure	la forme
pain, sorrow	la douleur

Note that forme is used in a variety of health-related phrases and expressions, such as **le club de forme/le club de remise en forme** (*health club*), **être en forme** (*to be fit, to be in shape*), **rester en forme** (*to stay in shape*), and **être en pleine/bonne forme** (*to be in good shape*).

 ## Conversation Practice 1

Re-read Conversation 1. Then say whether each sentence below is **vrai** (*true*) or **faux** (*false*). Next to each sentence, write down V for **vrai** or F for **faux**.

1. **Mme Laurent a du mal à marcher.** _____

2. **Mme Laurent est tombée.** _____

3. **Au club de forme, Mme Laurent a fait de la natation.** _____

4. **Le docteur dit que Mme Laurent s'est cassé la jambe.** _____

ANSWER KEY:
1. V (*Yes, she is having trouble walking.*) 2. F (*No, she didn't fall.*) 3. V (*Yes, she did go swimming at the health club.*) 4. F (*No, the doctor said she didn't break anything.*)

 ## Word Recall

Let's practice quantities. Match the quantities on the left to the correct English translations on the right.

1. un peu de	a. *a lot of*
2. beaucoup de	b. *more of*
3. moins de	c. *less of, fewer of*
4. plus de	d. *a little of*

ANSWER KEY:
1. d; 2. a; 3. c; 4. b

Grammar Builder 1
IRREGULAR SUBJUNCTIVE

▶ 16B Lesson 16 Grammar Builder 1 (CD 9, Track 18)

To form the subjunctive, most verbs that are irregular in the present tense follow the same pattern as verbs that are regular in the present tense: they drop the -ent from the present tense ils/elles form and add the appropriate subjunctive ending.

For example, to form the subjunctive of the irregular verb écrire (*to write*), simply drop the -ent from the ils/elles form in the present tense (écrivent) and then add the endings.

ÉCRIRE (*TO WRITE*) - **SUBJUNCTIVE**	
que j'écrive	que nous écrivions
que tu écrives	que vous écriviez
qu'il écrive	qu'ils écrivent
qu'elle écrive	qu'elles écrivent

However, there are exceptions.

For instance, if a verb has a different spelling for its nous and vous forms than for the rest of its forms in the present tense (such as elle achète vs. nous achetons), then that verb is usually conjugated a little differently in the subjunctive.

Examples of verbs with nous and vous spelling variations include, but are not limited to:

acheter	to buy
appeler	to call
jeter	to throw, to throw out/away
préférer	to prefer

prendre	to take, to have
comprendre	to understand
venir	to come
boire	to drink
croire	to believe
devoir	to have to, must, should, to owe
envoyer	to send
payer	to pay, to pay for
voir	to see

For these verbs, the **nous** and **vous** forms in the subjunctive are based on the present tense **nous** form instead of the **ils/elles** form. The rest of the forms (**je, tu, il/elle, ils/elles**) conjugate normally.

In other words, to conjugate the **nous** and **vous** forms of these types of verbs in the subjunctive, drop the **-ons** from the present tense **nous** form and then add the appropriate subjunctive ending (**-ions** or **-iez**).

For example, in the present tense, the **ils/elles** form of the verb **acheter** is **achètent**. So to create the **je** form of **acheter** in the subjunctive, you would drop the **-ent** from **achètent** and then add the **-e** subjunctive ending.

que j'achète
that I buy

However, to create the **nous** form of **acheter** in the subjunctive, you would drop the **-ons** from the **nous** form of **acheter** in the present tense (**achetons**), and then add the **-ions** subjunctive ending.

que nous achetions
that we buy

Now let's take a look at some more examples of verbs with nous and vous spelling variations.

Here is the full conjugation of prendre (*to take*) in the subjunctive. Remember that the ils/elles form of prendre in the present tense is prennent, but the nous form is prenons.

PRENDRE *(TO TAKE)* - **SUBJUNCTIVE**	
que je prenne	que nous prenions
que tu prennes	que vous preniez
qu'il prenne	qu'ils prennent
qu'elle prenne	qu'elles prennent

Don't forget that there are other verbs that conjugate like prendre, such as comprendre (*to understand*). Verbs that conjugate like prendre form the subjunctive in the same way. This is true for all verbs with nous and vous spelling variations.

Nous doutons qu'elle comprenne.
We doubt (that) she understands.

Now here is the full conjugation of venir (*to come*) in the subjunctive. Remember that the ils/elles form of venir in the present tense is viennent, but the nous form is venons.

VENIR *(TO COME)* - **SUBJUNCTIVE**	
que je vienne	que nous venions
que tu viennes	que vous veniez
qu'il vienne	qu'ils viennent
qu'elle vienne	qu'elles viennent

BOIRE *(TO DRINK)* - SUBJUNCTIVE

que je boive	que nous buvions
que tu boives	que vous buviez
qu'il boive	qu'ils boivent
qu'elle boive	qu'elles boivent

CROIRE *(TO BELIEVE)* - SUBJUNCTIVE

que je croie	que nous croyions
que tu croies	que vous croyiez
qu'il croie	qu'ils croient
qu'elle croie	qu'elles croient

DEVOIR *(TO HAVE TO, MUST, SHOULD, TO OWE)* - SUBJUNCTIVE

que je doive	que nous devions
que tu doives	que vous deviez
qu'il doive	qu'ils doivent
qu'elle doive	qu'elles doivent

ENVOYER *(TO SEND)* - SUBJUNCTIVE

que j'envoie	que nous envoyions
que tu envoies	que vous envoyiez
qu'il envoie	qu'ils envoient
qu'elle envoie	qu'elles envoient

VOIR *(TO SEE)* - SUBJUNCTIVE

que je voie	que nous voyions
que tu voies	que vous voyiez

VOIR (TO SEE) - SUBJUNCTIVE	
qu'il voie	qu'ils voient
qu'elle voie	qu'elles voient

Note that **manger** (*to eat*) and **commencer** (*to start, to begin*) do not belong to this group of irregular verbs in the subjunctive; those two verbs, and any verbs that conjugate like them, form the subjunctive normally.

Finally, there are also verbs that are completely irregular in the subjunctive. We'll look at them in Grammar Builder 2.

✎ Work Out 1

Translate the following sentences into English, with the subjunctive only expressing the present tense.

1. **Je voudrais que tu envoies cette lettre.** _____

   _____

2. **Il faut que vous croyiez.** _____

   _____

3. **Il préfère qu'elle vienne au restaurant.** _____

   _____

4. **Ils ne pensent pas que je doive aller à l'université.** _____

   _____

5. **Je vais partir avant que vous appeliez Hélène.** _____

   _____

ANSWER KEY:

1. *I would like you to send this/that letter.* 2. *It is necessary that you believe./You must/need to/have to believe.* 3. *He prefers (that) she come to the restaurant.* 4. *They don't think (that) I should/must/have to go to college.* 5. *I'm going to leave before you call Hélène.*

Conversation 2

In this dialogue, Anne and Nancy are discussing diets.

(▶) 16C Lesson 16 Conversation 2 (CD 9, Track 19)

Anne :	Eh bien, mon mari et moi, nous sommes en train de suivre un régime.
Nancy :	Comment ? Tu suis un régime ? Pourquoi faut-il que tu perdes du poids? Tu ne grossis pas, ma chère.
Anne :	Merci, Anne. Grâce à Dieu, je suis en bonne forme après tout le chocolat que je mange, mais il est nécessaire que mon mari perde cinq kilos.
Nancy :	Je doute que ce soit facile. Tu sais bien que les hommes n'aiment pas manger tout ce qui est bon pour eux.
Anne :	Il est important que je fasse des repas plus légers car il faut que mon mari maigrisse. C'est plus facile de le faire ensemble, tu sais.
Nancy :	Mon docteur voudrait aussi que nous perdions quelques kilos. Mais moi, j'adore les desserts.
Anne :	Il est possible que tu puisses manger des desserts s'ils sont faits avec de bons ingrédients, comme les fruits, par exemple.

Anne:	*Well, my husband and I, we are in the middle of following a diet.*
Nancy:	*What did you say? You're following a diet? Why do you need to lose some weight? You're not gaining weight, my dear.*
Anne:	*Thanks, Anne. Thank God (lit., Thanks to God), I am in good shape after all the chocolate that I eat, but my husband needs to lose five kilos (~eleven pounds).*

Nancy:	*I doubt that it will be easy. You know well that men don't like eating everything that is good for them (lit., all what is good for them).*
Anne:	*It's important that I make lighter meals because my husband needs to lose weight. It's easier to do it together, you know.*
Nancy:	*My doctor would also like us to lose some kilos. But me, I love desserts.*
Anne:	*Maybe (lit., It is possible that) you can eat desserts if they are made with good ingredients, like fruit, for example.*

Take It Further

There are a few more cases where the subjunctive is used. Unfortunately, they are a little more complicated than the ones you learned earlier. We will cover some of them briefly here.

1. The subjunctive is used after a relative pronoun (que or qui) if there is doubt or denial.

For example:

Nous cherchons une personne qui vende sa maison.
We're looking for a person who's selling his/her house.

There is doubt—this person may not be found—so the subjunctive is used. Now take a look at the following sentence:

Nous avons un ami qui vend sa maison.
We have a friend who's selling his house.

In this case, you don't use the subjunctive because there is no doubt. The person clearly exists.

Unit 4 Lesson 16: Conversations   289

2. The subjunctive is also used after a relative pronoun (**que** or **qui**) if it's preceded by a superlative (*the most, the best, the tallest*, etc.), unless you're stating a fact.

For instance, you would use the subjunctive here because you're expressing your opinion:

Paris est la plus belle ville que nous visitions.
Paris is the most beautiful city that we're visiting.

But you wouldn't use the subjunctive in this sentence because you're stating a fact:

Paris est la plus grande ville que nous visitons.
Paris is the biggest city that we're visiting.

3. Sometimes the subjunctive is used in certain exclamations or commands.

Qu'elle entre !
Let her enter!/Let her come in! (lit., That she enter!)

Vive la France !
Long live France! (lit., Live France!)

 ## Conversation Practice 2
Translate the following sentences into English.

1. **Tu suis un régime.** _____

2. **Je suis en bonne forme.** _____

3. **Tu ne grossis pas.** _____

4. C'est plus facile de le faire ensemble. _____

_____

ANSWER KEY:
1. *You're following a diet./You follow a diet.* 2. *I'm in good shape.* 3. *You're not gaining weight./You don't gain weight.* 4. *It's easier to do it together.*

✎ Word Recall

Remember greetings from *Essential* and *Intermediate French*? They're important to know, so let's review.

1. *How are you? (polite)* _____

2. *How are you? (familiar)* _____

3. *What's your name? (familiar)* _____

4. *What's your name? (polite)* _____

5. *Nice to meet you.* _____

ANSWER KEY:
1. **Comment allez-vous ?** 2. **Comment vas-tu ?** 3. **Comment t'appelles-tu ?** 4. **Comment vous appelez-vous ?** 5. **Enchanté/Enchantée (de faire votre connaissance).**

Grammar Builder 2
MORE IRREGULAR SUBJUNCTIVE

▶ 16D Lesson 16 Grammar Builder 2 (CD 9, Track 20)

As you know, there are some verbs that are completely irregular in the subjunctive. Unfortunately, they simply need to be memorized.

FAIRE *(TO DO, TO MAKE)* - **SUBJUNCTIVE**	
que je fasse	que nous fassions
que tu fasses	que vous fassiez

FAIRE *(TO DO, TO MAKE)* - **SUBJUNCTIVE**	
qu'il fasse	qu'ils fassent
qu'elle fasse	qu'elles fassent

POUVOIR *(CAN, TO BE ABLE TO)* - **SUBJUNCTIVE**	
que je puisse	que nous puissions
que tu puisses	que vous puissiez
qu'il puisse	qu'ils puissent
qu'elle puisse	qu'elles puissent

SAVOIR *(TO KNOW)* - **SUBJUNCTIVE**	
que je sache	que nous sachions
que tu saches	que vous sachiez
qu'il sache	qu'ils sachent
qu'elle sache	qu'elles sachent

For the following verbs, notice that the **nous** and **vous** forms are different from the rest of the forms.

VOULOIR *(TO WANT, TO WISH)* - **SUBJUNCTIVE**	
que je veuille	que nous voulions
que tu veuilles	que vous vouliez
qu'il veuille	qu'ils veuillent
qu'elle veuille	qu'elles veuillent

ALLER *(TO GO)* - **SUBJUNCTIVE**	
que j'aille	que nous allions
que tu ailles	que vous alliez
qu'il aille	qu'ils aillent

ALLER *(TO GO)* - **SUBJUNCTIVE**	
qu'elle aille	qu'elles aillent

Remember valoir (*to be worth*) from Take It Further? It's also irregular in the subjunctive, and it's formed in a similar way to aller: que je vaille, que tu vailles, qu'il/elle vaille, que nous valions, que vous valiez, qu'ils/elles vaillent.

Not surprisingly, être (*to be*) and avoir (*to have*) are completely irregular as well. However, they also have different endings from the normal subjunctive endings. Fortunately, they are the only verbs that have different endings in the subjunctive.

Here are avoir and être in the subjunctive:

AVOIR *(TO HAVE)* - **SUBJUNCTIVE**	
que j'aie	que nous ayons
que tu aies	que vous ayez
qu'il ait	qu'ils aient
qu'elle ait	qu'elles aient

ÊTRE *(TO BE)* - **SUBJUNCTIVE**	
que je sois	que nous soyons
que tu sois	que vous soyez
qu'il soit	qu'ils soient
qu'elle soit	qu'elles soient

Finally, let's look at some example sentences using irregular verbs in the subjunctive:

Il faut que tu sois à l'heure.
You have to be on time. (It is necessary that you be on time.)

Je ne crois pas qu'il puisse le faire.
I don't believe (that) he can do it.

J'ai peur qu'il ne sache pas la vérité.
I'm afraid (that) he doesn't know the truth.

✎ Work Out 2

Translate the following sentences into English, with the subjunctive only expressing the present tense.

1. Nous doutons qu'elle ait le livre. _____

2. Il faut que nous écrivions beaucoup. _____

3. Je suis heureux que tu puisses venir avec nous. _____

4. Bien qu'elle soit gentille, il n'est pas gentil. _____

5. Je ne veux pas que vous fassiez du jogging. _____

ANSWER KEY:
1. *We doubt (that) she has the book.* 2. *It is necessary that we write a lot./We must/need to/have to write a lot.* 3. *I am happy that you can come with us.* 4. *Although she is nice/kind, he is not nice/kind.* 5. *I don't want you to go jogging.*

✎ Drive It Home

A. Fill in the blanks with the subjunctive of être.

1. Je veux que tu _____ heureux. (*I want you to be happy.*)

2. Je veux qu'il _____ heureux. (*I want him to be happy.*)

3. Je veux que vous_____ heureux. (*I want you to be happy.*)

4. Je veux qu'elle_____ heureuse. (*I want her to be happy.*)

B. Now fill in the blanks with the subjunctive of aller.

1. **Il faut que nous** _____ **au cabinet médical.**

   (We need to go to the doctor's office.)

2. **Il faut qu'ils** _____ **au cabinet médical.**

   (They need to go to the doctor's office.)

3. **Il faut que j'**_____ **au cabinet médical.**

   (I need to go to the doctor's office.)

4. **Il faut que tu** _____ **au cabinet médical.**

   (You need to go to the doctor's office.)

C. Finally, fill in the blanks with the subjunctive of avoir.

1. **Je ne pense pas que vous** _____ **le verre.** *(I don't think you have the glass.)*

2. **Je ne pense pas qu'elle** _____ **le verre.** *(I don't think she has the glass.)*

3. **Je ne pense pas qu'elles** _____ **le verre.** *(I don't think they have the glass.)*

4. **Je ne pense pas que tu** _____ **le verre.** *(I don't think you have the glass.)*

ANSWER KEY:
A. 1. sois; 2. soit; 3. soyez; 4. soit
B. 1. allions; 2. aillent; 3. aille; 4. ailles
C. 1. ayez; 2. ait; 3. aient; 4. aies

Tip

Of course, the best way to learn when to use the subjunctive is simply by practicing as much as possible. Here are some more example sentences with the subjunctive:

Il faut qu'on aille au gymnase cet après-midi.
We need to go to the gym this afternoon.

Il faut que je fasse beaucoup d'exercice.
I need to do a lot of exercising.

Pour que je puisse être en forme, je vais au club de remise en forme.
So that I can be in shape, I go to the health club.

Il est nécessaire de bien manger pour que tu puisses être en bonne santé.
It is necessary to eat well so that you can be in good health.

Je voudrais bien que vous veniez avec nous.
I'd really like you to come with us.

Nous regrettons que vous ne puissiez pas venir.
We're sorry (that) you can't come.

Je doute que j'y aille.
I doubt that I'll go there.

Croyez-vous que ce soit possible ?
Do you believe it's possible?

Elles sont contentes que vous soyez ici.
They are happy (that) you're here.

Nous cherchons quelqu'un qui puisse voyager.
We're looking for someone who can travel.

Qu'ils viennent !
Let them come! (lit., That they come!)

Votre société fait les meilleurs produits que je connaisse.
Your company makes the best products (that) I know.

How Did You Do?

Let's see how you did! By now, you should be able to:

☐ Talk about what you need to *buy*, *take*, or *see*
(Still unsure? Jump back to page 283)

☐ Say what you have to *be* or what you doubt someone *can* do
(Still unsure? Jump back to page 291)

Unit 4 Essentials

Don't forget to go to **www.livinglanguage.com/languagelab** to access your free online tools for this lesson: audiovisual flashcards, and interactive games and quizzes.

Vocabulary Essentials

PARTS OF THE BODY

body		neck	
head		shoulder	
eye		back	
eyes		arm	
nose		hand	
mouth		leg	
ear		knee	
tooth		foot	

[Pg. 234] (If you're stuck, visit this page to review!)

TO HAVE PAIN OR TO HURT

to have pain in, to ache, to have an ache, to have a sore something	
to have trouble (doing something)	
to hurt	

[Pg. 237]

Advanced French

HEALTH

illness, disease		common cold	
medical checkup		fever	
doctor's office		flu	
doctor		virus	
patient		allergy	
x-ray		infection	
diagnosis		care	

[Pg. 238]

INJURIES AND DISABILITIES

to break one's arm/leg	
to sprain one's ankle	
to walk with a cane	
to walk with crutches	
wheelchair	
to be disabled	
to have Alzheimer's disease	
to have Parkinson's disease	
to be deaf	
to use sign language	
to be paralyzed	
to wear contact lenses	
to be blind	
to need a seeing-eye dog	

[Pg. 246]

EXERCISE

exercise		stationary bike	
gym		workout, training	
health club		to be sweating	
to train		heartbeat	
treadmill		to be fit, to be in shape	

[Pg. 251]

AT THE DOCTOR'S OFFICE

I would like to make an appointment.	
What's the matter? (lit., What is there?)	
What happened to you? (pl./fml.)	
What should I do?	
The doctor gives a prescription. (lit., The doctor makes a prescription.)	
I have trouble swallowing.	
I have a sore throat.	
He has a headache.	
My nose is stuffed up./I have a stuffy nose.	

[Pg. 259]

EMERGENCIES

emergency situations	
It's necessary to have a first-aid kit.	
to have an accident	
Call the emergency medical service.	
The ambulance is arriving.	
He needs a blood transfusion.	
It's a superficial injury.	
It's not serious.	
Do you have insurance?	
Take a pill/a tablet/a capsule.	
Sometimes there are side effects.	
It's a burn.	
It's a cut.	
The dentist is going to replace the filling.	
It's necessary to have a tooth pulled.	

[Pg. 265]

Grammar Essentials

RECIPROCAL VERBS

When a verb uses a plural reflexive pronoun to mean *each other*, it is known as a reciprocal verb, such as **s'aimer** (*to like/love each other*) and **se dire** (*to tell each other, to say to each other*).

DIRECT OBJECTS AND AVOIR

If a verb that uses **avoir** is *preceded* by a direct object noun or pronoun, then that verb's past participle must agree in gender and number with the direct object noun or pronoun.

FORMING THE SUBJUNCTIVE

1. Drop the **-ent** from the **ils/elles** form of the verb in the present tense.
2. Add the following endings:

PRONOUN	ENDING	PRONOUN	ENDING
je	-e	nous	-ions
tu	-es	vous	-iez
il	-e	ils	-ent
elle	-e	elles	-ent

3. The subjunctive usually follows the conjunction **que** (*that*).
4. This form of the subjunctive, known as the "present subjunctive," is used for both the present tense and the future tense.

PARLER *(TO SPEAK)* - **SUBJUNCTIVE**			
that I speak	**que je parle**	*that we speak*	**que nous parlions**
that you speak (infml.)	**que tu parles**	*that you speak (pl./fml.)*	**que vous parliez**
that he speak	**qu'il parle**	*that they speak (m.)*	**qu'ils parlent**
that she speak	**qu'elle parle**	*that they speak (f.)*	**qu'elles parlent**

FINIR *(TO FINISH)* **- SUBJUNCTIVE**

that I finish	que je finisse	*that we finish*	que nous finissions
that you finish (infml.)	que tu finisses	*that you finish (pl./fml.)*	que vous finissiez
that he finish	qu'il finisse	*that they finish (m.)*	qu'ils finissent
that she finish	qu'elle finisse	*that they finish (f.)*	qu'elles finissent

RÉPONDRE *(TO ANSWER, TO RESPOND)* **- SUBJUNCTIVE**

that I answer	que je réponde	*that we answer*	que nous répondions
that you answer (infml.)	que tu répondes	*that you answer (pl./fml.)*	que vous répondiez
that he answer	qu'il réponde	*that they answer (m.)*	qu'ils répondent
that she answer	qu'elle réponde	*that they answer (f.)*	qu'elles répondent

5. Some verbs that are irregular in the present tense, such as écrire *(to write)*, still form the subjunctive regularly.

ÉCRIRE *(TO WRITE)* **- SUBJUNCTIVE**

that I write	que j'écrive	*that we write*	que nous écrivions
that you write (infml.)	que tu écrives	*that you write (pl./fml.)*	que vous écriviez
that he write	qu'il écrive	*that they write (m.)*	qu'ils écrivent
that she write	qu'elle écrive	*that they write (f.)*	qu'elles écrivent

THE SUBJUNCTIVE OF VERBS WITH SPELLING VARIATIONS

Verbs that have a different spelling for their nous and vous forms than for the rest of their forms in the present tense conjugate the subjunctive differently. To conjugate the nous and vous forms of these types of verbs in the subjunctive, drop the -ons from the present tense nous form and then add the appropriate subjunctive ending.

ACHETER (TO BUY) - SUBJUNCTIVE			
that I buy	que j'achète	that we buy	que nous achetions
that you buy (infml.)	que tu achètes	that you buy (pl./fml.)	que vous achetiez
that he buy	qu'il achète	that they buy (m.)	qu'ils achètent
that she buy	qu'elle achète	that they buy (f.)	qu'elles achètent

PRENDRE (TO TAKE) - SUBJUNCTIVE			
that I take	que je prenne	that we take	que nous prenions
that you take (infml.)	que tu prennes	that you take (pl./fml.)	que vous preniez
that he take	qu'il prenne	that they take (m.)	qu'ils prennent
that she take	qu'elle prenne	that they take (f.)	qu'elles prennent

Other verbs with these spelling variations include: appeler (to call), jeter (to throw, to throw out/away), préférer (to prefer), comprendre (to understand), venir (to come), boire (to drink), croire (to believe), devoir (to have to, must, should, to owe), payer (to pay, to pay for), and voir (to see).

MORE IRREGULAR VERBS IN THE SUBJUNCTIVE

ALLER *(TO GO)* - **SUBJUNCTIVE**

that I go	que j'aille	*that we go*	que nous allions
that you go (infml.)	que tu ailles	*that you go (pl./fml.)*	que vous alliez
that he go	qu'il aille	*that they go (m.)*	qu'ils aillent
that she go	qu'elle aille	*that they go (f.)*	qu'elles aillent

AVOIR *(TO HAVE)* - **SUBJUNCTIVE**

that I have	que j'aie	*that we have*	que nous ayons
that you have (infml.)	que tu aies	*that you have (pl./fml.)*	que vous ayez
that he have	qu'il ait	*that they have (m.)*	qu'ils aient
that she have	qu'elle ait	*that they have (f.)*	qu'elles aient

ÊTRE *(TO BE)* - **SUBJUNCTIVE**

that I be	que je sois	*that we be*	que nous soyons
that you be (infml.)	que tu sois	*that you be (pl./fml.)*	que vous soyez
that he be	qu'il soit	*that they be (m.)*	qu'ils soient
that she is	qu'elle soit	*that they be (f.)*	qu'elles soient

FAIRE *(TO DO, TO MAKE)* - **SUBJUNCTIVE**

that I make	que je fasse	*that we make*	que nous fassions
that you make (infml.)	que tu fasses	*that you make (pl./fml.)*	que vous fassiez
that he make	qu'il fasse	*that they make (m.)*	qu'ils fassent

FAIRE *(TO DO, TO MAKE)* - **SUBJUNCTIVE**			
that she make	qu'elle fasse	*that they make (f.)*	qu'elles fassent

POUVOIR *(CAN, TO BE ABLE TO)* - **SUBJUNCTIVE**			
that I can	que je puisse	*that we can*	que nous puissions
that you can (infml.)	que tu puisses	*that you can (pl./fml.)*	que vous puissiez
that he can	qu'il puisse	*that they can (m.)*	qu'ils puissent
that she can	qu'elle puisse	*that they can (f.)*	qu'elles puissent

SAVOIR *(TO KNOW)* - **SUBJUNCTIVE**			
that I know	que je sache	*that we know*	que nous sachions
that you know (infml.)	que tu saches	*that you know (pl./fml.)*	que vous sachiez
that he know	qu'il sache	*that they know (m.)*	qu'ils sachent
that she know	qu'elle sache	*that they know (f.)*	qu'elles sachent

VOULOIR *(TO WANT)* - **SUBJUNCTIVE**			
that I want	que je veuille	*that we want*	que nous voulions
that you want (infml.)	que tu veuilles	*that you want (pl./fml.)*	que vous vouliez
that he want	qu'il veuille	*that they want (m.)*	qu'ils veuillent
that she want	qu'elle veuille	*that they want (f.)*	qu'elles veuillent

Advanced French

USING THE SUBJUNCTIVE

The subjunctive is used after:

1. verbs of command, request, permission, or other expressions imposing your will on someone else + que

to request that, to ask that	demander que	*to order that*	ordonner que
to prevent from, to keep from	empêcher que	*to allow that*	permettre que
to demand that, to require that	exiger que	*to suggest that*	suggérer que

2. verbs or expressions of doubt, denial, uncertainty, or possibility + que

to doubt that	douter que
it seems that	il semble que
it is possible that	il est probable que

3. verbs or expressions of approval, disapproval, or preference + que

to prefer that (lit., to like better that)	aimer mieux que
to recommend that	recommander que
to prefer that	préférer que
it is preferable that	il est préférable que

4. verbs or expressions of wishing, want, or desire + que

to desire that, to want that, to wish that	désirer que
to want that, to wish that	vouloir que
to wish that	souhaiter que

5. verbs of thinking or believing when they are negative or in the form of a question + que.

to think that	penser que
to believe that	croire que
to find that, to think that	trouver que

6. verbs or expressions of necessity or need + que

it is necessary that	il faut que
to need for	avoir besoin que

7. expressions of urgency or importance + que

it is urgent that	il est urgent que
it is important that	il est important que
it is essential that	il est essentiel que

8. expressions of emotion, such as joy, fear, sorrow, or regret + que

9. specific conjunctions with que

in order that, so that	afin que, pour que	although	bien que, quoique
before	avant que	without	sans que
unless	à moins que... ne	until	jusqu'à ce que

10. The subjunctive is **only** used when the subject of the verb before que is different from the subject of the verb after que.

OTHER VERBS

SUIVRE (TO FOLLOW) - PRESENT			
I follow	je suis	we follow	nous suivons
you follow (infml.)	tu suis	you follow (pl./fml.)	vous suivez
he follows	il suit	they follow (m.)	ils suivent
she follows	elle suit	they follow (f.)	elles suivent
Past Participle: suivi			

Unit 4 Quiz

You've made it to the very last quiz! Félicitations !

Once you successfully complete this quiz, you'll be done with the entire program and ready to go out and speak French naturally and conversationally.

Ready?

A. Match English words on the left to the correct French translations on the right.

1. *eye*	a. **la tête**
2. *head*	b. **la bouche**
3. *nose*	c. **l'œil**
4. *mouth*	d. **le dos**
5. *back*	e. **le nez**

B. Translate the following sentences into English.

1. J'ai un rhume. _____

2. J'ai la grippe. _____

3. J'ai mal à la tête. _____

4. J'ai mal à la gorge. _____

5. J'ai mal aux dents. _____

C. Conjugate the following verbs in the subjunctive.

1. que j' _____ (aller)

2. que tu _____ (être)

3. qu'il _____ (avoir)

4. que nous _____ (acheter)

5. qu'elles _____ (vendre)

D. Translate the following sentences into English. Only translate the subjunctive in the present tense.

1. 1. J'ai suggéré qu'elle fasse ses devoirs. _____
   _____

2. Nous doutons qu'elle puisse le faire. _____
   _____

3. Elle voudrait que vous leur répondiez. _____
   _____

4. Pensez-vous qu'il veuille venir au restaurant ? _____
   _____

5. J'ai peur que vous ne compreniez pas. _____
   _____

ANSWER KEY:
A. 1. c; 2. a; 3. e; 4. b; 5. d
B. 1. I have a cold. 2. I have the flu. 3. I have a headache. 4. I have a sore throat. 5. I have a toothache.
C. 1. aille; 2. sois; 3. ait; 4. achetions; 5. vendent
D. 1. I suggested (that) she do her homework. 2. We doubt (that) she can do it. 3. She would like you to respond to/answer them. 3. Do you think (that) he wants to come to the restaurant? 5. I'm afraid (that) you don't understand.

How Did You Do?

Give yourself a point for every correct answer, then use the following key to determine whether or not you're ready to move on:

0-7 points: It's probably best to go back and study the lessons again to make sure you understood everything completely. Take your time; it's not a race! Make sure you spend time reviewing the vocabulary and reading through each grammar note carefully.

8-16 points: If the questions you missed were in Section A or B, you may want to review the vocabulary again; if you missed answers mostly in Section C or D, check the Unit 4 Essentials to make sure you have your conjugations and other grammar basics down.

17-20 points: Wow, congratulations! You made it through the entire program successfully! However, don't forget to come back and review as much as you can. This is one of the keys to learning a new language—not just holding it temporarily in your short-term memory, but making it stick in your long-term memory. Go back over old lists and example sentences. Test yourself with flashcards. Listen to the audio from previous lessons. Just practice, practice, practice.

Bonne chance ! (Good luck!)

_____ **Points**

Pronunciation Guide

Consonants

Note that the letter h can act as either a vowel or a consonant. See the end of the Pronunciation Guide for more information.

FRENCH	APPROXIMATE SOUND	PHONETIC SYMBOL	EXAMPLES
b, d, f, k, m, n, p, t, v, z	same as in English	same as in English	
ç	*s*	[s]	français [frah(n)-seh] (*French*)
c before a, o, u	*k*	[k]	cave [kahv] (*cellar*)
c before e, i, y	*s*	[s]	cinéma [see-nay-mah] (*movie theater*)
ch	*sh*	[sh]	chaud [shoh] (*hot*)
g before a, o, u	*g* in *game*	[g]	gâteau [gah-toh] (*cake*)
g before e, i, y	*s* in *measure*	[zh]	âge [ahzh] (*age*)
gn	*ni* in *onion*	[ny]	agneau [ah-nyoh] (*lamb*)
j	*s* in *measure*	[zh]	jeu [zhuh] (*game*)
l	*l*	[l]	lent [lah(n)] (*slow*)
l when it's at the end of the word and follows i	*y* in *yes*	[y]	fauteuil [foh-tuhy] (*armchair*)
ll	*ll* in *ill*	[l]	elle [ehl] (*she*), ville [veel] (*town*)
ll between i and another vowel	*y* in *yes*	[y]	fille [feey] (*girl, daughter*), papillon [pah-pee-yoh(n)] (*butterfly*)

FRENCH	APPROXIMATE SOUND	PHONETIC SYMBOL	EXAMPLES
qu, final q	k	[k]	qui [kee] (who), cinq [sa(n)k] (five)
r	pronounced in the back of the mouth, like a light gargling sound	[r]	Paris [pah-ree] (Paris)
s between vowels	z in zebra	[z]	maison [meh-zoh(n)] (house)
s at the beginning of a word or before/after a consonant	s	[s]	salle [sahl] (hall, room), course [koors] (errand)
ss	s	[s]	tasse [tahs] (cup)
th	t	[t]	thé [tay] (tea)
w	v	[v]	wagon-lit [vah-goh(n)-lee] (sleeping car)
x usually before a vowel	x in exact	[gz]	exact [ehgz-ahkt] (exact)
x before a consonant or final e	x in exterior	[ks]	extérieur [ehks-tay-ree-uhr] (outside)

Keep in mind that most final consonants are silent in French, as with the -s in Paris [pah-ree] (Paris). However, there are five letters that are often (but not always) pronounced when final: c, f, l, q, and r.

French speakers also pronounce some final consonants when the next word begins with a vowel or silent h (see the end of the Pronunciation Guide for more information on the "silent h"). This is known as liaison [lyeh-zoh(n)] (link).

For example, the -s in nous [noo] (we) normally isn't pronounced. However, if it's followed by a word that begins with a vowel, such as allons [ah-loh(n)], then you do pronounce it: nous allons [noo zah-loh(n)] (we go). Notice that, in liaison, the s or x is pronounced z and it is "linked" to the following word: [zah-loh(n)]. Here's another example of liaison: un grand arbre [uh(n) grah(n) tahr-bruh] (a big tree). Normally, the -d in grand [grah(n)] is not pronounced, but, in liaison, it is pronounced t and linked to the following word.

Vowels

FRENCH	APPROXIMATE SOUND	PHONETIC SYMBOL	EXAMPLES
a, à, â	*a* in *father*	[ah]	laver [lah-vay] (*to wash*), à [ah] (*in, to, at*)
é, er, ez (end of a word), et	*ay* in *lay*	[ay]	été [ay-tay] (*summer*), aller [ah-lay] (*to go*), ballet [bah-lay] (*ballet*)
è, ê, ei, ai, aî	*e* in *bed*, with relaxed lips	[eh]	père [pehr] (*father*), forêt [foh-reh] (*forest*), faire [fehr] (*to do*)

FRENCH	APPROXIMATE SOUND	PHONETIC SYMBOL	EXAMPLES
e without an accent (and not combined with another vowel or r, z, t)	a in *above*, or e in *bed* with relaxed lips, or silent	[uh] *or* [eh] or silent at end of word	le [luh] *(the)*, belle [behl] *(beautiful)*, danse [dah(n)s] *(dance)*
eu, œu followed by a consonant sound	u in *fur* with lips very rounded and loose	[uh]	cœur [kuhr] *(heart)*
eu, œu not followed by any sound	u in *fur* with lips very rounded and tight	[uh]	feu [fuh] *(fire)*
eille, ey	ey in *hey*	[ehy]	bouteille [boo-tehy] *(bottle)*
euille, œil	a in *above* + y in *yesterday*	[uhy]	œil [uhy] *(eye)*
i	ee in *beet*	[ee]	ici [ee-see] *(here)*
i plus vowel	ee in *beet* + y in *yesterday*	[y]	violon [vyoh-loh(n)] *(violin)*
o, au, eau, ô	o in *both*	[oh]	mot [moh] *(word)*, eau [oh] *(water)*, hôtel [oh-tehl] *(hotel)*
oi	wa in *watt*	[wah]	moi [mwah] *(me)*
ou	oo in *boot*	[oo]	vous [voo] *(you)*
ou *before a vowel*	w in *week*	[w]	ouest [wehst] *(west)*, oui [wee] *(yes)*
oy	wa in *watt* + y in *yesterday*	[wahy]	foyer [fwahy-ay] *(home)*

FRENCH	APPROXIMATE SOUND	PHONETIC SYMBOL	EXAMPLES
u	keep your lips rounded as you pronounce *ee* in *beet*	[ew]	**tu** [tew] *(you)*
ui	*wee* in *week*	[wee]	**lui** [lwee] *(he, him, her)*

Nasal Vowels

FRENCH	APPROXIMATE SOUND	PHONETIC SYMBOL	EXAMPLES
an/en or am/em	*a* in *balm*, pronounced through both the mouth and the nose	[ah(n)] or [ah(m)]	**France** [frah(n)s] *(France),* **entrer** [ah(n)-tray] *(to enter),* **emmener** [ah(m)-muh-nay] *(to take along)*
in/yn/ain/ein or im/ym/aim/eim	*a* in *mad*, pronounced through both the mouth and the nose	[a(n)] or [a(m)]	**vin** [va(n)] *(wine),* **vain** [va(n)] *(vain),* **sympa** [sa(m)-pah] *(cool, nice, good),* **faim** [fa(m)] *(hunger)*
ien	*ee* in *beet* + *y* in *yesterday* + nasal *a* in *mad*	[ya(n)]	**rien** [rya(n)] *(nothing)*
oin	*w* + nasal *a* in *mad*	[wa(n)]	**loin** [lwa(n)] *(far)*

FRENCH	APPROXIMATE SOUND	PHONETIC SYMBOL	EXAMPLES
on or om	*o* in *song,* pronounced through both the mouth and the nose	[oh(n)] or [oh(m)]	bon [boh(n)] (*good*), tomber [toh(m)-bay] (*to fall*)
ion	*ee* in *beet* + *y* in *yesterday* + nasal *o* in *song*	[yoh(n)]	station [stah-syoh(n)] (*station*)
un or um	*u* in *lung,* pronounced through both the mouth and the nose	[uh(n)] or [uh(m)]	un [uh(n)] (*one, a/ an*), parfum [pahr-fuh(m)] (*perfume*)

The Letter H

In French, the letter h is not pronounced. For example, huit (*eight*) would be pronounced [weet].

However, there are actually two different types of h in French: the silent or mute h and the aspirated h. While you wouldn't pronounce either one, they behave differently.

The silent h acts like a vowel. For example, words like le, la, se, de, and so on become "contracted" (l', s', d', etc.) before a silent h:

l'homme (le + homme)	*the man*
s'habiller (se + habiller)	*to get dressed*

Also, you usually use liaison with a silent h. For instance, les hommes would be pronounced [lay zohm].

However, the aspirated h acts like a consonant. Words like le, la, se, de, etc. do **not** become l', s', d', and so on before an aspirated h:

| le homard | *the lobster* |
| se hâter | *to rush* |

Also, you do not use liaison with an aspirated h: les homards would be pronounced [lay oh-mahr].

Most h are silent, not aspirated. Still, there are many words that begin with an aspirated h. Unfortunately, there isn't an easy way to tell which are which. Just start by learning the common ones, and then continue memorizing others that you come across.

Apart from homme and habiller, here are some other examples of common words that begin with a silent h: habiter (*to live*), heure (*hour*), heureux/heureuse (*happy*), hier (*yesterday*), hôpital (*hospital*), horaire (*schedule*), and huile (*oil*). Apart from homard and hâter, here are some other examples of common words that begin with an aspirated h: huit (*eight*), héros (*hero*), haine (*hatred*), hasard (*chance*), hâte (*haste*), haut (*high*), honte (*shame*), and hors (*outside*).

Grammar Summary

Here is a brief snapshot of French grammar from *Essential* and *Intermediate French*. Keep in mind that there are exceptions to many grammar rules. For a more comprehensive grammar summary, please visit www.livinglanguage.com.

1. NUMBERS

CARDINAL		ORDINAL	
un/une	one	premier/première	first
deux	two	deuxième, second/seconde	second
trois	three	troisième	third
quatre	four	quatrième	fourth
cinq	five	cinquième	fifth
six	six	sixième	sixth
sept	seven	septième	seventh
huit	eight	huitième	eighth
neuf	nine	neuvième	ninth
dix	ten	dixième	tenth

2. ARTICLES

	DEFINITE		INDEFINITE	
	Singular	Plural	Singular	Plural
Masculine	le	les	un	des
Feminine	la	les	une	des

Note that l' is used instead of le and la before words beginning with a vowel or silent h.

3. CONTRACTIONS

de + le = du (*some/of the, masculine*)

de + les = des (*some/of the, plural*)

à + le = au (*to/at/in the, masculine*)

à + les = aux (*to/at/in the, plural*)

There is no contraction with la or l'. In a negative sentence, de la, de l', du, and des change to de/d'.

4. PLURALS

Most nouns add -s to form the plural. If a noun ends in -s, -x, or -z in the singular, there is no change in the plural.

Nouns ending in -eau or -eu, and some nouns ending in -ou, add -x instead of -s to form the plural. Many nouns ending in -al and -ail change to -aux in the plural.

5. ADJECTIVES

Adjectives agree with the nouns they modify in gender and number; that is, they are masculine if the noun is masculine, plural if the noun is plural, etc.

a. The feminine of an adjective is normally formed by adding -e to the masculine singular.

b. If the masculine singular already ends in -e, the adjective has the same form in the feminine.

c. Some adjectives double the final consonant of the masculine singular form and then add -e to form the feminine.

Advanced French

d. If the masculine singular ends in -x, change the ending to -se to form the feminine.

e. If the masculine singular ends in -f, change the ending to -ve to form the feminine.

f. If the masculine singular ends in -er, change the ending to -ère to form the feminine.

g. If the masculine singular ends in -et, change the ending to -ète or -ette to form the feminine.

h. The plural of adjectives is usually formed by adding -s to the masculine or feminine singular form. But if the adjective ends in -s or -x in the masculine singular, the masculine plural stays the same.

i. Most masculine adjectives ending in -al in the masculine singular, change the ending to -aux in the masculine plural.

Adjectives usually come after the noun. However, adjectives of beauty, age, goodness, and size (B-A-G-S adjectives) usually come before the noun.

6. POSSESSIVE ADJECTIVES

Possessive adjectives agree in gender and number with the possession.

BEFORE SINGULAR NOUNS		BEFORE PLURAL NOUNS	
Masculine	Feminine	Masculine and Feminine	
mon	ma	mes	*my*
ton	ta	tes	*your (familiar)*
son	sa	ses	*his, her, its*
notre	notre	nos	*our*
votre	votre	vos	*your (polite/plural)*
leur	leur	leurs	*their*

Before feminine singular nouns beginning with a vowel or silent h, use mon, ton, and son.

7. COMPARISONS

Most adjectives form the comparative with plus (*more*) and moins (*less*), using que where English uses *than*. To express *as ... as*, use aussi and que.

To express the superlative of something, use le/la/les + plus + adjective to express superiority (*the most, -est*) and le/la/les + moins + adjective to express inferiority (*the least*).

8. PRONOUNS

	SUBJECT	DIRECT OBJECT	INDIRECT OBJECT	STRESSED	REFLEXIVE
1st singular	je/j'	me/m'	me/m'	moi	me/m'
2nd singular	tu	te/t'	te/t'	toi	te/t'
3rd masculine singular	il	le/l'	lui	lui	se/s'
3rd feminine singular	elle	la/l'	lui	elle	se/s'
1st plural	nous	nous	nous	nous	nous
2nd plural	vous	vous	vous	vous	vous
3rd masculine plural	ils	les	leur	eux	se/s'

	SUBJECT	DIRECT OBJECT	INDIRECT OBJECT	STRESSED	REFLEXIVE
3rd feminine plural	elles	les	leur	elles	se/s'

On is an indefinite subject pronoun that means *we, one,* or *people/you/they in general.*

Stressed pronouns are generally used after prepositions (avec moi, etc.) or for emphasis (moi, j'ai vingt ans).

9. ORDER OF PRONOUNS

In sentences or negative commands, place pronouns in the following order:

subject pronouns	me/m' te/t' se/s' nous vous	le la l' les	lui leur	y	en	verb

In the positive imperative, place pronouns in the following order:

positive imperative form of verb	le la les	m' moi t' toi lui nous vous leur	y	en

10. QUESTION WORDS

où	where	de quel/quelle/ quels/quelles + noun	what/of what + noun
qu'est-ce que	what	combien (de)	how much, how many
quel/quelle, quels/quelles	which, what	à quelle heure	at what time
qui	who	pourquoi	why
comment	how	quand	when

11. DEMONSTRATIVES ADJECTIVES

Masculine Singular	ce	this, that
Masculine Singular (before a vowel or silent h)	cet	this, that
Feminine Singular	cette	this, that
Masculine Plural	ces	these, those
Feminine Plural	ces	these, those

When it is necessary to distinguish between *this* and *that*, -ci and -là are added to the noun: **Donnez-moi ce livre-ci.** (*Give me this book.*)

12. NEGATION

A sentence is made negative by placing **ne** before the verb and **pas** after it. When placed before a vowel or silent **h**, **ne** becomes **n'**.

To form the negative of the past tense, place **ne** (**n'**) and **pas** around the present tense form of **avoir** or **être**. To form a negative statement with a reflexive verb, place **ne** after the subject pronoun but before the reflexive pronoun, and then place **pas** immediately after the verb.

13. ADVERBS

Adverbs are usually placed after the verb. In the past tense, they're placed after the past participle. However, adverbs of quality (**bien, mal**), quantity (**beaucoup**) and frequency (**toujours**), along with some other adverbs, come before the past participle.

Most adverbs are formed from their corresponding adjectives. If the adjective ends in -e in the masculine singular, just add **-ment** to the masculine singular form. If the adjective ends in a consonant in the masculine singular, add **-ment** to the feminine singular form.

14. THE SUBJUNCTIVE

The subjunctive is used after:

a. verbs of command, request, permission, or other expressions imposing your will on someone else + **que**

b. verbs or expressions of doubt, denial, uncertainty, or possibility + **que**

c. verbs or expressions of approval, disapproval, or preference + **que**

d. verbs or expressions of wishing, want, or desire + **que**

e. verbs of thinking or believing when they are negative or in the form of a question + **que**

f. verbs or expressions of necessity or need + **que**

g. expressions of urgency or importance + **que**

h. expressions of emotion, such as joy, fear, sorrow, or regret + **que**

i. specific conjunctions with **que**

j. a relative pronoun (**que** or **qui**) if there is doubt or denial

k. a relative pronoun (que or qui) if it's preceded by a superlative, unless you're stating a fact

Sometimes the subjunctive is used in certain exclamations or commands: Vive la France ! (*Long live France!*).

15. REGULAR VERBS

There are three types of regular French verbs:

TYPE	EXAMPLE
verbs ending in -er	parler (*to speak*)
verbs ending in -re	vendre (*to sell*)
verbs ending in -ir	finir (*to finish*)

Here are the full conjugations of each example.

parler
to speak, to talk

je	nous
tu	vous
il/elle/on	ils/elles

Present		Imperative	
parle	parlons		Parlons !
parles	parlez	Parle !	Parlez !
parle	parlent		

Past		Imperfect	
ai parlé	avons parlé	parlais	parlions
as parlé	avez parlé	parlais	parliez
a parlé	ont parlé	parlait	parlaient

Future		Conditional	
parlerai	parlerons	parlerais	parlerions
parleras	parlerez	parlerais	parleriez
parlera	parleront	parlerait	parleraient

Future Perfect		Past Conditional	
aurai parlé	aurons parlé	aurais parlé	aurions parlé
auras parlé	aurez parlé	aurais parlé	auriez parlé
aura parlé	auront parlé	aurait parlé	auraient parlé

Past Perfect		Subjunctive	
avais parlé	avions parlé	parle	parlions
avais parlé	aviez parlé	parles	parliez
avait parlé	avaient parlé	parle	parlent

vendre
to sell

je	nous
tu	vous
il/elle/on	ils/elles

Present

vends	vendons
vends	vendez
vend	vendent

Imperative

	Vendons !
Vends !	Vendez !

Past

ai vendu	avons vendu
as vendu	avez vendu
a vendu	ont vendu

Imperfect

vendais	vendions
vendais	vendiez
vendait	vendaient

Future

vendrai	vendrons
vendras	vendrez
vendra	vendront

Conditional

vendrais	vendrions
vendrais	vendriez
vendrait	vendraient

Future Perfect

aurai vendu	aurons vendu
auras vendu	aurez vendu
aura vendu	auront vendu

Past Conditional

aurais vendu	aurions vendu
aurais vendu	auriez vendu
aurait vendu	auraient vendu

Past Perfect

avais vendu	avions vendu
avais vendu	aviez vendu
avait vendu	avaient vendu

Subjunctive

vende	vendions
vendes	vendiez
vende	vendent

finir
to finish

je	nous
tu	vous
il/elle/on	ils/elles

Present		Imperative	
finis	finissons		Finissons !
finis	finissez	Finis !	Finissez !
finit	finissent		

Past		Imperfect	
ai fini	avons fini	finissais	finissions
as fini	avez fini	finissais	finissiez
a fini	ont fini	finissait	finissaient

Future		Conditional	
finirai	finirons	finirais	finirions
finiras	finirez	finirais	finiriez
finira	finiront	finirait	finiraient

Future Perfect		Past Conditional	
aurai fini	aurons fini	aurais fini	aurions fini
auras fini	aurez fini	aurais fini	auriez fini
aura fini	auront fini	aurait fini	auraient fini

Past Perfect		Subjunctive	
avais fini	avions fini	finisse	finissions
avais fini	aviez fini	finisses	finissiez
avait fini	avaient fini	finisse	finissent

16. COMMON IRREGULAR VERBS

aller
to go

je	nous
tu	vous
il/elle/on	ils/elles

Present		Imperative	
vais	allons		Allons !
vas	allez	Va !	Allez !
va	vont		

Past		Imperfect	
suis allé(e)	sommes allé(e)s	allais	allions
es allé(e)	êtes allé(e)(s)	allais	alliez
est allé(e)	sont allé(e)s	allait	allaient

Future		Conditional	
irai	irons	irais	irions
iras	irez	irais	iriez
ira	iront	irait	iraient

Future Perfect		Past Conditional	
serai allé(e)	serons allé(e)s	serais allé(e)	serions allé(e)s
seras allé(e)	serez allé(e)(s)	serais allé(e)	seriez allé(e)(s)
sera allé(e)	seront allé(e)s	serait allé(e)	seraient allé(e)s

Past Perfect		Subjunctive	
étais allé(e)	étions allé(e)s	aille	allions
étais allé(e)	étiez allé(e)(s)	ailles	alliez
était allé(e)	étaient allé(e)s	aille	aillent

avoir
to have

je	nous
tu	vous
il/elle/on	ils/elles

Present		Imperative	
ai	avons		Ayons !
as	avez	Aie !	Ayez !
a	ont		

Past		Imperfect	
ai eu	avons eu	avais	avions
as eu	avez eu	avais	aviez
a eu	ont eu	avait	avaient

Future		Conditional	
aurai	aurons	aurais	aurions
auras	aurez	aurais	auriez
aura	auront	aurait	auraient

Future Perfect		Past Conditional	
aurai eu	aurons eu	aurais eu	aurions eu
auras eu	aurez eu	aurais eu	auriez eu
aura eu	auront eu	aurait eu	auraient eu

Past Perfect		Subjunctive	
avais eu	avions eu	aie	ayons
avais eu	aviez eu	aies	ayez
avait eu	avaient eu	ait	aient

être
to be

je	nous
tu	vous
il/elle/on	ils/elles

Present		Imperative	
suis	sommes		Soyons !
es	êtes	Sois !	Soyez !
est	sont		

Past		Imperfect	
ai été	avons été	étais	étions
as été	avez été	étais	étiez
a été	ont été	était	étaient

Future		Conditional	
serai	serons	serais	serions
seras	serez	serais	seriez
sera	seront	serais	seraient

Future Perfect		Past Conditional	
aurai été	aurons été	aurais été	aurions été
auras été	aurez été	aurais été	auriez été
aura été	auront été	aurait été	auraient été

Past Perfect		Subjunctive	
avais été	avions été	sois	soyons
avais été	aviez été	sois	soyez
avait été	avaient été	soit	soient

faire
to do, to make

je	nous
tu	vous
il/elle/ on	ils/elles

Present		Imperative	
fais	faisons		Faisons !
fais	faites	Fais !	Faites !
fait	font		

Past		Imperfect	
ai fait	avons fait	faisais	faisions
as fait	avez fait	faisais	faisiez
a fait	ont fait	faisait	faisaient

Future		Conditional	
ferai	ferons	ferais	ferions
feras	ferez	ferais	feriez
fera	feront	ferait	feraient

Future Perfect		Past Conditional	
aurai fait	aurons fait	aurais fait	aurions fait
auras fait	aurez fait	aurais fait	auriez fait
aura fait	auront fait	aurait fait	auraient fait

Past Perfect		Subjunctive	
avais fait	avions fait	fasse	fassions
avais fait	aviez fait	fasses	fassiez
avait fait	avaient fait	fasse	fassent

Glossary

Note that the following abbreviations will be used in this glossary:
(m.) = masculine, (f.) = feminine, (sg.) = singular, (pl.) = plural, (fml.) = formal/
polite, (infml.) = informal/familiar. If a word has two grammatical genders, (m./f.)
or (f./m.) is used.

French-English

A

à *in, at, to*
  à la / à l' / au / aux (f./m. or f. before a vowel or silent h/m./pl.) *in/at/to the*
  à cause de *because of, as a result of, due to (in a negative way)*
  à côté de *next to*
  à côté *at the side, on the side, to the side*
  à plein temps *full-time*
  à temps partiel *part-time*
  à la retraite *retired*
  à quelle heure ? *at what time?*
  à gauche *on the left, to the left, at the left*
  à droite *on the right, to the right, at the right*
  à moins que... ne *unless*
  à mon avis *in my opinion*
  à travers *through, across*
  à l'heure *on time*
  à la maison *at the house, at home*
  à pied *on foot, by foot*
  À votre santé ! *To your health!*
  À la prochaine ! *See you later!*
  À plus tard ! *See you later!*
  À plus ! *See you later!* (infml.)
  À tout à l'heure ! *See you later!*
  À bientôt ! *See you soon!*
  À table ! *Dinner's ready!/The food is ready!* (lit., To the table!)
abdomen (m.) *abdomen*
abdominaux (m. pl.) *sit-ups*
Absolument ! *Absolutely!*
accessoires (m. pl.) *accessories*
accident (m.) *accident*
accompagner *to accompany*
  plat (m.) d'accompagnement *side dish*

accord (m.) *agreement*
  D'accord. *Okay./All right.*
acheter *to buy*
acteur / actrice (m./f.) *actor/actress*
actif / active (m./f.) *active*
action (f.) *action*
  film (m.) d'action *action film*
activement *actively*
activité (f.) *activity*
  activités de plein air *outdoor activities*
  activités extra-scolaires / parascolaires *extracurricular activities*
addition (f.) *check, bill*
admirer *to admire*
adolescent / adolescente (m./f.) *adolescent, teenager*
adorer *to love, to adore*
adulte (m./f.) *adult, grown-up*
aéroport (m.) *airport*
affaires (f. pl.) *business, belongings*
  homme / femme (m./f.) d'affaires *businessman/woman*
afin que *in order that, so that*
âge (m.) *age*
  personne (f.) âgée *elderly person*
agent / agente de police (m./f.) *policeman/policewoman*
agir *to act (to behave)*
agneau (m.) *lamb*
  carré (m.) d'agneau rôti *roast rack of lamb*
agréable *pleasant, enjoyable*
Ah bon... *Oh really .../Oh okay ...*
aider *to help*
  Pouvez-vous m'aider, s'il vous plaît ? *Can you help me, please?*
aigre *sour*
aiguille (f.) *needle*
ailleurs *elsewhere*

aimable *kind (nice)*
aimer *to like, to love*
  J'aime (bien)... *I (do) like ...*
  J'aime ça. *I like that./I love that.*
  Je n'aime pas... *I do not like ...*
  aimer mieux *to prefer*
aîné / aînée (m./f.) *oldest child*
alcool (m.) *alcohol*
Algérie (f.) *Algeria*
algérien / algérienne (m./f.) *Algerian*
Allemagne (f.) *Germany*
allemand / allemande (m./f.) *German*
aller *to go*
  aller visiter *to go sightseeing*
  aller à ravir à quelqu'un *to look great on someone, to suit someone well*
  Allons-y. *Let's go.*
  On y va. *Let's go.* (infml.)
  Comment allez-vous ? *How are you?* (pl./fml.)
  Comment vas-tu ? *How are you?* (infml.)
  Je vais très bien. *I'm very well.*
  Va ! *Go!* (infml.)
  Allez ! *Go!* (pl./fml.)
  Vas-y ! *Go there!/Go on!/Go ahead!* (infml.)
aller simple (m.) *one-way*
allergie (f.) *allergy*
allergique *allergic*
aller-retour (m.) *round-trip*
  Je voudrais un billet aller-retour. *I would like a round-trip ticket.*
alliance (f.) *wedding ring*
Allô. *Hello. (only on the phone)*
allonger *to lay down, to lie down*
Alors... *Well ... /So ... /Then ...*
  Alors là... *So then ... , Well, well, well!*
alpinisme (m.) *(mountain) climbing*
amande (f.) *almond*
ambulance (f.) *ambulance*
américain / américaine (m./f.) *American*
ami / amie (m./f.) *friend*
  petit ami / petite amie (m./f.) *boyfriend/ girlfriend*
amical / amicale (m./f.) *friendly*
amusant / amusante (m./f.) *amusing, funny*
amuser *to entertain*
  s'amuser *to have a good time, to enjoy oneself, to have fun*
  Je m'amuse. *I'm having a good time./I'm having fun.*
an (m.) *year*
  jour (m.) de l'An *New Year's Day*
  Nouvel An *New Year*
  avoir... ans *to be ... years old*
ancien / ancienne (m./f.) *old, former, ancient*
anglais (m.) *English language*
  en anglais *in English*
anglais / anglaise (m./f.) *English*
Angleterre (f.) *England*
animal (m.) *animal*
anneau (m.) *ring*
année (f.) *year*
  mois (m. pl.) de l'année *months of the year*
  Bonne Année ! *Happy New Year!*
  année dernière *last year*
  année scolaire *academic year*
anniversaire (m.) *birthday, anniversary*
  Joyeux / Bon anniversaire ! *Happy birthday!/Happy anniversary!*
annoncer *to announce*
antibiotiques (m. pl.) *antibiotics*
anti-inflammatoire *anti-inflammatory*
août *August*
apéritif *drink served before the meal*
appareil (m.) *device, telephone*
  Qui est à l'appareil ? *Who is it?/Who's calling? (on the phone)*
  appareil photo *camera*
appartement (m.) *apartment*
appeler *to call*
  s'appeler *to be called (to call oneself)*
appétit (m.) *appetite*
  Bon appétit ! *Enjoy your meal! (lit., Good appetite!)*
apporter *to bring*
apprendre *to learn*
  apprendre par cœur *to learn by heart*
  J'apprends le français. *I'm learning French.*
après *after, afterwards*
après-demain *the day after tomorrow*
après-midi (m./f.) *afternoon*
arbre (m.) *tree*
Arc (m.) de Triomphe *Arc de Triomphe (Arch of Triumph)*
architecte (m./f.) *architect*
argent (m.) *money, cash, silver*
armoire (f.) *wardrobe, cabinet*

armoire à pharmacie *medicine cabinet*
arracher (une dent) *to pull (a tooth)*
arrêt (m.) *stop*
  arrêt de bus / d'autobus *bus stop*
arriver *to arrive, to get somewhere, to reach, to happen*
  arriver à (+ verb) *to be able to (do something), to manage to (do something)*
  arriver à (+ destination) *to arrive (somewhere), to get to (a destination)*
  heure (f.) d'arrivée *arrival time*
art (m.) *art*
artiste (m./f.) *artist*
assez *quite, enough*
assiette (f.) *plate*
assis / assise (m./f.) *sitting (down), seated*
assistant / assistante (m./f.) *assistant*
assister à (un cours) *to attend (a class), to take (a class)*
assurance (f.) *insurance*
athlétisme (m.) *track (and field)*
attaque (f.) cérébrale *stroke*
attendre *to wait (for), to expect*
au *to/at/in the (m.)*
  Au revoir. *Good-bye.*
  au bout de *at the end of*
  au pied de *at the foot of*
  au bord de *at the edge of (at the border of)*
  au milieu de *in the middle of*
  au bureau *at the office*
  au travail *at work*
  au collège *in middle school*
  au lycée *in high school*
auberge (f.) *inn*
  auberge de jeunesse *youth hostel*
aujourd'hui *today*
auparavant *before*
  deux mois auparavant *two months before*
aussi *also, too, as, just as*
  aussi… que *as … as*
  moins… que *not as … as*
Australie (f.) *Australia*
australien / australienne (m./f.) *Australian*
autant *as much, as many*
  autant de *as many as*
auteur / auteure (m./f.) *author*
auto(mobile) (f.) *car, automobile*
autobus (m.) *bus*

arrêt (m.) d'autobus *bus stop*
autocar (m.) *bus*
automne (m.) *fall, autumn*
  en automne *in (the) fall, in autumn*
autour de *around*
autre *other, else*
  d'autre *else*
  un / une autre (m./f.) *another*
  de l'autre côté de *on the other side of*
  autre chose *something else, anything else*
  ne… rien d'autre *nothing else, anything else*
  quelqu'un d'autre *someone else*
autrefois *formerly, in the past*
aux *to/at/in the (pl.)*
  aux États-Unis *to the United States*
avancer *to advance*
avant *before*
  deux mois avant *two months before*
  d'avant *before last*
  semaine (f.) d'avant *the week before last*
  avant que *before*
avant-hier *the day before yesterday*
avec *with*
  Avec plaisir. *With pleasure.*
  sortir avec *to go out with (to date)*
avenue (f.) *avenue*
aveugle *blind*
  être aveugle *to be blind*
avion (m.) *airplane*
avis (m.) *opinion*
  à mon avis *in my opinion*
avocat / avocate (m./f.) *lawyer*
avoir *to have*
  avoir besoin de *to need*
  avoir besoin que *to need for*
  avoir envie de *to feel like*
  avoir chaud *to be hot/warm*
  avoir froid *to be cold*
  avoir faim *to be hungry*
  avoir soif *to be thirsty*
  avoir hâte *to look forward to (can't wait)*
  avoir honte *to be ashamed*
  avoir lieu *to take place, to be held*
  avoir peur *to be afraid*
  avoir raison *to be right*
  avoir tort *to be wrong*
  avoir sommeil *to be sleepy*
  avoir… ans *to be … years old*

avoir le temps *to have (the) time*
avoir du mal à *to have trouble (doing something)*
avoir mal à *to ache, to have pain in, to have a sore (something)*
avoir un accident *to have an accident*
avoir une entrevue *to have an interview*
avril *April*

B

baccalauréat / bac (m.) *baccalauréat (an exam for students wishing to continue their education beyond high school)*
bague (f.) *ring*
  bague de fiançailles *engagement ring*
  bague en diamant *diamond ring*
baguette (f.) *baguette (French bread), chopstick*
baignoire (f.) *bathtub*
balai (m.) *broom*
balle (f.) *ball (small – tennis, etc.)*
ballet (m.) *ballet*
ballon (m.) *ball (large – basketball, etc.)*
banane (f.) *banana*
bandage (m.) *bandage*
banlieue (f.) *suburbs*
  de banlieue *suburban*
banque (f.) *bank*
  employé de banque / employée de banque (m./f.) *bank clerk*
banquier / banquière (m./f.) *banker*
bar (m.) *counter*
bas (m.) *stocking (hose)*
bas / basse (m./f.) *low*
  en bas *downstairs, down below*
baseball (m.) *baseball*
basket (f.) *sneaker, tennis shoe*
basket(-ball) (m.) *basketball*
bateau (m.) *boat, ship*
bâtiment (m.) *building*
  ouvrier en bâtiment / ouvrière en bâtiment (m./f.) *construction worker*
bâtir *to build*
battement (m.) de cœur *heartbeat*
batterie (f.) *drums*
beau / bel / belle (m./m. before a vowel or silent h/f.) *beautiful, handsome, nice*
  Il fait beau. *It's beautiful (outside).*
Beaubourg *Beaubourg (area in Paris and another name for the Pompidou Center)*
beaucoup *many, a lot, much*
  beaucoup de *a lot of, many*
beau-fils (m.) *stepson, son-in-law*
beau-père (m.) *father-in-law, stepfather*
beauté (f.) *beauty*
  institut (m.) de beauté *beauty parlor, beauty salon*
bébé (m.) *baby*
beige *beige, tan (color)*
belge *Belgian*
Belgique (f.) *Belgium*
belle / beau / bel (f./m./m. before a vowel or silent h) *beautiful, handsome, nice*
belle-fille (f.) *stepdaughter, daughter-in-law*
belle-mère (f.) *mother-in-law, stepmother*
Ben... *Oh well ... /Well ...(infml.)*
béquilles (f. pl.) *crutches*
  marcher avec des béquilles *walk with crutches (to)*
besoin (m.) *need*
  avoir besoin de *to need (lit., to have need of)*
beurre (m.) *butter*
  livre (f.) de beurre *pound of butter*
  radis (m. pl.) au beurre *rosette-cut radishes served with butter on top (lit., radishes in butter)*
bibliothèque (f.) *library, bookshelf*
bicyclette (f.) *bicycle*
  monter à bicyclette *to go bike riding, to ride a bike*
bidet (m.) *bidet*
bien *well, good, fine, really, very*
  Ça va bien. *It's going well.*
  très bien *very good, very well*
  Bien sûr. *Of course.*
  Eh bien... *Oh well ... /Well ...*
  J'aime bien... *I like ...*
  Je veux bien... *I want ... /I do want ...*
  Je voudrais bien... *I would like ...*
  J'ai bien... *I do have ...*
  Merci bien. *Thank you very much.*
  Bien entendu. *I do understand./Completely understood./Of course.*
  ou bien *or even, or else, either, or*
  et bien plus *and even more, and much more*
  bien au contraire *quite the opposite, quite the contrary*

Glossary

bien habillé / habillée (m./f.) *well-dressed*
bien que *although*
bientôt *soon*
À bientôt ! *See you soon!*
Bienvenue. *Welcome.*
bière (f.) *beer*
bijou (m.) *jewel*
bijoux (m. pl.) *jewelry*
billard (m.) *pool, billiards*
billet (m.) *ticket, banknote, bill (currency)*
distributeur (m.) de billets *ATM*
biologie (f.) *biology*
bisque (f.) *bisque (creamy soup)*
bisque de homard *lobster bisque*
bizarre *strange, bizarre*
C'est bizarre. *It's strange.*
blanc / blanche (m./f.) *white*
vin (m.) blanc *white wine*
blouse (f.) blanche *white coat (doctor's coat)*
blancs (m. pl.) (d'œufs) *egg whites*
blessé / blessée (m./f.) *wounded*
blesser *to hurt*
se blesser *to hurt oneself*
blessure (f.) *injury*
blessure superficielle *superficial injury*
bleu / bleue (m./f.) *blue*
truite (f.) au bleu *trout cooked in wine and vinegar*
blond / blonde (m./f.) *blonde*
blouse (f.) *blouse, coat*
blouse blanche *white coat (doctor's coat)*
bœuf (m.) *beef*
rôti (m.) de bœuf *roast beef*
boire *to drink*
bois (m.) *wood*
en bois *wooden*
Bois de Vincennes *Bois de Vincennes (Vincennes Wood – a large park in Paris)*
Bois de Boulogne *Bois de Boulogne (Boulogne Wood – a large park in Paris)*
boisson (f.) *drink*
boisson gazeuse *soft drink*
boîte (f.) *club, nightclub, box*
boîte de nuit *nightclub*
sortir en boîte *to go out to clubs, to go out clubbing*
boîte de conserve (f.) *can*
boîte (en carton) *carton, can (food)*

bon / bonne (m./f.) *good*
très bon / bonne (m./f.) *very good*
Bon appétit. *Bon appetit.*
Bonne chance. *Good luck.*
Bon anniversaire ! *Happy birthday!/Happy anniversary!*
Bonne Année ! *Happy New Year!*
Bonne nuit ! *Good night!*
Bonnes Fêtes ! *Happy Holidays!*
Ah bon... *Oh really .../Oh okay ...*
moins bon / bonne *not as good*
bon marché *inexpensive, a good buy*
bonbons (m. pl.) *(pieces of) candy*
bonhomme (m.) de neige *snowman*
Bonjour. *Hello./Good day.*
Bonsoir. *Good evening.*
bord (m.) *border, edge*
au bord de *at the edge of (at the border of)*
botte (f.) *bundle, bunch*
botte d'asperges *bunch of asparagus*
bouche (f.) *mouth*
boucherie (f.) *butcher shop*
boucle (f.) d'oreille *earring*
boulangerie (f.) *bakery*
boulevard (m.) *boulevard*
bouquet (m.) *bouquet*
boulot (m.) *job, work*
bout (m.) *end*
au bout de *at the end of*
bouteille (f.) *bottle*
bouteille de champagne *bottle of champagne*
boutique (f.) *boutique*
boxe (f.) *boxing*
bracelet (m.) *bracelet*
bras (m.) *arm*
brave *good, courageous, brave*
Bravo. *Well done.*
Brésil (m.) *Brazil*
brésilien / brésilienne (m./f.) *Brazilian*
bricoler *to tinker, to fiddle with things, to fix/ repair things*
brioche *sweet bun*
brique (f.) *carton (for milk/juice), brick (construction)*
brochure (f.) *brochure*
bronzé / bronzée (m./f.) *tan/tanned (from the sun)*
bronzer *to tan, to get a tan*

brosser *to brush*
  se brosser *to brush oneself (hair, teeth, etc.)*
brouillard (m.) *fog*
brouiller *to scramble*
  œufs (m. pl.) **brouillés** *scrambled eggs*
brûlure (f.) *burn*
brun / brune (m./f.) *brown*
brut / brute (m./f.) *dry (alcohol)*
bulletin (m.) **scolaire** *report card*
bureau (m.) *office, desk*
  bureau de poste *post office*
  bureau de change *currency exchange office*
bus (m.) *bus*
  arrêt (m.) **de bus** *bus stop*
but (m.) *goal*

C

c'est *this is, that is, it is*
  C'est nuageux. *It's cloudy.*
  C'est tout ? *Is that all?*
  C'est tout. *That's all.*
  Qu'est-ce que c'est ? *What is this/that?*
  C'est délicieux ! *It's delicious!*
  C'est ennuyeux. *It's boring.*
  C'est bizarre. *It's strange.*
  C'est étrange. *It's strange.*
  C'est parfait. *It's perfect.*
  C'est mauvais. *That's bad.*
ça / c' *this, that, it*
  (Comment) ça va ? *How's it going?/How are you?*
  Ça va. *I'm fine./It's going fine.*
  Ça va bien. *It's going well.*
  Ça va mal. *It's not going well./It's going badly.*
  Ça fait… *That makes …/That is …*
  Ça coûte… *That costs …*
  J'aime ça. *I like that./I love that.*
  Ça suffit. *That's enough.*
cabines (f. pl.) **d'essayage** *dressing rooms*
cabinet (m.) **médical** *doctor's office*
câble (m.) *cable*
cache-cache (m.) *hide and seek*
  jouer à cache-cache *to play hide and seek*
cachet (m.) *tablet*
cadet / cadette (m./f.) *youngest child*
café (m.) *café, coffee shop, coffee*
  café-crème (m.) *coffee with cream*
cafétéria (f.) *cafeteria (general)*

cafetière (f.) *coffeemaker*
cahier (m.) *notebook*
caisse (f.) *cash register*
calcul (m.) *calculus*
caleçon (m.) *underpants*
calme *quiet, calm*
camion (m.) *truck*
camper *to go camping*
camping (m.) *camping*
Canada (m.) *Canada*
canadien / canadienne (m./f.) *Canadian*
canapé (m.) *sofa, couch*
canard (m.) *duck*
  canard à l'orange *duck à l'orange, duck with orange sauce*
canne (f.) *cane*
cantine (f.) *school cafeteria*
capsule (f.) *capsule*
carafe (f.) *pitcher*
  carafe d'eau *pitcher of water*
  carafe de vin *pitcher of wine*
caramel (m.) *caramel*
  crème (f.) **caramel** *creamy dessert made with caramel*
carotte (f.) *carrot*
carré (m.) *square, rack (of meat)*
  carré d'agneau (rôti) *(roast) rack of lamb*
carte (f.) *menu, card, map*
  carte des vins *wine list*
  carte de la ville *map of the city*
  carte du métro *map of the subway*
  cartes (pl.) **à jouer** *playing cards*
  La carte, s'il vous plaît. *The menu, please.*
carton (m.) *carton*
cas (m. pl.) **d'urgence** *emergency situations*
casque (m.) *helmet*
casquette (f.) *cap*
casser *to break*
  se casser le bras / la jambe *to break one's arm/leg*
cassis (m.) *black currant*
cathédrale (f.) *cathedral*
  Cathédrale Notre-Dame *Notre Dame Cathedral*
cause (f.) *cause*
  à cause de *because of, as a result of, due to (in a negative way)*
cave (f.) *cellar*

CD-ROM (m.) *CD-ROM*

ce / cet / cette (m./m. before a vowel or silent h/f.) *this, that*
  ce soir *tonight, this evening*

ceinture (f.) *belt*

célèbre *famous*

célébrer *to celebrate*

céleri (m.) *celery*

célibataire *single*

celui-ci / celle-ci (m./f.) *this one, this one here*

celui-là / celle-là (m./f.) *that one, that one there*

ceux-ci / celles-ci (m. pl./f. pl.) *these ones, these ones here*

ceux-là / celles-là (m. pl./f. pl.) *those ones, those ones there*

cent *hundred*

cent (m.) *cent*

centre (m.) *center*
  centre d'informations *information center*
  centre commercial *mall*
  Centre National d'Art et de Culture Georges-Pompidou (Centre Pompidou) *National Center of Art and Culture Georges-Pompidou (Pompidou Center)*

cercle (m.) *club*

cerise (f.) *cherry*

certain / certaine (m./f.) *certain*
  il est certain que *it is certain that*

certainement *certainly*

cerveau (m.) *brain*

ces *these, those*

cesser *to stop, to cease*

cette / ce / cet (f./m./m. before a vowel or silent h) *this, that*

chacun / chacune (m./f.) *each, each one*

chaîne (f.) hi-fi *sound system*

chaise (f.) *chair*
  chaise roulante *wheelchair*

chambre (f.) (à coucher) *bedroom*

champ (m.) *field*

champagne (m.) *champagne*
  bouteille (f.) de champagne *bottle of champagne*

champignon (m.) *mushroom*

champion / championne (m./f.) *champion*

chance (f.) *luck*
  Pas de chance ! *No luck!*
  Bonne chance ! *Good luck!*

changer *to change, to exchange*
  changer de chaîne *to change channels*
  bureau (m.) de change *currency exchange office*

chanson (f.) *song*

chanter *to sing*

chanteur / chanteuse (m./f.) *singer*

chapeau (m.) *hat*

chaque *each, every*

charcuterie (f.) *delicatessen (store that sells prepared meats)*

charmant / charmante (m./f.) *charming*

charpentier (m.) *carpenter*

chasse (f.) *hunting*

château (m.) *castle*
  château de sable *sandcastle*
  faire un château de sable *to make/build a sandcastle*

chaud / chaude (m./f.) *hot, warm*
  Il fait chaud. *It's hot./It's warm.*
  avoir chaud *to be hot/warm (person)*
  chocolat (m.) chaud *hot chocolate*

chauffeur (m.) de taxi *taxi driver*

chaussette (f.) *sock*

chaussure (f.) *shoe*
  chaussure de basket / tennis *sneaker, tennis shoe*

chef (m.) *boss*

chemin (m.) *path, way*

chemise (f.) *shirt*

chemisier (m.) *blouse*

chèque (m.) *check*
  chèque de voyage *traveler's check*

cher / chère (m./f.) *dear, expensive*

chercher *to look for*

chéri / chérie (m./f.) *honey, dear, darling*

cheval (m.) *horse*
  monter à cheval *to ride a horse, to go horseback riding*

cheveux (m. pl.) *hair*
  cheveu (m.) *hair (single strand)*
  avoir les cheveux bruns / blonds / roux / noirs *to have brown/blond/red/black hair*

cheville (f.) *ankle*

chez *at someone's house/place*
  chez moi *at my house, at home*

chien (m.) *dog*

chien d'aveugle *seeing-eye dog*
chimie (f.) *chemistry*
Chine (f.) *China*
chinois (m.) *Chinese language*
chinois / chinoise (m./f.) *Chinese*
chocolat (m.) *chocolate*
   gâteau (m.) au chocolat *chocolate cake*
   mousse (f.) au chocolat *chocolate mousse*
   glace (f.) au chocolat *chocolate ice cream*
   chocolat (m.) chaud *hot chocolate*
choisir *to choose*
choix (m.) *choice*
chômage (m.) *unemployment*
   au chômage *unemployed*
chose (f.) *thing*
   Pas grand-chose. *Not a lot.*
   autre chose *something else, anything else*
ci *this, here*
cidre (m.) *cider*
ciel (m.) *sky*
cil (m.) *eyelash*
cinéma (m.) *movie theater, the movies*
cinq *five*
cinquante *fifty*
cinquième *fifth*
circuit (m.) en bus *bus tour*
circulation (f.) *traffic*
cirque (m.) *circus*
citron (m.) *lemon*
   citron vert *lime*
citrouille (f.) *pumpkin*
   tarte (f.) à la citrouille *pumpkin pie*
clam (m.) *clam*
clarinette (f.) *clarinet*
classe (f.) *class, grade, classroom*
   classe terminale *final year of high school*
clavier (m.) *keyboard*
client / cliente (m./f.) *client*
club (m.) *club (organization)*
   centre/club de remise en forme *health club*
cochon (m.) *pig*
code (m.) vestimentaire *dress code*
cœur (m.) *heart*
   battement (m.) de cœur *heartbeat*
   apprendre par cœur *to learn by heart*
coin (m.) *neighborhood, corner*
coïncidence (f.) *coincidence*
   Quelle coïncidence ! *What a coincidence!*

collection (f.) *collection*
collectionner *to collect*
collège (m.) *secondary school, junior high school, middle school*
collègue / collègue (m./f.) *colleague*
collier (m.) *necklace*
colline (f.) *hill*
combien *how many, how much*
   C'est combien, s'il vous plaît ? *That's how much, please?/It's how much, please?*
comédie (f.) *comedy*
   comédie romantique *romantic comedy*
   comédie musicale *musical*
   comédie de situation *sitcom*
commander *to order*
comme *like, as, how*
   Comme ci, comme ça. *So-so.*
commencer *to begin, to start*
comment *how*
   Comment ? *Pardon?/What did you say?/How?*
   (Comment) ça va ? *How's it going?/How are you?*
   Comment allez-vous ? *How are you?* (pl./fml.)
   Comment vas-tu ? *How are you?* (infml.)
   Comment vous appelez-vous ? *What's your name?* (pl./fml.)
   Comment t'appelles-tu ? *What's your name?* (infml.)
commercial / commerciale (m./f.) *commercial*
   centre (m.) commercial *mall*
compétition (f.) *competition, contest*
complet (m., fml.) *man's suit*
   complet-veston *three-piece suit*
compléter *to complete*
compliqué / compliquée (m./f.) *complicated*
comprendre *to understand*
   Je ne comprends pas. *I don't understand.*
comprimé (m.) *tablet, pill*
comptabilité (f.) *accounting*
   service (m.) de comptabilité *accounting department*
comptable / comptable (m./f.) *accountant*
comptoir (m.) *counter*
concert (m.) *concert*
concombre (m.) *cucumber*
concours (m.) *competititon, contest*
conduire *to drive*
confiserie (f.) *candy store*

pâtisserie-confiserie (f.) *pastry and candy store*

confiture (f.) *jelly, jam, marmalade*

confortable *comfortable*

connaissance (f.) *acquaintance*

Enchanté / Enchantée (de faire votre connaissance). *Pleased to meet you./Nice to meet you.*

Je suis ravi / ravie de faire votre connaissance. *I'm delighted to make your acquaintance.*

connaître *to know, to be familiar with*

consommé (m.) *consommé (clear soup made from stock)*

consommé aux vermicelles *noodle soup (vermicelli pasta consommé)*

construire *to construct*

consulter *to consult*

consulter l'annuaire *to consult a phone book*

contraire *opposite, contrary*

bien au contraire *quite the opposite, quite the contrary*

cool *cool (great)*

copain / copine (m./f.) *boyfriend/girlfriend*

coq (m.) *rooster*

coq au vin *chicken/rooster cooked in wine*

coque (f.) *shell*

œuf (m.) à la coque *soft-boiled egg*

coquilles (f. pl.) Saint-Jacques *scallops*

corps (m.) *body*

corps humain *human body*

parties (f. pl.) du corps *body parts*

costume (m.) *suit*

côte (f.) *chop, rib, coast*

côte de porc *pork chop*

côté (m.) *side*

à côté *at the side, on the side, to the side*

à côté de *next to*

de l'autre côté de *on the other side of*

coton (m.) *cotton*

cou (m.) *neck (necks)*

coucher *to lay down, to put someone to bed*

se coucher *to go to bed, to lie down (to lie oneself down)*

chambre (f.) (à coucher) *bedroom*

coude (m.) *elbow*

couloir (m.) *hallway, corridor/hall*

coupure (f.) *cut*

cour (f.) de récréation *schoolyard, playground*

courir *to run*

courir le marathon *to run the marathon*

courriel (m.) *e-mail*

courrier (m.) électronique *e-mail*

cours (m.) *course, class*

cours de français *French class*

cours de danse *dance class*

réussir à un cours *to pass a class, to do well in a class*

course (f.) *errand, run, race*

course à pied *running*

faire des / les courses *to shop*

course automobile *auto racing, car racing*

court / courte (m./f.) *short*

cousin / cousine (m./f.) *cousin*

couteau (m.) *knife*

coûter *to cost*

Combien ça coûte, s'il vous plaît ? *How much does that cost, please?*

couture (f.) *sewing*

haute couture *high fashion*

couturier (m.) *fashion designer*

couvert (m.) *table setting*

cravate (f.) *tie*

crémant (m.) *type of French sparkling wine*

crème (f.) *cream, creamy dessert*

crème à raser *shaving cream*

crème caramel *creamy dessert made with caramel*

crème chantilly *whipped cream (that is flavored and sweetened)*

crème de marrons *chestnut paste*

crêpe (f.) *crêpe (tissue-thin pancake)*

crêpe Suzette *Crêpe suzette (crêpe with sugar, orange, and liqueur)*

crevettes (f. pl.) *shrimp*

crise (f.) cardiaque *heart attack*

croire *to believe*

croissant *croissant*

croque-madame (m.) *grilled ham and cheese sandwich with an egg on top*

croque-monsieur (m.) *grilled ham and cheese sandwich*

cru / crue (m./f.) *raw*

crudités (f. pl.) *crudités (French appetizer of raw, mixed vegetables)*

cruel / cruelle (m./f.) *cruel*

cuiller / cuillère (f.) *spoon*
cuir (m.) *leather*
cuisine (f.) *kitchen, cooking*
  faire la cuisine *to cook, to do the cooking*
cuisiner *to cook*
cuisinier / cuisinière (m./f.) *cook*
cuisinière (f.) *stove, cook*
cyclisme (m.) *cycling*

D

dame (f.) *lady*
dames (f. pl.) *checkers*
dans *in, into*
  dans un mois *next month, in one month*
  dans une semaine *next week, in one week*
  dans deux semaines *the week after next, in two weeks*
danse (f.) *dancing, dance*
danser *to dance*
danseur / danseuse (m./f.) *dancer*
  danseur / danseuse de ballet, ballerine *ballet dancer*
date (f.) *date*
de / d' *of, for, from*
  de la / de l' / du / des (f./m. or f. before a vowel or silent h/m./pl.) *of the, some*
  d'ici *from here, by, until*
  d'ici là *by then, from now on, from now until, until then*
  D'accord. *Okay./All right.*
  D'abord... *First ...*
  De rien. *You're welcome./It's nothing.*
  de l'autre côté de *on the other side of*
  de ma part *on my behalf, from me, on my part*
  de la part de *on behalf of, from (someone)*
  C'est de la part de qui ? *Who's calling? (on the phone)*
  de quel / quelle ? (m./f.) *what?/of what?*
  de temps en temps *from time to time, occasionally*
  de toute façon *at any rate, in any case, anyhow*
debout *standing (up)*
débutant / débutante (m./f.) *beginner*
décembre *December*
décider *to decide*
  se décider *to make up one's mind, to be decided, to be resolved (to do something)*

décontracté / décontractée (m./f.) *casual*
décrocher *to pick up (the phone)*
défendre *to defend*
défiler *to march*
degré (m.) *degree*
dehors *outside*
déjà *already*
déjeuner *to have lunch*
déjeuner (m.) *lunch*
  petit déjeuner (m.) *breakfast (lit., little lunch)*
délicieux / délicieuse (m./f.) *delicious*
demain *tomorrow*
  après-demain *the day after tomorrow*
demander *to ask, to ask for*
  se demander *to wonder, to ask oneself*
déménager *to move out*
demi / demie (m./f.) *half*
  ... et demie *half past ...*
demi-heure (f.) *half hour*
dent (f.) *tooth*
dentiste (m./f.) *dentist*
déodorant (m.) *deodorant*
départ (m.) *departure*
  heure (f.) du départ *departure time*
dépêcher *to dispatch*
  se dépêcher *to hurry*
depuis *since, for*
  depuis quand ? *since when?*
  depuis combien de temps ? *(for) how long?*
dernier / dernière (m./f.) *last, final, latest*
  lundi dernier *last Monday*
  mois (m.) dernier *last month*
  été (m.) dernier *last summer*
  nuit (f.) dernière *last night*
  année (f.) dernière *last year*
  la dernière fois *the last time, the final time*
derrière *behind*
des *some (pl.), of the (pl.), plural of un / une*
descendre *to go down, to come down, to descend*
  Où dois-je descendre ? *Where do I have to get off?/Where should I get off?*
description (f.) *description*
désert (m.) *desert*
désirer *to want, to wish*
désobéir *to disobey*
désolé / désolée (m./f.) *sorry*
  Je suis désolé / désolée. *I am sorry.*
dessert (m.) *dessert*

dessin (m.) *drawing*
dessin animé *animated movie*
dessous *underneath*
dessus *on top*
détester *to hate, to detest*
deux *two*
  deux fois *twice, two times*
deuxième *second*
  deuxième base (f.) *second base*
devant *in front (of), ahead, before*
devenir *to become*
devoir *to have to, must, should, to owe*
devoirs (m. pl.) *homework*
diagnostic (m.) *diagnosis*
diamant (m.) *diamond*
  bague (f.) en diamant *diamond ring*
d'ici *from here, by, until*
  d'ici demain *by tomorrow, until tomorrow*
  d'ici la fin de la semaine *by the end of the week, until the end of the week*
  d'ici là *by then, from now on, from now until, until then*
dieu (m.) *god*
  Mon dieu ! *My god!*
différent / différente (m./f.) *different*
difficile *difficult*
dimanche *Sunday*
dîner *to dine, to have dinner*
dîner (m.) *dinner*
diplôme (m.) *diploma*
  diplôme universitaire *college degree*
dire *to say, to tell*
  Dis donc ! *Man!/You don't say!/Say! (lit., Say so!)*
directeur / directrice (m./f.) *director, manager*
  directeur / directrice du personnel *human resources manager, personnel manager*
direction (f.) *direction, way, management*
discothèque (f.) *(night)club*
distributeur (m.) de billets *ATM*
divertissement (m.) *entertainment*
divorce (m.) *divorce*
divorcer *to get a divorce*
dix *ten*
dix-huit *eighteen*
dixième *tenth*
dix-neuf *nineteen*
dix-sept *seventeen*

docteur / doctoresse (m./f.) *doctor*
document (m.) *document*
documentaire (m.) *documentary*
doigt (m.) *finger*
  doigt de pied *toe*
donc *so, then, therefore*
  Dis donc ! *Man!/You don't say!/Say! (lit., Say so!)*
donner *to give, to show*
  donner un coup de fil *to make a phone call (lit., to give/pass a hit of the wire)* (infml.)
  donner un coup de pied *to kick (lit., to give a kick)*
dont *whom, whose, of which, of whom*
dos (m.) *back*
doublé / doublée (m./f.) *dubbed*
doucement *gently, softly, sweetly*
douche (f.) *shower*
  gel (m.) douche *shower gel*
douleur (f.) *pain, sorrow*
douter que *to doubt that*
doux / douce (m./f.) *sweet, gentle, soft*
douzaine (f.) *dozen*
  douzaine d'œufs *dozen eggs*
douze *twelve*
drame (m.) *drama*
  drame d'époque *period drama*
drapeau (m.) *flag*
droit *straight*
  tout droit *straight ahead*
  Il faut aller tout droit. *You must go straight ahead.*
droite (f.) *right (opposite of left)*
  à droite *on the right, to the right, at the right*
  rive (f.) droite *right bank*
drôle *funny*
  si drôle *so funny*
du / de l' / de la / des (m./m. or f. before a vowel or silent h/f./pl.) *some, of the*
dur / dure (m./f.) *hard*
  œuf (m.) dur *hard-boiled egg (lit., hard egg)*

E

eau (f.) *water*
  eau de cologne *cologne*
  eau de Javel *bleach*
  eau minérale *mineral water*
  carafe (f.) d'eau *pitcher of water*

écharpe (f.) *scarf (long)*
échecs (m. pl.) *chess*
échouer à (un examen / cours) *to fail (a test/ class)*
éclair (m.) *lightning, éclair (type of cream-filled pastry)*
école (f.) *school*
   école maternelle *nursery school, preschool*
   école primaire *elementary school, primary school*
écossais / écossaise (m./f.) *Scottish*
Écosse (f.) *Scotland*
écouter *to listen (to)*
écran (m.) *monitor, screen*
écrire *to write*
écrivain (m.) (sometimes: écrivaine, f.) *writer*
effet (m.) secondaire *side effect*
effrayant / effrayante (m./f.) *scary*
égal / égale (m./f.) *equal*
église (f.) *church*
électricien (m.) *electrician*
élégant / élégante (m./f.) *elegant*
éléphant (m.) *elephant*
élève (m./f.) *student, pupil*
elle *she, it* (f.), *her*
elles *they* (f.), *it* (f. pl.), *them* (f.)
e-mail (m.) *e-mail*
émission (f.) *television program*
emmener *to take (someone) along*
emploi (m.) *employment, job*
  emploi régulier *steady job*
  emploi saisonnier *summer job*
  sans emploi *unemployed*
employé / employée (m./f.) *employee, worker*
  employé de banque / employée de banque *bank clerk*
employer *to use, to employ*
en *in, into, to, some, of it, of them*
  en effet *really, indeed*
  en avance *early*
  en face de *across from, facing*
  en général *in general, generally, usually*
  en haut *upstairs, up above*
  en bas *downstairs, down below*
  en retard *late*
  en solde *on sale*
  en grève *on strike*
  en tenue de soirée *formal, in formal dress/ attire*
Enchanté. / Enchantée. (m./f.) *Pleased to meet you./Nice to meet you.*
encore *again, still, more*
  ne... pas encore *not yet*
enfant (m./f.) *child*
enfin *finally*
enlever *to remove, to take off*
ennuyer *to annoy, to bore (someone)*
  s'ennuyer *to get bored, to be bored*
  C'est ennuyeux. *It's boring.*
énorme *enormous*
enseignant / enseignante (m./f.) *teacher*
enseigner *to teach*
ensemble *together*
ensemble (m.) *outfit*
ensuite *then, next*
entendre *to understand, to hear*
  Entendu. *All right./Understood.*
  s'entendre avec *get along with (to)*
  s'entendre bien avec *get along well with (to)*
entraînement (m.) *workout, training*
entraîneur (m.) *coach*
entre *between*
entrée (f.) *appetizer, entrance*
entrer *to enter, to come in*
  Entre ! / Entrez ! *Come in! (infml./pl., fml.)*
entrevue (f.) *interview*
envie (f.) *desire*
  avoir envie de *to feel like (lit., to have desire for)*
envoyer *to send, to throw*
  envoyer en pièce jointe *to attach a file*
  envoyer un fichier *to send a file*
  envoyer un mail / mèl / e-mail / courriel / courrier électronique *to send an e-mail*
épaule (f.) *shoulder*
épicerie (f.) *grocery store*
épinards (m. pl.) *spinach*
éponger *to mop, to soak up*
épouser (quelqu'un) *to marry (someone)*
équipe (f.) *team*
  équipe de rugby *rugby team*
équitation (f.) *horseback riding*
  faire de l'équitation *to go horseback riding*
erreur (f.) *mistake*
escaliers (m. pl.) *stairs*
escargots (m. pl.) *snails, escargots*

Espagne (f.) *Spain*
espagnol (m.) *Spanish language*
espagnol / espagnole (m./f.) *Spanish*
espérer *to hope*
essai (m.) *touchdown*
essayer *to try, to try on/out*
essentiel / essentielle (m./f.) *essential*
 il est essentiel que *it is essential that*
est (m.) *east*
est-ce...? *is it ...?*
esthéticien / esthéticienne (m./f.) *beautician*
estomac (m.) *stomach, abdomen*
et *and*
étage (m.) *floor (as in, second floor, third floor, etc.)*
 premier étage *first floor (one floor above the ground floor)*
étagère (f.) *shelf, bookshelf*
étang (m.) *pond*
état (m.) *state*
 États-Unis (m. pl.) *United States*
été (m.) *summer*
 en été *in (the) summer*
 été dernier *last summer*
étoile (f.) *star*
étrange *strange*
 C'est étrange. *It's strange.*
être *to be*
 peut-être *maybe, possibly*
 être fiancé / fiancée (à) (m./f.) *to be engaged (to)*
 être aveugle *to be blind*
 être en forme *to be fit, to be in shape*
 être en pleine / bonne forme *to be in good shape*
 être en pleine expansion *to be growing (business)*
 être en sueur *to be sweating*
 être en nage *to be sweating*
 être en train de *to be in the middle of, to be in the process of*
 être handicapé / handicapée (m./f.) *to be disabled*
 être malade *to be sick*
 être occupé / occupée (m./f.) *to be busy*
 être paralysé / paralysée (m./f.) *to be paralyzed*
 être sans emploi, être sans travail *to be unemployed*
 être sourd / sourde (m./f.) *to be deaf*
 être membre de *to be a member of*
être (m.) humain *human being*
étudiant / étudiante (m./f.) *student*
 étudiant / étudiante en médecine *medical student*
étudier *to study*
euro (m.) *euro*
européen / européenne (m./f.) *European Union* (f.) européenne *European Union*
eux *them* (m.)
évier (m.) *sink*
 évier de la cuisine *kitchen sink*
exact / exacte (m./f.) *exact, correct*
examen (m.) *test, exam, examination*
 rater un examen *to fail a test*
 échouer à un examen *to fail a test*
 réussir à un examen *to pass a test*
 examen médical *medical checkup*
examiner *to examine*
excellent / excellente (m./f.) *excellent*
excursion (f.) *tour, excursion*
 excursion en autocar *bus tour*
excuser *to excuse*
 Excusez-moi. *Excuse me.*
exiger que *to demand that*
expression (f.) *expression*
extérieur (m.) *outside, exterior*
extra *great*
extra-scolaire *extracurricular*
 activités (f. pl.) extra-scolaires *extracurricular activities*

F

face (f.) *face, side*
 en face de *across from, facing*
facile *easy*
facilement *easily*
façon (f.) *way, manner, fashion*
 de toute façon *at any rate, in any case, anyhow*
faible *weak*
faim (f.) *hunger*
 avoir faim *to be hungry*
faire *to do, to make*
 faire la cuisine *to do the cooking, to cook*
 faire la lessive *to do the laundry*

faire la vaisselle *to do the dishes*

faire le ménage *to do the house cleaning, to clean the house*

faire les / des courses *to do the shopping, to go shopping, to shop*

faire des achats *to run errands*

faire la queue *to wait in line*

faire un tour *to take/do a tour*

faire du sport *to play a sport, to do a sport*

faire du foot(ball) *to play soccer, to do soccer*

faire match nul *to tie (in a game/match)*

faire de la natation *to go swimming, to swim*

faire du ski *to ski, to go skiing*

faire du ski nautique *to water-ski, to go water-skiing*

faire de la plongée sous-marine *to go scuba diving*

faire une promenade *to take a walk*

faire une réservation *to make a reservation*

faire des réservations *to make reservations*

faire de l'équitation *to do horseback riding, to go horseback riding*

faire de la musculation *to do strength training, to lift weights, to do bodybuilding*

faire du camping *to camp, to go camping*

faire de la marche *to go hiking*

faire du jogging *to go jogging*

faire du vélo d'appartement *to ride a stationary bike*

faire du yoga *to do yoga*

faire mal *to hurt*

faire partie de *to be a member of*

faire un château de sable *to make/build a sandcastle*

faire un pique-nique *to go on a picnic*

faire (la) grève *to strike*

faire une demande d'emploi *to apply for a job*

faire une faute / erreur *to make a mistake*

faire suivre *to forward*

Ça fait... *That makes ... / That is ...*

Il fait beau. *It's beautiful (outside).*

Il fait chaud. *It's hot./It's warm.*

Il fait froid. *It's cold.*

Il fait (du) soleil. *It's sunny.*

Il fait du vent. *It's windy.*

falloir *to be necessary*

il faut *it's necessary to, you have/need to, you must*

il faut que *it is necessary that*

s'il le faut *if necessary, if needed*

famille (f.) *family*

faute (f.) *mistake*

faute d'orthographe *spelling mistake*

fauteuil (m.) *armchair*

faux / fausse (m./f.) *false, wrong*

favori / favorite (m./f.) *favorite*

Félicitations. *Congratulations.*

femme (f.) *woman, wife*

femme d'affaires *businesswoman*

femme au foyer *homemaker* (f.)

fenêtre (f.) *window*

fer (m.) à repasser *iron*

fermer *to close*

fermer un fichier *to close a file*

fermier / fermière (m./f.) *farmer*

fête (f.) *party, festival, holiday*

fête nationale *national holiday*

Bonnes / Joyeuses Fêtes ! *Happy Holidays!*

feu (m.) *fire*

feuilleton (m.) (télévisé) *TV series*

février *February*

fiancé / fiancée (m./f.) *fiancé/fiancée*

être fiancé / fiancée (à) *to be engaged (to)*

bague (f.) de fiançailles *engagement ring*

fichier (m.) *file*

fier / fière (m./f.) *proud*

fièvre (f.) *fever*

figure (f.) *face*

fille (f.) *girl, daughter*

fille unique *only child* (f.)

film (m.) *movie, film*

film d'action *action film*

film policier *crime drama/film, detective drama/film*

film à suspense *thriller*

film d'épouvante *horror movie*

fils (m.) *son*

fils unique *only child* (m.)

fin (f.) *end*

fin du match *end of the game, end of the match*

Vivement la fin de la journée ! *Can't wait for the end of the day!*

finir *to finish*

firme (f.) *company, firm*

fleur (f.) *flower*

flûte (f.) *flute*
fois (f.) *time*
   une fois *once, one time*
   la dernière fois *the last time, the final time*
fonctionnaire / fonctionnaire (m./f.) *civil servant*
foot(ball) (m.) *soccer*
football (m.) américain *(American) football*
footballeur / footballeuse (m./f.) *soccer player*
forêt (f.) *forest*
forme (f.) *form, shape, figure*
Formidable. *Fantastic.*
fort / forte (m./f.) *strong*
foulard (m.) *scarf (fashion)*
foule (f.) *crowd*
four (m.) *oven*
fourchette (f.) *fork*
foyer (m.) *home*
   homme au foyer / femme au foyer (m./f.) *homemaker*
fraise (f.) *strawberry*
   glace (f.) à la fraise *strawberry ice cream*
   tarte (f.) aux fraises *strawberry pie*
français (m.) *French language*
   en français *in French*
français / française (m./f.) *French*
France (f.) *France*
franchement *frankly, honestly*
fréquemment *frequently*
frère (m.) *brother*
frites (f. pl.) *french fries*
   moules (f. pl.) frites *mussels and fries*
   poulet (m.) frites *chicken and fries*
   steak (m.) frites *steak and fries*
froid / froide (m./f.) *cold*
   Il fait froid. *It's cold.*
   avoir froid *to be cold (person)*
fromage (m.) *cheese*
   sandwich (m.) au fromage *cheese sandwich*
   sandwich (m.) jambon-fromage *ham and cheese sandwich*
   tranche (f.) de fromage *slice of cheese*
front (m.) *forehead*
fruit (m.) *fruit*
   salade (f.) de fruits *fruit salad*

G

gagner *to win, to earn*
   gagner de l'argent *to earn money*
   gagner un match *to win a game, to win a match*
galerie (f.) *gallery*
gant (m.) *glove*
garage (m.) *garage*
garçon (m.) *boy*
gare (f.) *train station*
gastronomie (f.) *gastronomy*
gâteau (m.) *cake*
   gâteau au chocolat *chocolate cake*
gauche (f.) *left*
   à gauche *on the left, to the left, at the left*
   rive (f.) gauche *left bank*
gaufre (f.) *waffle*
gel (m.) douche *shower gel*
général / générale (m./f.) *general*
généralement *generally*
généreux / généreuse (m./f.) *generous*
genou (m.) *knee*
genre *kind, type, genre*
gens (m. pl.) *people*
gentil / gentille (m./f.) *nice, kind*
géométrie (f.) *geometry*
gérant / gérante (m./f.) *manager*
glace (f.) *ice cream, ice*
   glace à la vanille *vanilla ice cream*
   glace à la fraise *strawberry ice cream*
   glace au chocolat *chocolate ice cream*
   hockey (m.) sur glace *ice hockey*
   patin (m.) à glace *ice skating, ice skate*
   patinage (m.) sur glace *ice skating*
golf (m.) *golf*
gorge (f.) *throat*
gourmand (m.) *lover of food, gourmand*
gourmet (m.) *gourmet, lover of fine food*
goût (m.) *taste*
grâce à... *thanks to ...*
grain (m.) de beauté *mole*
grammaire (f.) *grammar*
gramme (m.) *gram*
grand / grande (m./f.) *big, large, tall*
   grand magasin (m.) *department store*
   grandes vacances (f. pl.) *summer vacation*
   Pas grand-chose. *Not a lot.*

grandir *to grow*

grand-mère (f.) *grandmother*

grand-parent (m.) *grandparent*

grand-père (m.) *grandfather*

gratiné / gratinée (m./f.) *topped with browned cheese (and possibly also breadcrumbs)*

grave *serious*

    Ce n'est pas grave. *It's not serious./It's not a problem./It's not a big deal./Don't worry about it.*

grec / grecque (m./f.) *Greek*

Grèce (f.) *Greece*

grêle (f.) *hail*

    Il grêle. *It's hailing.*

grève (m.) *strike*

    en grève *on strike*

    faire (la) grève *to strike*

grippe (f.) *flu*

gros / grosse (m./f.) *fat*

grossir *to gain weight*

groupe (m.) **de musique** *band*

guérir *to cure, to get better*

guichet (m.) *ticket window, counter, window, box office*

    guichet automatique *ATM*

guichetier (m.) *clerk (at the window/counter), teller*

guide (m.) *guide*

guitare (f.) *guitar*

gym / gymnastique (f.) *gym (physical education), gymnastics*

gymnase (m.) *gym (place)*

H

habillé / habillée (m./f.) *dressed*

    bien habillé / habillée (m./f.) *well-dressed*

habiller *to dress*

    s'habiller *to dress oneself, to get dressed*

habiter *to live*

habitude (f.) *habit*

    d'habitude *usually*

haie (f.) *hurdle*

haine (f.) *hatred*

haltérophilie (f.) *weight lifting*

handicapé / handicapée (m./f.) *disabled*

Hanoukka / Hanoucca (f.) *Hanukkah*

haricot (m.) *bean*

    haricot vert *green bean*

hasard (m.) *chance*

hâte (f.) *haste*

    avoir hâte *to look forward to (can't wait)*

hâter *to hasten*

    se hâter *to rush*

haut / haute (m./f.) *high*

    en haut *upstairs, up above*

    haute couture *high fashion*

hériter *to inherit*

héros / héroïne (m./f.) *hero/heroine*

heure (f.) *hour*

    Quelle heure est-il ? *What time is it?*

    heure du départ *departure time*

    heure de l'arrivée *arrival time*

    à l'heure *on time*

    à quelle heure ? *at what time?*

    À tout à l'heure ! *See you later!*

heureusement *happily, fortunately*

heureux / heureuse (m./f.) *happy*

hier *yesterday*

    avant-hier *the day before yesterday*

    hier soir *last night*

histoire (f.) *story, history, tale*

hiver (m.) *winter*

    en hiver *in (the) winter*

hockey (m.) *hockey*

    hockey sur glace *ice hockey*

homard (m.) *lobster*

    bisque (f.) **de homard** *lobster bisque*

homme (m.) *man*

    homme d'affaires *businessman*

    homme au foyer *homemaker* (m.)

honte (f.) *shame*

    avoir honte *to be ashamed*

hôpital (m.) *hospital*

horaire (m.) *schedule*

horrible *horrible*

hors *outside*

hors-d'œuvre (m.) *appetizer*

hôtel (m.) *hotel*

    hôtel de ville *city hall, town hall, municipal building*

huile (f.) *oil*

huit *eight*

huitième *eighth*

huître (f.) *oyster*

humain / humaine (m./f.) *human, humane*

    être (m.) **humain** *human being*

I

ici *here*
  d'ici *from here, by, until*
  d'ici là *by then, from now on, from now until, until then*
  par ici *this way*
idée (f.) *idea*
  Quelle bonne idée ! *What a good idea!*
il *he, it* (m.)
  Il fait beau. *It's beautiful (outside).*
  Il fait chaud. *It's hot./It's warm.*
  Il fait froid. *It's cold.*
  Il fait (du) soleil. *It's sunny.*
  Il fait du vent. *It's windy.*
  Il grêle. *It's hailing.*
  Il neige. *It's snowing.*
  Il pleut. *It's raining./It rains.*
  Il est temps de... *It is time to .../Now is the time to ...*
  il faut *it's necessary to, you have/need to, you must*
  il faut que *it is necessary that*
  il vaut mieux *it is better, it would be better*
  il vaut mieux que *it is better that, it would be better that*
  il est certain que *it is certain that*
  il est vrai que *it is true that*
  il est possible que *it is possible that*
  il est probable que *it is probable that*
  il semble que *it seems that*
  il est urgent que *it is urgent that*
  il est essentiel que *it is essential that*
  il est important que *it is important that*
  il est nécessaire que *it is necessary that*
  il est préférable que *it is preferable that*
il y a *there is/are, ago*
  il y avait *there was/were*
  Il n'y a pas de quoi. *You're welcome.*
  Il y a du soleil. *It's sunny.*
  Il y a du vent. *It's windy.*
Île (f.) de la Cité *Île de la Cité (City Island)*
ils *they (m./mixed), it* (m. pl.)
immeuble (m.) *apartment building, office building*
imperméable (m.) *raincoat*
important / importante (m./f.) *important*
  il est important que *it is important that*

importer *to matter*
  n'importe quoi / qui / où *whatever/whoever/wherever, anything/anyone/anywhere*
imprimante (f.) *printer*
Inde (f.) *India*
indien / indienne (m./f.) *Indian*
individu (m.) *individual*
infection (f.) *infection*
infirmier / infirmière (m./f.) *nurse*
inflammation (f.) *inflammation*
informaticien / informaticienne (m./f.) *computer programmer*
informatique (f.) *IT, computer science*
  service (m.) d'informatique *IT department*
ingénieur (m.) *engineer*
injection (f.) *shot, injection*
inquiet / inquiète (m./f.) *worried (anxious)*
institut (m.) de beauté *beauty parlor, beauty salon*
instructions (f. pl.) *instructions*
intelligent / intelligente (m./f.) *intelligent*
intéressant / intéressante (m./f.) *interesting*
intéresser *to interest*
  s'intéresser à *to be interested in*
  Ça m'intéresse. *That interests me.*
  Ça ne m'intéresse pas. *That doesn't interest me.*
Internet (m.) *internet*
interrompre *to interrupt*
intersection (f.) *intersection*
inviter *to invite*
irlandais / irlandaise (m./f.) *Irish*
Irlande (f.) *Ireland*
Italie (f.) *Italy*
italien / italienne (m./f.) *Italian*

J

jamais *ever, never*
  ne... jamais *never*
jambe (f.) *leg*
jambon (m.) *ham*
  sandwich (m.) au jambon *ham sandwich*
  sandwich (m.) jambon-fromage *ham and cheese sandwich*
janvier *January*
Japon (m.) *Japan*
japonais / japonaise (m./f.) *Japanese*
jardin (m.) *garden*

jaune *yellow*

je / j' *I*

  Je m'appelle... *My name is ... / I am called ...*

  Je ne comprends pas. *I don't understand.*

  Je vais très bien. *I'm very well.*

  Je veux... *I want ...*

  Je voudrais... *I would like ...*

  Je te présente... / Je vous présente... *Let me introduce ... (infml./pl., fml.)*

  Je vous en prie. *You're welcome. (fml.)*

  Je suis ravi / ravie de faire votre connaissance. *I'm delighted to make your acquaintance.*

jean (m.) *jeans*

jeter *to throw, to throw out/away*

jeu (m.) *game*

  jeu électronique *electronic game*

  jeu vidéo *video game*

  jeu de cartes *card game*

jeudi *Thursday*

jeune *young*

Joconde (f.) *Mona Lisa*

joli / jolie (m./f.) *nice, pretty*

joue (f.) *cheek*

jouer *to play, to perform, to act*

  jouer à cache-cache *to play hide and seek*

  jouer un match *to play a game, to play a match*

  cartes (f. pl.) à jouer *playing cards*

joueur / joueuse (m./f.) *player (games, sports, etc.)*

jour (m.) *day*

  jour de l'An *New Year's Day*

  jours (pl.) de la semaine *days of the week*

journal (m.) *newspaper*

journaliste (m./f.) *journalist*

journée (f.) *day*

  Vivement la fin de la journée ! *Can't wait for the end of the day!*

joyeux / joyeuse (m./f.) *joyful, cheerful*

  Joyeuses Fêtes ! *Happy Holidays!*

  Joyeux anniversaire ! *Happy birthday!/ Happy anniversary!*

  Joyeux Noël ! *Merry Christmas!*

juillet *july*

  14 (Quatorze) Juillet *Bastille Day, July 14th (France's national holiday)*

juin *June*

jupe (f.) *skirt*

juridique *legal (related to the law)*

  service (m.) juridique *legal department*

  langage (m.) juridique *legal language, legal terminology*

jus (m.) *juice*

  brique (f.) de jus d'orange *carton of orange juice*

jusqu'à *to, until, up to, up until*

  jusqu'à ce que *until*

juste *just, only*

K

kilo (m.) *kilo*

kilomètre (m.) *kilometer*

kir (m.) *white wine with black currant liqueur*

  kir royal *champagne with black currant liqueur*

L

là *there*

  là-bas *over there, there*

la / l' / le / les (f./m. or f. before a vowel or silent h/m./pl.) *the*

  la / le / les moins... *the least ...*

  la / le / les plus... *the most ...*

la / l' *her, it (f. direct object pronoun)*

laboratoire (m.) *laboratory*

lac (m.) *lake*

laid / laide (m./f.) *ugly*

laisser *to leave, to let (someone do something), to let go*

  Je voudrais laisser un message. *I would like to leave a message.*

lait (m.) *milk*

  verre (m.) de lait *glass of milk*

laitue (f.) *lettuce*

lampadaire (m.) *streetlight*

lampe (f.) *lamp*

lancer les dés *to roll the dice*

langage (m.) *language*

  langage des signes *sign language*

  langage courant *everyday language*

  langage du corps *body language*

  langage enfantin *baby talk (baby language)*

  langage familier *informal language, familiar language*

  langage soutenu *formal language*

langage grossier *bad language*
langage juridique *legal language, legal terminology,*
langage de programmation informatique *programming language*
langue (f.) *language, tongue*
  langue étrangère *foreign language*
laquelle / lequel (f./m.) *which*
large *wide*
lavabo (m.) *sink*
lave-linge (m.) *washing machine*
laver *to wash*
  se laver *to wash up, to wash oneself*
lave-vaisselle (m.) *dishwasher*
le / l' / la / les (m./m. or f. before a vowel or silent h/f./pl.) *the*
  le / la / les moins... *the least ...*
  le / la / les plus... *the most ...*
le / l' *him, it* (m. direct object pronoun)
leçon (f.) *lesson*
lecteur (m.) *player (CDs, DVDs, etc.), drive (computer)*
  lecteur de CD *CD player*
  lecteur de DVD *DVD player*
  lecteur de CD-ROM *CD-ROM drive*
lecture *reading*
léger / légère (m./f.) *light*
légèrement *lightly*
légume (m.) *vegetable*
lent / lente (m./f.) *slow*
lentement *slowly*
  Parlez plus lentement, s'il vous plaît. *Speak slower/more slowly, please.*
lentille (f.) *lens*
  lentilles (pl.) de contact *contact lenses*
lequel / laquelle (m./f.) *which*
les *the* (pl.)
  les moins... *the least ...* (pl.)
  les plus... *the most ...* (pl.)
les *them, it* (pl. direct object pronoun)
lessive (f.) *laundry detergent*
lettre (f.) *letter*
leur *their, to them/it* (pl.) (indirect object pronoun)
leurs *their* (pl.)
lever *to lift, to raise, to pick up*
  se lever *to get up, to rise (to get oneself up)*
liaison (f.) *link*
librairie (f.) *bookstore*

libre *free*
licence (f.) *bachelor's degree*
lieu (m.) *place*
  avoir lieu *to take place, to be held (lit., to have place)*
liquide (m.) vaisselle *dishwashing detergent*
lire *to read*
lit (m.) *bed*
littérature (f.) *literature*
  littérature anglaise *English literature*
livre (f.) *pound*
  livre de beurre *pound of butter*
livre (m.) *book*
  livre scolaire *textbook*
logiciel (m.) *software*
loin *far*
  loin d'ici *far from here*
  plus loin *farther*
loisirs (m. pl.) *leisure activities, recreation*
long / longue (m./f.) *long*
  le long de *along, alongside*
longtemps *long time, for a long time, long*
  il y a longtemps *a long time ago*
loup (f.) *wolf*
Louvre (m.) *Louvre*
  musée (m.) du Louvre *Louvre museum*
lui *him, to him/her/it* (indirect object pronoun)
lundi *Monday*
  lundi dernier *last Monday*
lune (f.) *moon*
lunettes (f. pl.) *(eye)glasses*
  lunettes de soleil *sunglasses*
lustre (m.) *chandelier*
Lutèce (f.) *Lutetia (old name for Paris)*
lutte (f.) *wrestling*
lycée (m.) *high school*
lycéen / lycéenne (m./f.) *high school student*

 M

M. *Mr.*
ma / mon / mes (f./m./pl.) *my*
macaron (m.) *meringue cookie*
machine (f.) à laver *washing machine*
madame *ma'am, Mrs., Ms., madam*
  mesdames *ladies*
mademoiselle *miss*
  mesdemoiselles *misses*
magasin (m.) *store*

grand magasin *department store*
magasin d'électronique *electronics store*
magasin de chaussures *shoe store*
magasin de vêtements *clothing store*
magazine (m.) *magazine*
magnifique *magnificent*
mai *May*
maigrir *to lose weight*
mail (m.) *e-mail*
maillot (m.) (de bain) *bathing suit, bathing trunks*
maillot (m.) de corps *undershirt*
main (f.) *hand*
maintenant *now*
maire (m.) *mayor*
mairie (f.) *city hall, municipal building*
mais *but*
maïs (m.) *corn*
maison *homemade*
maison (f.) *house, home*
   à la maison *at the house, at home*
maître-nageur (f.) *lifeguard*
maîtrise (f.) *master's degree*
mal *badly, bad, wrong*
   Ça va mal. *It's going badly./It's not going well.*
malade *sick*
maladie (f.) *illness, disease*
   maladie d'Alzheimer *Alzheimer's disease*
   maladie de Parkinson *Parkinson's disease*
malheureusement *unfortunately, unhappily*
malheureux / malheureuse (m./f.) *unfortunate, unhappy*
maman *Mom, Mommy*
manger *to eat*
   salle (f.) à manger *dining room*
manifestant / manifestante (m./f.) *demonstrator, protestor*
manifestation (f.) *demonstration, protest*
manifester *to demonstrate, to protest*
manteau (m.) *coat*
marchand / marchande (m./f.) *merchant, vendor, dealer*
marché (m.) *market*
   bon marché *inexpensive, a good buy*
marcher *to walk*
   marcher avec des béquilles *to walk with crutches*
   marcher avec une canne *to walk with a cane*

mardi *Tuesday*
mare (f.) *pond*
mari (m.) *husband*
marié / mariée (m./f.) *married*
Maroc (m.) *Morocco*
marocain / marocaine (m./f.) *Moroccan*
marquer *to score*
marron *brown*
marron (m.) *chestnut*
   crème (f.) de marrons *chestnut paste*
   marrons (pl.) glacés *sugar-coated chestnuts*
mars *March*
master (m.) *master's degree*
match (m.) *match, game*
mathématiques (f. pl.) *math*
maths (f. pl.) *math*
matière (f.) *subject*
   matière difficile *difficult subject*
matin (m.) *morning*
matinée (f.) *morning*
mauvais / mauvaise (m./f.) *bad*
   C'est mauvais. *That's bad.*
   plus mauvais / mauvaise *worse*
   le / la plus mauvais / mauvaise *the worst*
   moins mauvais / mauvaise *not as bad*
me / m' *myself (reflexive pronoun), me (direct object pronoun), to me (indirect object pronoun)*
   Je m'appelle... *My name is .../I am called...*
médecin (m.) *doctor*
médecine (f.) *medicine*
meilleur / meilleure (m./f.) *better, best*
   le / la meilleur / meilleure *the best*
mèl (m.) *e-mail*
melon (m.) *melon, cantaloupe*
membre (m.) *member*
même *same, even*
mémoire (f.) *memory*
menacer *to threaten*
ménage (m.) *house cleaning*
   faire le ménage *to clean the house, to do the house cleaning*
mener *to lead*
menthe (f.) *mint*
   menthe à l'eau *water with mint syrup*
menton (m.) *chin*
menu (m.) *menu*
   Le menu, s'il vous plaît. *The menu, please.*
mer (f.) *sea*

merci *thank you*
  Merci bien. *Thank you very much.*
mercredi *Wednesday*
mère (f.) *mother*
mes / mon / ma (pl./m./f.) *my*
mesdames *ladies*
mesdemoiselles *misses*
message (m.) instantané *instant message*
messieurs *gentlemen*
métro (m.) *subway, metro*
  station (f.) de métro *subway station*
  plan (m.) du métro *map of the subway*
  carte (f.) du métro *map of the subway*
mettre *to put, to put on*
  mettre à la poste *to mail, to put in the mail*
meubles (m. pl.) *furniture (in general)*
  meuble (m.) *a piece of furniture*
mexicain / mexicaine (m./f.) *Mexican*
Mexique (m.) *Mexico*
micro-ondes (m.) *microwave (oven)*
midi (m.) *noon*
  Il est midi. *It is noon.*
miel (m.) *honey*
mieux *better*
  il vaut mieux (que) *it is better (that), it would be better (that)*
milieu (m.) *middle*
  au milieu de *in the middle of*
mille *thousand*
milliard *billion*
milliardaire (m./f.) *billionaire*
million *million*
millionnaire (m./f.) *millionaire*
mince *thin*
minéral / minérale (m./f.) *mineral*
  eau (f.) minérale *mineral water*
minuit (m.) *midnight*
  Il est minuit. *It is midnight.*
miroir (m.) *mirror*
mi-temps (f.) *halftime*
mixer (m.) *blender*
Mlle *Miss*
Mme *Mrs., Ms.*
modem (m.) *modem*
moi *me*
moins *less, minus, fewer, not as*
  ... moins le quart *quarter to ...*
  moins de *less*

moins... que *less ... than, not as ... as*
le / la moins... *the least ...*
moins bon / bonne (m./f.) *not as good*
moins mauvais / mauvaise (m./f.) *not as bad*
à moins que... ne *unless*
mois (m.) *month*
  dans un mois *next month, in one month*
  mois prochain *next month*
  mois dernier *last month*
  deux mois auparavant *two months before*
  deux mois avant *two months before*
  mois (pl.) de l'année *months of the year*
moment (m.) *moment*
mon / ma / mes (m./f./pl.) *my*
monde (m.) *world, people*
  tout le monde *everyone*
monnaie (f.) *change, coins, currency*
monsieur *sir, Mr.*
  messieurs *gentlemen*
montagne (f.) *mountain*
monter *to go up, to come up, to rise*
  monter à bicyclette *to go bike riding, to ride a bike*
  monter à cheval *to go horseback riding, to ride a horse*
montre (f.) *watch*
montrer *to show*
monument (m.) *monument*
moquette (f.) *carpet*
morceau (m.) *piece, bite*
mosquée (f.) *mosque*
mot (m.) *word*
moto (f.) *motorcycle, motorcycling*
motocyclette (f.) *motorcycle*
mouchoir (m.) *handkerchief, tissue*
moule (f.) *mussel*
  moules (pl.) frites *mussels and fries*
mourir *to die*
mousse (f.) *mousse*
  mousse au chocolat *chocolate mousse*
moutarde (f.) *mustard*
  moutarde de Dijon *Dijon mustard*
mur (m.) *wall*
muscle (m.) *muscle*
musclé / musclée (m./f.) *muscular (person)*
musculaire *muscular (medical term)*
musculation (f.) *bodybuilding, strength training, weight lifting*

faire de la musculation *to do strength training, to lift weights, to do bodybuilding*
musée (m.) *museum*
  Musée du Louvre *Louvre Museum*
  Musée d'Orsay *Orsay Museum*
musicien / musicienne (m./f.) *musician*
musique (f.) *music*
mystérieux / mystérieuse (m./f.) *mysterious*

N

nager *to swim*
naître *to be born*
nappe (f.) *tablecloth*
natation (f.) *swimming*
  faire de la natation *to go swimming*
nation (f.) *nation*
national / nationale (m./f.) *national*
  fête (f.) nationale *national holiday*
nationalité (f.) *nationality*
naturel / naturelle (m./f.) *natural*
naturellement *naturally*
ne / n'... pas *not*
  n'est-ce pas ? *isn't it?, isn't that so?, right?*
  ne... jamais *never*
  ne... plus *no longer, no more, any more, anymore*
  ne... pas encore *not yet*
  ne... rien *nothing, anything*
  ne... rien d'autre *nothing else, anything else*
  il est nécessaire que *it is necessary that*
nécessaire *necessary*
neige (f.) *snow*
  vacances (f. pl.) de neige *winter vacation*
neiger *to snow*
  Il neige. *It's snowing.*
nettoyer *to clean*
neuf *nine*
neuf (m.) *new*
  Rien de neuf. *Nothing new.*
  Quoi de neuf ? *What's up?/What's new?*
neuvième *ninth*
neveu (m.) *nephew*
nez (m.) *nose*
nièce (f.) *niece*
Noël (m.) *Christmas*
  Joyeux Noël ! *Merry Christmas!*
  réveillon (m.) de Noël *Christmas Eve*
  veille (f.) de Noël *Christmas Eve*

noir / noire (m./f.) *black*
noisette (f.) *hazelnut*
nom (m.) *name*
  sous quel nom ? *under what name?*
nombre (m.) *number*
non *no*
nord (m.) *north*
normalement *usually*
note (f.) *grade, note*
notre / nos (m. or f./pl.) *our*
nourrir *to feed*
nourriture (f.) *food*
nous *we, us, ourselves* (reflexive pronoun), *to us* (indirect object pronoun), *each other*
nouveau / nouvel / nouvelle (m./m. before a vowel or silent h/f.) *new*
  Nouvel An (m.) *New Year*
nouveau-né (m.) *newborn*
nouvelles (f. pl.) *news (the news)*
novembre *November*
nuage (m.) *cloud*
nuageux / nuageuse (m./f.) *cloudy*
  C'est nuageux. *It's cloudy.*
nuit (f.) *night*
  Bonne nuit ! *Good night!*
  nuit dernière *last night*
nul / nulle (m./f.) *no, nil, null*
  nulle part *nowhere, anywhere*
numéro (m.) de téléphone *phone number*

O

obéir *to obey*
occupé / occupée (m./f.) *busy*
océan (m.) *ocean*
octobre *October*
œil (m.) (yeux, pl.) *eye (eyes)*
œuf (m.) *egg*
  œuf poché *poached egg*
  œuf au plat, œuf sur le plat *fried egg (over easy egg)*
  œuf à la coque *soft-boiled egg*
  œuf dur *hard-boiled egg (lit., hard egg)*
  œufs (pl.) brouillés *scrambled eggs*
  blancs (m. pl.) (d'œufs) *egg whites*
  douzaine (f.) d'œufs *dozen eggs*
Oh là là ! *Wow!/Oh dear!*
oignon (m.) *onion*
  soupe (f.) à l'oignon *onion soup*

omelette (f.) *omelette*
  omelette aux champignons *mushroom omelette*
on *we* (infml.), *people in general, one* (pronoun), *you* (general), *they* (general)
  On y va. *Let's go.* (infml.)
oncle (m.) *uncle*
ongle (m.) *fingernail*
  ongle de pied *toenail*
onze *eleven*
onzième *eleventh*
opéra (m.) *opera*
or (m.) *gold*
orage (m.) *storm*
orange *orange (color)*
orange (f.) *orange (fruit)*
  brique (f.) **de jus d'orange** *carton of orange juice*
  canard (m.) **à l'orange** *duck à l'orange, duck with orange sauce*
ordinateur (m.) *computer*
ordonnance (f.) *prescription*
oreille (f.) *ear*
  boucle (f.) **d'oreille** *earring*
organiser *to organize*
  organiser une fête *to have a party*
original / originale (m./f.) *original*
origine (f.) *origin*
orteil (m.) *toe*
orthographe (f.) *spelling*
os (m.) *bone*
ou *or*
  ou bien *or even, or else, either, or*
où *where*
  Où sont les toilettes ? *Where is the restroom?*
  Où se trouve... ? / Où est... ? *Where is ... ?*
  n'importe où *wherever, anywhere*
ouest (m.) *west*
oui *yes*
ouragan (m.) *hurricane*
ouvrier / ouvrière (m./f.) *worker*
  ouvrier / ouvrière en bâtiment *construction worker*
ouvrir *to open*
  ouvrir un fichier *to open a file*

P

page (f.) **web** *webpage*
pain (m.) *bread*
paire (f.) *pair*
  Ça coûte trois euros la paire. *That's three euros per pair.*
palourde (f.) *clam*
panier (m.) *basket*
  panier de fraises *basket of strawberries*
pansement (m.) *bandage*
pantalon (m.) *pants*
papa *Dad, Daddy*
papier (m.) *paper*
  papier hygiénique *toilet paper*
papillon (m.) *butterfly*
paquebot (m.) *cruise ship, ocean liner*
par *by, through, per*
  par ici *this way*
  par là *that way*
  par cœur *by heart*
paralysé / paralysée (m./f.) *paralyzed*
parapluie (m.) *umbrella*
parascolaire *extracurricular*
  activités (f. pl.) **parascolaires** *extracurricular activities*
parc (m.) *park*
parce que *because*
parcours (m.) **de golf** *golf course*
pardon *pardon (me), excuse me*
parent (m.) *relative, parent*
parfait / parfaite (m./f.) *perfect*
  C'est parfait. *It's perfect.*
parfois *sometimes*
parfum (m.) *flavor, fragrance, perfume*
Paris *Paris*
parisien / parisienne (m./f.) *Parisian*
parler *to speak, to talk*
  Parlez plus lentement, s'il vous plaît. *Speak slower/more slowly, please.*
  Je parle un peu français. *I speak a little French.*
part (f.) *part, share, slice (cake, pie, pizza)*
  de la part de *on behalf of, from (someone)*
  de ma part *on my behalf, from me, on my part*
  nulle part *nowhere, anywhere*
partenaire / partenaire (m./f.) *partner*
partie (f.) *party*

partiel / partielle *partial*
  à temps partiel *part-time*
partir *to leave, to go away*
partout *everywhere*
pas *not*
  ne... pas *not*
  pas du tout *not at all*
  Pas mal. *Not bad.*
  Pas grand-chose. *Not a lot.*
passeport (m.) *passport*
passer *to pass, to go past, to spend (time)*
  Je vous le / la passe. *I'm getting him/her for
    you. (lit., I'm passing him/her to you.)*
  passer un coup de fil *to make a phone call
    (lit., to pass a hit of the wire)* (infml.)
  passer (un examen) *to take (a test)*
  passer du temps *to spend time*
passe-temps (m.) *hobby, pastime*
passionnant / passionnante (m./f.) *exciting*
pâté (m.) *pâté (spreadable purée of meat)*
  pâté de foie gras *goose liver pâté*
patient / patiente (m./f.) *patient*
  Sois patient. *Be patient.* (infml.)
  Soyez patient. *Be patient.* (pl./fml.)
patin (m.) *skating, skate*
  patin à glace *ice skating, ice skate*
patinage (m.) sur glace *ice skating*
pâtisserie (f.) *pastry shop, pastry*
  pâtisserie-confiserie (f.) *pastry and candy
    store*
patron / patronne (m./f.) *boss*
pauvre *unfortunate, poor, impoverished*
payer *to pay, to pay for*
peau (f.) *skin*
pêche (f.) *peach, fishing*
  pêche Melba *peaches with ice cream*
peindre *to paint*
peinture (f.) *painting*
pendant *during*
  pendant que *while*
pendule (f.) *grandfather clock*
penser *to think*
perdre *to lose*
  perdre du temps *to waste time*
  perdre votre / ton temps *to waste your time*
  perdre un match *to lose a game, to lose a
    match*
perdu / perdue (m./f.) *lost*

Je suis perdu / perdue. *I'm lost.*
père (m.) *father*
permettre *to allow, to permit*
personne (f.) *person, no one, nobody*
  personne âgée *elderly person*
  ne / n'... personne *no one, anyone, nobody,
    anybody*
  pour quatre personnes *for four people, for a
    party of four*
personnel (m.) *staff*
peser *to weigh*
petit / petite (m./f.) *small, little, short*
  petit ami / petite amie (m./f.) *boyfriend/
    girlfriend*
  petit déjeuner (m.) *breakfast*
  prendre le petit déjeuner *to have breakfast*
  petits pois (m. pl.) *(green) peas (lit., little peas)*
peu *little, bit*
  peu de *little, few*
  un peu *a little*
  peu amical / peu amicale (m./f.) *unfriendly*
peur (f.) *fear*
  avoir peur *to be afraid (lit, to have fear)*
peut-être *maybe, possibly*
pharmacie (f.) *pharmacy, drugstore*
pharmacien / pharmacienne (m./f.) *pharmacist*
photo (f.) *photo*
  Pourriez-vous nous prendre en photo,
    s'il vous plaît ? *Can you take our picture
    (photo)?*
phrase (f.) *phrase*
physique (f.) *physics*
pièce (f.) *room, play (theater), piece, coin*
  pièce jointe *attachment*
pied (m.) *foot*
  à pied *on foot, by foot*
  au pied de *at the foot of*
  doigt (m.) de pied *toe*
  ongle (m.) de pied *toenail*
pilule (f.) *pill*
pique-nique (m.) *picnic*
piqûre (f.) *shot, injection*
pire *worse*
  le / la pire *the worst*
piste (f.) *trail, ski slope, track*
  piste pour débutants *bunny slope/hill,
    beginners' slope/hill*
placard (m.) *cupboard, closet*

Glossary   359

place (f.) *place, seat, ticket, room*
plafond (m.) *ceiling*
plage (f.) *beach*
plaire *to please*
  s'il te plaît *please* (infml.)
  s'il vous plaît *please* (pl./fml.)
plaisir (m.) *pleasure*
  Avec plaisir. *With pleasure.*
plan (m.) *map, plan*
  plan de la ville *map of the city*
  plan du métro *map of the subway*
planche (f.) *board*
  planche à repasser *ironing board*
  planche à roulettes *skateboard*
plante (f.) *plant*
plastique (m.) *plastic*
  en plastique *made of plastic*
plat (m.) *dish*
  plat principal *main dish/course*
  plat d'accompagnement *side dish*
plein / pleine (m./f.) *full, solid*
  à plein temps *full-time*
  activités (f. pl.) de plein air *outdoor activities*
  être en pleine expansion *to be growing (business)*
  être en pleine forme *to be in good shape*
pleuvoir *to rain*
  Il pleut. *It's raining./It rains.*
plombage (m.) *filling (tooth)*
plombier (m.) *plumber*
plongée (f.) sous-marine *scuba diving*
  faire de la plongée sous-marine *to go scuba diving*
plonger *to dive*
  plonger dans la piscine *to dive in(to) the pool*
pluie (f.) *rain*
plus *more*
  plus loin *farther*
  le / la plus proche *the nearest, the closest*
  À plus tard ! *See you later!*
  À plus ! *See you later!* (infml.)
  et bien plus *and even more, and much more*
  ne... plus *no longer, no more, any more, anymore*
  plus de *more*
  plus... que *more ... than*
  plus mauvais / mauvaise (m./f.) *worse*
  le / la plus... *the most ...*

plusieurs *several*
pneu (m.) *tire*
pocher *to poach*
  œuf (m.) poché *poached egg*
poème (m.) *poem*
poignet (m.) *wrist*
pointure (f.) *shoe size*
poire (f.) *pear*
poireau (m.) *leek*
pois (m. pl.) *peas*
  petits pois *(green) peas (lit., little peas)*
poisson (m.) *fish*
poitrine (f.) *chest*
poivre (m.) *pepper (condiment)*
poivron (m.) *pepper (vegetable)*
poli / polie (m./f.) *polite*
policier / femme policier (m./f.) *policeman/woman*
policier / policière (m./f.) *police, detective (adjective)*
  film (m.) policier *detective drama/film, crime drama/film*
poliment *politely*
politique (f.) *politics*
pomme (f.) *apple*
  pomme de terre *potato*
  tarte (f.) aux pommes *apple pie*
  purée (f.) de pommes de terre *mashed potatoes*
  pommes (pl.) de terre en robe des champs *boiled potatoes in their skins, baked potatoes*
pompes (f. pl.) *push-ups*
pont (m.) *bridge*
porc (m.) *pork, pig*
  côte (f.) de porc *pork chop*
portable (m.) *cell phone*
porte (f.) *door*
porter *to carry, to wear*
portugais / portugaise (m./f.) *Portuguese*
Portugal (m.) *Portugal*
posséder *to own*
possible *possible*
  il est possible que *it is possible that*
  Ce n'est pas possible ! *I don't believe it!/ Oh man!/It's not possible! (disappointment, anger)*
poste (f.) *post office, mail*

bureau (m.) de poste *post office*
poste (m.) *telephone extension*
poste (m.) de police *police station*
pot (m.) *drink* (infml.)
potage (m.) *soup*
poubelle (f.) *garbage, trash can*
poudre (f.) *powder*
poulet (m.) *chicken*
  poulet frites *chicken and fries*
poumon (m.) *lung*
pour *for, to*
  pour que *in order that, so that*
pourquoi *why*
pouvoir *to be able to, can*
  Puis-je vous aider ? *Can I help you?*
praliné / pralinée (m./f.) *filled with hazelnut or almond ganache*
pratiquer *to practice*
précédent / précédente (m./f.) *before last*
  semaine (f.) précédente *the week before last*
précis / précise (m./f.) *sharp, exact, precise*
  à midi précis *exactly at noon (at noon sharp)*
préférable *preferable*
  il est préférable que *it is preferable that*
préféré / préférée (m./f.) *favorite*
préférer *to prefer*
  préférer que *to prefer that*
premier / première (m./f.) *first*
  premier étage (m.) *first floor (one floor above the ground floor)*
  première base (f.) *first base*
prendre *to take, to have (food/drink)*
  prendre un bain *to take a bath*
  prendre une douche *to take a shower*
  prendre un verre *to have a drink*
  prendre le petit déjeuner *to have breakfast*
  prendre une chambre *to check in*
  prendre rendez-vous *to make an appointment*
  prendre un bain de soleil *to sunbathe (lit., to take a bath of sun)*
  prendre une photo *to take a picture (photo)*
  Pourriez-vous nous prendre en photo, s'il vous plaît ? *Can you take our picture please?*
préparer *to prepare, to make, to cook*
près *close, near*
  tout près *very close, very near*

près d'ici *nearby, near here, close to here*
présenter *to introduce, to show, to present*
  Je te présente… / Je vous présente… *Let me introduce …* (infml./pl., fml.)
prêt / prête (m./f.) *ready*
prier *to ask, to beg, to pray*
  Je vous en prie. *You're welcome.* (fml.)
principal / principale (m./f.) *principal (main)*
  plat (m.) principal *main course*
printemps (m.) *spring*
  au printemps *in (the) spring*
probable *probable*
  il est probable que *it is probable that*
probablement *probably*
prochain / prochaine (m./f.) *next*
  mois (m.) prochain *next month*
  semaine (f.) prochaine *next week*
  À la prochaine ! *See you later! (Until next time!)*
proche *near, nearby, close*
  le / la plus proche *the nearest, the closest*
produire *to produce*
prof (m./f.) *professor, teacher* (infml.)
professeur / professeure (m./f.) *professor, teacher*
profession (f.) *profession*
progrès (m.) *progress*
projeter *to plan*
promenade (f.) *walk*
  faire une promenade *to take a walk*
promener *to take someone or something for a walk*
  se promener *to take a walk*
propre *clean, own*
protéger *to protect*
prune (f.) *plum*
pubs / publicités (f. pl.) *commercials*
puis *then*
pull(-over) (m.) *sweater*
punir *to punish*
purée (f.) *purée*
  purée de pommes de terre *mashed potatoes*
pyjama (m.) *pajamas*

Q

qu'est-ce qui/que… *what …*
quai (m.) *platform, quay, bank (of a river)*
quand *when*

quarante *forty*
quart (m.) *quarter*
  ... et quart *quarter after/past ...*
  ... moins le quart *quarter to ...*
quartier (m.) *neighborhood, quarter, area*
quatorze *fourteen*
quatre *four*
quatre-vingt-dix *ninety*
quatre-vingts *eighty*
quatrième *fourth*
que *what, that, which, whom, than*
  qu'est-ce que ? *what?*
  Qu'est-ce que c'est ? *What is this/that?*
  plus... que *more ... than*
  moins... que *less ... than, not as ... as*
  aussi... que *as ... as*
quel / quelle (m./f.) *which, what*
  à quelle heure ? *at what time?*
  de quel / quelle ? (m./f.) *what?/of what?*
  Quel temps fait-il aujourd'hui ? *What is the weather today?*
  Quelle heure est-il ? *What time is it?*
  Quel soulagement ! *What a relief!*
  Quelle coïncidence ! *What a coincidence!*
  Quelle bonne idée ! *What a good idea!*
quelque *some, any*
  quelqu'un *someone, somebody*
  quelqu'un d'autre *someone else*
  quelque chose *something*
quelquefois *sometimes*
question (f.) *question*
queue (m.) *line, tail*
  faire la queue *to wait in line*
qui *who, that*
  Qui est à l'appareil ? *Who is it?/Who's calling? (on the phone)*
  Qui est-ce ? *Who is it?*
  à qui *to whom*
  avec qui *with whom*
  chez qui *at whose house*
  de qui *from whom, of whom, about whom*
  pour qui *for whom*
  n'importe qui *whoever, anyone*
quiche (f.) *quiche (baked dish made with eggs and cream)*
  quiche lorraine *type of quiche made with bacon*
quincaillerie (f.) *hardware store*

quinze *fifteen*
quinzième *fifteenth*
quitter *to leave, to depart, to quit*
  Ne quittez pas, s'il vous plaît. *Hold on, please. (lit., Don't leave, please.)*
quoi *what*
  Quoi de neuf ? *What's up?/What's new?*
  n'importe quoi *whatever, anything*
quoique *although*
quotidien / quotidienne (m./f.) *everyday, daily*

R

raccrocher *to hang up*
radio(graphie) (f.) *x-ray*
radis (m.) *radish*
  radis au beurre *rosette-cut radishes served with butter on top (lit., radishes in butter)*
raisin (m.) *grape(s)*
raison (f.) *reason*
  avoir raison *to be right (lit., to have reason)*
Ramadan (m.) *Ramadan*
ranger *to put away*
rapide *quick*
rappeler *to call back*
rarement *rarely*
rasoir (m.) *razor*
rater (un examen) *to fail (a test)*
ravi / ravie (m./f.) *delighted, charmed*
  Je suis ravi / ravie de faire votre connaissance. *I'm delighted to make your acquaintance.*
réception (f.) *reception desk*
recette (f.) *recipe*
recevoir une piqûre *to get a shot*
recommander *to recommend*
  recommander que *to recommend that*
récré(ation) (f.) *recess, break*
réfléchir *to think, to reflect*
réfrigérateur (m.) *refrigerator*
regarder *to watch, to look at*
régler sa note *to check out*
rejeter *to reject*
remise (f.) *discount*
remplir *to fill (in)*
rencontrer (une personne/quelqu'un) *to meet (a person/someone)*
rendez-vous (m.) *meeting, appointment, date*
  prendre rendez-vous *to make an*

appointment

rendre *to return*

rendre visite à *to visit, to pay a visit (to a person)*

rentrée (f.) *back-to-school*

rentrer *to go home, to come home, to return, to come back (in), to go in*

repas (m.) *meal*

répéter *to repeat*

Répétez, s'il vous plaît. *Repeat (that), please.*

répondre *to answer, to respond, to reply*

répondre au téléphone *to answer the phone*

reposer *to rest*

se reposer *to rest (oneself), to relax*

réservation (f.) *reservation*

faire une réservation *to make a reservation*

faire des réservations *to make reservations*

réserver *to reserve*

restaurant (m.) *restaurant*

reste (f.) *rest (what's left)*

rester *to stay*

rester en forme *to stay in shape*

résultats (m. pl.) *results*

retard (m.) *delay*

en retard *late*

retourner *to return*

retraite (f.) *retirement*

à la retraite *retired*

réunion (f.) *meeting, reunion*

réussir *to succeed, to do well*

réussir à (un examen / cours) *to pass (a test/a class), to do well in (a test/a class)*

réveiller *to wake (someone)*

se réveiller *to wake up (to wake oneself up)*

réveillon (m.) (du jour de l'An) *New Year's Eve*

réveillon (m.) de Noël *Christmas Eve*

revenir *to come back, to return*

réverbère (m.) *lamppost*

revue (f.) *magazine*

rez-de-chaussée (m.) *ground floor*

rhume (m.) *(common) cold*

riche *rich*

rideau (m.) *curtain*

rien *nothing, anything*

ne... rien *nothing, anything*

De rien. *You're welcome./It's nothing.*

Rien de neuf. *Nothing new.*

Rien de particulier. *Nothing much.*

ne... rien d'autre *nothing else, anything else*

rive (f.) droite *right bank*

rive (f.) gauche *left bank*

rivière (f.) *river*

riz (m.) *rice*

robe (f.) *dress*

rocher (m.) *rock*

rôle (m.) *role, part (in a play, movie, etc.)*

romantique *romantic*

rompre *to break*

rondelle (f.) *(round) slice of (cucumber, banana, sausage, etc.)*

rose *pink*

rosé *rosé*

vin (m.) rosé *rosé wine*

rose (f.) *rose*

rôti (m.) *roast, joint (of meat)*

rôti de bœuf *roast beef*

rôti / rôtie (m./f.) *roast(ed)*

carré (m.) d'agneau rôti *roast rack of lamb*

rouge *red*

vin (m.) rouge *red wine*

rougir *to blush, to redden*

rue (f.) *street*

rural / rurale (m./f.) *rural*

russe *Russian*

Russie (f.) *Russia*

S

s'aimer *to like/love each other*

s'amuser *to have a good time, to enjoy oneself, to have fun*

s'appeler *to be called, to call oneself*

Comment vous appelez-vous ? *What's your name? (pl./fml.)*

Comment t'appelles-tu ? *What's your name? (infml.)*

Je m'appelle... *My name is ... /I am called ...*

s'embrasser *to hug (each other), to kiss (each other)*

s'ennuyer *to get bored, to be bored*

s'entraîner *to train*

s'habiller *to get dressed, to dress oneself*

s'il le faut *if necessary, if needed*

s'il te plaît / s'il vous plaît *please (infml./pl., fml.) (lit., if it pleases you)*

sa / son / ses (f./m./pl.) *his, her, its*

sable (m.) *sand*

château (m.) de sable *sandcastle*
faire un château de sable *to make/build a sandcastle*
sac (m.) *purse, bag*
Sacré-Cœur (m.) *Sacré Cœur (Sacred Heart)*
Saint-Sylvestre (f.) *New Year's Eve*
salade (f.) *salad*
salade de fruits *fruit salad*
salade verte *green salad*
salade niçoise *niçoise salad*
saladier (m.) *bowl*
salaire (m.) *salary*
sale *dirty*
salé / salée (m./f.) *savory, salty*
salle (f.) *room, hall*
salle à manger *dining room*
salle de bains *bathroom, washroom*
salle de classe *classroom*
salle de réunion *meeting room*
salon (m.) *parlor, living room*
Salut. *Hello./Hi./Bye./See you later!*
samedi *Saturday*
sandwich (m.) *sandwich*
sandwich au jambon *ham sandwich*
sandwich au fromage *cheese sandwich*
sandwich jambon-fromage *ham and cheese sandwich*
sang (m.) *blood*
sans *without*
sans que *without*
santé (f.) *health*
À votre santé ! *To your health!*
en bonne santé *healthy*
sardines (f. pl.) *sardines*
sardines sauce tomate *sardines in tomato sauce*
sarrasin (m.) *buckwheat*
sauce (f.) *sauce*
sardines (f. pl.) sauce tomate *sardines in tomato sauce*
saucisse (f.) *sausage*
sauter *to jump, to sauté*
sauter une haie *to jump a hurdle*
sauvegarder un document *to save a document*
sauveteur (m.) *lifeguard*
savoir *to know*
Je ne sais pas. *I don't know.*
savon (m.) *soap*

saxophone (m.) *saxophone*
science (f.) *science*
score (m.) *score*
score final *final score*
sculpture (f.) *sculpture*
se / s' *himself, herself, themselves, oneself, each other* (reflexive pronoun)
s'amuser *to have a good time, to enjoy oneself, to have fun*
s'appeler *to be called, to call oneself*
s'ennuyer *to get bored, to be bored*
s'habiller *to get dressed, to dress oneself*
se blesser *to hurt oneself*
se brosser *to brush oneself (hair, teeth, etc.)*
se casser le bras / la jambe *to break one's arm/leg*
se coucher *to go to bed, to lie down (to lie oneself down)*
se décider *to make up one's mind, to be decided, to be resolved (to do something)*
se demander *to wonder, to ask oneself*
se dépêcher *to hurry*
se faire une élongation *to pull a muscle*
se fouler la cheville *to sprain one's ankle*
se hâter *to rush*
se laver *to wash up, to wash oneself*
se lever *to get up, to rise (to get oneself up)*
se promener *to take a walk*
se raser *to shave*
se rendre *to surrender*
se rendre à (+ evidence, an argument, etc.) *to give in to, to yield to*
se rendre à (+ location) *to take oneself to (a place), to go to (a place)*
se rendre compte (de) *to notice, to realize, to make oneself aware*
se rendre heureux / heureuse (m./f.) *to make oneself happy*
se rendre malade *to make oneself sick*
se reposer *to rest (oneself), to relax*
se réveiller *to wake up (to wake oneself up)*
se souvenir *to remember*
se tromper *to be mistaken, to make a mistake*
se trouver *to find oneself (somewhere), to be situated*
se comprendre *to understand each other*
se connaître *to know each other*
se dire *to tell each other, to say to each other*

se disputer *to argue (with each other)*
se fiancer *to get engaged (to each other)*
se marier *to get married (to each other)*
se parler *to speak to each other*
se regarder *to look at each other, to watch each other*
se téléphoner *to call each other*
se voir *to see each other*
sèche-linge (m.) *dryer*
second / seconde (m./f.) *second*
secrétaire (m./f.) *secretary*
seize *sixteen*
séjour (m.) *trip, stay, sojourn*
sel (m.) *salt*
semaine (f.) *week*
   dans une semaine *next week, in one week*
   semaine prochaine *next week*
   semaine précédente *the week before last*
   semaine suivante *the week after next*
   semaine d'avant *the week before last*
   semaine d'après *the week after next*
   jours (m. pl.) de la semaine *days of the week*
sembler *seem (to)*
   il semble que *it seems that*
sept *seven*
septembre *September*
septième *seventh*
sérieux / sérieuse (m./f.) *serious*
serveur / serveuse (m./f.) *waiter/waitress, server*
service (m.) *department*
   service de comptabilité *accounting department*
   service d'informatique *IT department*
   service financier *finance department*
   service des ventes *sales department*
   service juridique *legal department*
   service de marketing *marketing department*
   service des relations publiques *public relations (PR) department*
   service du courrier *shipping department, mail room*
   service clientèle / client *customer service department*
serviette (f.) *napkin, towel, briefcase*
   serviette de bain *bath towel*
ses / son / sa (pl./m./f.) *his, her, its*
seul / seule (m./f.) *alone*

seulement *only*
shampooing (m.) *shampoo*
si *if, yes (negative)*
   s'il te plaît / s'il vous plaît *please* (infml./pl., fml.) *(lit., if it pleases you)*
simple *simple*
   aller simple *one-way*
sincère *sincere*
sirop (m.) de cassis *black currant syrup*
site (m.) web *website*
six *six*
sixième *sixth*
skateboard (m.) *skateboard*
ski (m.) *skiing*
   faire du ski *to ski, to go skiing*
   ski nautique *water-skiing*
skier *to ski*
social / sociale (m./f.) *social*
société (f.) *company, firm*
sœur (f.) *sister*
soie (f.) *silk*
soif (f.) *thirst*
   avoir soif *to be thirsty*
soin (m.) *care*
soir (m.) *evening, night*
   ce soir *tonight, this evening*
   hier soir *last night*
   Bonsoir ! *Good evening!*
soirée (f.) *party, evening, night*
soixante *sixty*
soixante-dix *seventy*
sol (m.) *floor (of a room)*
sole (f.) *sole (fish)*
   sole meunière *sole covered in flour and sautéed in butter*
soleil (m.) *sun*
   Il fait (du) soleil. / Il y a du soleil. *It's sunny.*
   lunettes (f. pl.) de soleil *sunglasses*
solex (m.) *moped*
sommeil (m.) *sleep*
   avoir sommeil *to be sleepy (lit., to have sleep)*
son / sa / ses (m./f./pl.) *his, her, its*
sonner *to ring*
sortie (f.) *exit*
sortir *to go out, to leave, to come out*
   sortir avec *to go out with, to date*
   sortir en boîte *to go out to clubs, to go out clubbing*

soudain *suddenly*
  tout à coup, tout d'un coup *all of a sudden*
souhaiter *to wish*
soulagement (m.) *relief*
  Quel soulagement ! *What a relief!*
soulever un haltère *to lift a dumbbell*
soupe (f.) *soup*
  soupe à l'oignon *onion soup*
souper *to have a late dinner*
souper (m.) *late dinner*
sourcil (m.) *eyebrow*
sourd / sourde (m./f.) *deaf*
sourire (m.) *smile*
souris (f.) *mouse*
sous *under*
  sous quel nom ? *under what name?*
sous-titre (m.) *subtitle*
sous-vêtements (m. pl.) *underwear*
souvenir (m.) *souvenir, memory*
souvent *often*
spécialité (f.) *specialty*
spectateur / spectatrice (m./f.) *spectator*
sport (m.) *sport*
  faire du sport *to play sports, to do sports*
sportif / sportive (m./f.) *athletic*
stade (m.) *stadium*
  stade de foot *soccer stadium*
station (f.) *station*
  station de métro *subway station, metro station*
  station de sports d'hiver *ski resort*
statue (f.) *statue*
steak (m.) *steak*
  steak frites *steak and fries*
sucre (m.) *sugar*
sucré / sucrée (m./f.) *sweet*
sud (m.) *south*
sueur (f.) *sweat*
suggérer *to suggest*
suisse *Swiss*
Suisse (f.) *Switzerland*
suite (f.) *rest, next part, what happens next*
  Vivement la suite ! *Can't wait for the rest!/Can't wait for what happens next!*
suivant / suivante (m./f.) *following, after next*
  semaine (f.) suivante *the week after next*
suivre *to follow*
  suivre un cours *to take a class*

sujet (m.) *subject*
super *super, great*
  Super ! *Great!*
supermarché (m.) *supermarket*
supporteur / supportrice (m./f.) *fan (sports)*
supprimer *to delete*
sur *on*
sûr / sûre (m./f.) *sure, certain*
  Bien sûr ! *Of course!*
surf (m.) *surfing*
  surf sur neige *snowboarding (lit., surfing on snow)*
surprendre *to surprise*
surtout *mostly, above all, especially*
sympa *cool, nice, good*
  très sympa *very cool/nice/good*
sympathique *friendly (nice)*
synagogue (f.) *synagogue*

T

ta / ton / tes (f./m./pl.) *your* (infml.)
table (f.) *table*
  table pour deux *table for two*
  À table ! *Dinner's ready!* (lit., *To the table!*)
tableau (m.) *painting*
taille (f.) *size (clothing)*
tailleur (m.) *suit (woman's)*
talc (m.) *powder*
talentueux / talentueuse (m./f.) *talented*
tante (f.) *aunt*
tapis (m.) *rug*
  tapis de course, tapis de jogging *treadmill*
tard *late*
  À plus tard ! *See you later!*
tarte (f.) *pie, tart*
  tarte aux fraises *strawberry pie*
  tarte aux pommes *apple pie*
  tarte à la citrouille *pumpkin pie*
tartine (f.) *bread with various spreads*
tasse (f.) *cup*
  tasse de thé *cup of tea*
taxi (m.) *taxi, cab*
te / t' *yourself* (infml., reflexive pronoun), *you* (infml., direct object pronoun), *to you* (infml., indirect object pronoun)
télé(vision) (f.) *television, TV*
télécopieur (m.) *fax machine*
téléphone (m.) *telephone*

(téléphone) portable *cell phone*
répondre au téléphone *to answer the phone*
numéro (m.) de téléphone *phone number*
téléphoner *to phone, to call, to make a phone call*
télévision (f.) *television*
température (f.) *temperature*
temple (m.) *temple*
temps *time, weather*
  Quel temps fait-il aujourd'hui ? *What's the weather today?*
  Je n'ai pas le temps. *I don't have (the) time.*
  à plein temps *full-time*
  à temps partiel *part-time*
  temps libre *free time*
  perdre du temps *waste time (to)*
  perdre votre / ton temps *waste your time (to)*
tendon (m.) *tendon*
tenir *to hold*
tennis (m.) *tennis*
tenue (f.) *outfit*
  en tenue de soirée *formal, in formal dress/ attire*
terminer *to finish, to end*
terrain (m.) de golf *golf course*
terre (f.) *land, earth*
tes / ton / ta (pl./m./f.) *your* (infml.)
tête (f.) *head*
thé (m.) *tea*
  tasse (f.) de thé *cup of tea*
théâtre (m.) *theater*
théière (f.) *teakettle, teapot*
thriller (m.) *thriller*
Tiens ! *Say!/Hey! (surprise)*
timbre (m.) *stamp*
tiroir (m.) *drawer*
tisane (f.) *herbal tea*
toi *you* (infml.)
toilettes (f. pl.) *toilet, restroom*
  Où sont les toilettes ? *Where is the restroom?*
tomate (f.) *tomato*
  sardines (f. pl.) sauce tomate *sardines in tomato sauce*
tomber *to fall*
  tomber malade *to get sick*
ton / ta / tes (m./f./pl.) *your* (infml.)
tonnerre (m.) *thunder*
tort (m.) *wrong*
  avoir tort *to be wrong (lit., to have wrong)*

tôt *early*
touchdown (m.) *touchdown*
toujours *always, still*
tour (f.) *tower*
  Tour Eiffel *Eiffel Tower*
tour (m.) *tour, turn*
touriste (m./f.) *tourist*
tourner *to turn*
tout / toute / tous / toutes (m./f./m. pl./f. pl.) *all, every*
  tout le monde *everyone*
  tout droit *straight ahead*
  pas du tout *not at all*
  C'est tout ? *Is that all?*
  C'est tout. *That's all.*
  À tout à l'heure ! *See you later!*
tractions (f. pl.) *pull-ups*
train (m.) *train*
  train à grande vitesse (TGV) *high-speed train*
tranche (f.) *slice (bread, cheese)*
  tranche de fromage *slice of cheese*
transfusion (f.) de sang *blood transfusion*
transport (m.) *transportation*
travail (m.) *work*
travailler *to work*
  travailler dur *to work hard*
travers (m.) *beam, quirk*
  à travers *through, across*
traverser *to cross, to go across*
treize *thirteen*
trente *thirty*
très *very*
  très bien *very good, very well*
  très bon / bonne (m./f.) *very good*
tricher *to cheat*
tricot (m.) *knitting, sweater*
trillion *trillion*
triste *sad*
trois *three*
troisième *third*
  troisième base (f.) *third base*
tromper *to deceive*
  se tromper *to be mistaken, to make a mistake*
trop *too, too much*
  trop de *too much*
trottoir (m.) *sidewalk*
trousse (f.) de secours *first-aid kit*

trouver *to find*
　se trouver *to find oneself (somewhere), to be situated*
　trouver que *to find that, to think that*
　Où se trouve... ? *Where is ... ?*
truite (f.) *trout*
　truite au bleu *trout cooked in wine and vinegar*
T-shirt (m.) *t-shirt*
tu *you* (infml.)

U

un / une (m./f.) (plural of un / une is des) *a, an, one*
　un peu *a little*
　une fois *once, one time*
Union (f.) européenne *European Union*
université (f.) *university, college*
urbain / urbaine (m./f.) *urban*
urgent / urgente (m./f.) *urgent*
　il est urgent que *it is urgent that*
usine (f.) *factory*
utiliser *to use*
　utiliser le langage des signes *to use sign language*

V

vacances (f. pl.) *vacation*
　grandes vacances *summer vacation*
　vacances d'hiver *winter vacation*
vaccin (m.) *vaccine*
vain / vaine (m./f.) *vain*
valoir *to be worth*
　valoir la peine *to be worth the trouble*
　il vaut mieux (que) *it would be better (that), it is better (that)*
vanille (f.) *vanilla*
　glace (f.) à la vanille *vanilla ice cream*
Vas-y ! (infml.) *Go there!/Go on!/Go ahead!*
veau (m.) *veal*
veille (f.) de *the day before*
　veille de Noël *Christmas Eve*
vélo (m.) *bike*
　vélo d'appartement *stationary bike*
vélomoteur (m.) *moped*
vendeur / vendeuse (m./f.) *salesman/woman*
vendre *to sell*
vendredi *Friday*

venir *to come*
vent (m.) *wind*
　Il fait du vent. / Il y a du vent. *It's windy.*
ventre (m.) *belly, stomach (general term)*
vermicelle (m.) *vermicelli pasta*
　consommé (m.) aux vermicelles *noodle soup (vermicelli pasta consommé)*
verre (m.) *glass, lens*
　prendre un verre *to have a drink*
　verre de lait *glass of milk*
　verres (pl.) de contact *contact lenses*
vers *around, about*
version (f.) *version*
　version française (v.f.) *French version of a film (dubbed into French)*
　version originale (v.o.) *original version of a film (not dubbed into French)*
vert / verte (m./f.) *green*
　citron (m.) vert *lime*
　haricots (m. pl.) verts *green beans*
　salade (f.) verte *green salad*
veste (f.) *jacket*
veston (m.) *jacket*
vêtements (m. pl.) *clothes, clothing*
vétérinaire (m.) *veterinarian*
viande (f.) *meat*
vie (f.) *life*
vietnamien / vietnamienne (m./f.) *Vietnamese*
vieux / vieil / vieille (m./m. before a vowel or silent h/f.) *old, elderly, outdated*
village (m.) *village*
ville (f.) *town, city*
　plan (m.) de la ville *map of the city*
　carte (f.) de la ville *map of the city*
　hôtel (m.) de ville *city hall, town hall, municipal building*
vin (m.) *wine*
　vin rouge / blanc / rosé / mousseux *red/white/rosé/sparkling wine*
　carafe (f.) de vin *pitcher of wine*
　coq (m.) au vin *chicken/rooster cooked in wine*
vingt *twenty*
vingtième *twentieth*
violet / violette (m./f.) *violet, purple*
violon (m.) *violin*
violoncelle (m.) *cello*
virus (m.) *virus*
visage (m.) *face*

visite (f.) guidée *guided tour*
visiter *to visit (a place)*
vite *quickly*
vivement *strongly*
 Vivement la fin de la journée ! *Can't wait for the end of the day!*
 Vivement la suite ! *Can't wait for the rest!/ Can't wait for what happens next!*
vocabulaire (m.) *vocabulary*
voici *here is/are, here it is/they are*
voie (f.) *track, lane*
voilà *there is/are, here is/are, there it is/they are, here it is/they are*
voile (f.) *sail/sailing*
 faire de la voile *sailing*
voir *to see*
voiture (f.) *car*
volaille (f.) *poultry*
volley(-ball) (m.) *volleyball*
votre / vos (m. or f./pl.) *your (pl./fml.)*
vouloir *to want, to wish*
 Je veux (bien)... *I (do) want ...*
 Je voudrais (bien)... *I would like ...*
 Que voulez-vous ? *What do you want?*
vous *you (pl./fml.), yourself (fml., reflexive pronoun), yourselves (reflexive pronoun), to you (pl./fml., indirect object pronoun), each other*
voyage (m.) *voyage, trip, travel*
 chèque (m.) de voyage *traveler's check*
voyager *to travel*
vrai / vraie (m./f.) *true, real*
 il est vrai que *it is true that*
vraiment *truly, really*

W

wagon (m.) *car (on a train)*
 wagon-lit (m.) *sleeping/sleeper car*
week-end (m.) *weekend*
western (m.) *western*

Y

y *there*
 il y a *there is/are, ago*
 il y avait *there was/were*
yeux (m. pl.) (œil, sg.) *eyes (eye)*
 avoir les yeux bleus / bruns / verts *to have blue/brown/green eyes*
yoga (m.) *yoga*

Z

zéro *zero*
zoo (m.) *zoo*

English-French

A

a, an *un / une* (m./f.) (plural of *un / une* is *des*)
 a little *un peu*
 a lot *beaucoup*
 a lot of *beaucoup de*
abdomen *ventre* (m.), *abdomen* (m.)
able to (to be) *pouvoir, arriver à (+ verb)*
above all *surtout*
Absolutely! *Absolument !*
academic year *année* (f.) *scolaire*
accessories *accessoires* (m. pl.)
accident *accident* (m.)
accompany (to) *accompagner*
accountant *comptable / comptable* (m./f.)
accounting *comptabilité* (f.)
 accounting department *service* (m.) *de comptabilité*
ache (to) *avoir mal à*
across *à travers*
 across from *en face de*
act (to) *agir, jouer*
action *action* (f.)
 action film/movie *film* (m.) *d'action*
active *actif / active* (m./f.)
actively *activement*
actor/actress *acteur / actrice* (m./f.)
admire (to) *admirer*
adolescent *adolescent / adolescente* (m./f.)
adore (to) *adorer*
adult *adulte* (m./f.)
advance (to) *avancer*
afraid (to be) *avoir peur*
after *après*
 after next *suivant / suivante* (m./f.), *d'après*
afternoon *après-midi* (m./f.)
afterwards *après*
again *encore*
age *âge* (m.)
ago *il y a*
ahead *devant*
airplane *avion* (m.)

airport *aéroport* (m.)

alcohol *alcool* (m.)

Algeria *Algérie* (f.)

Algerian *algérien / algérienne* (m./f.)

all *tout / toute / tous / toutes* (m./f./m. pl./f. pl.)

   Is that all? *C'est tout ?*

   That's all. *C'est tout.*

   All right. *D'accord. / Entendu.*

allergic *allergique*

allergy *allergie* (f.)

allow (to) *permettre*

almond *amande* (f.)

   filled with hazelnut or almond ganache *praliné / pralinée* (m./f.)

alone *seul / seule* (m./f.)

along(side) *le long de*

already *déjà*

also *aussi*

although *bien que, quoique*

always *toujours*

ambulance *ambulance* (f.)

American *américain / américaine* (m./f.)

amusing *amusant / amusante* (m./f.)

and *et*

animal *animal* (m.)

animated movie *film* (m.) *dessin animé*

ankle *cheville* (f.)

   to sprain one's ankle *se fouler la cheville*

anniversary *anniversaire* (m.)

   Happy anniversary! *Joyeux / Bon anniversaire !*

announce (to) *annoncer*

annoy (to) *ennuyer*

another *un / une autre* (m./f.)

answer (to) *répondre*

   answer the phone (to) *répondre au téléphone*

antibiotics *antibiotiques* (m. pl.)

anti-inflammatory *anti-inflammatoire*

anxious *inquiet / inquiète* (m./f.)

any *quelque, du*

   in any case, at any rate *de toute façon*

anybody, anyone *personne, ne... personne, n'importe qui*

anyhow *de toute façon*

anymore, any more *ne... plus*

anything *rien, ne... rien, n'importe quoi*

   anything else *autre chose, ne... rien d'autre*

anywhere *nulle part, n'importe où*

apartment *appartement* (m.)

   apartment building *immeuble* (m.)

appetizer *entrée* (f.), *hors-d'œuvre* (m.)

apple *pomme* (f.)

   apple pie *tarte* (f.) *aux pommes*

apply for a job (to) *faire une demande d'emploi*

appointment *rendez-vous* (m.)

April *avril*

Arc de Triomphe (Arch of Triumph) *Arc* (m.) *de Triomphe*

architect *architecte* (m./f.)

area *quartier* (m.)

argue (with each other) (to) *se disputer*

arm *bras* (m.)

armchair *fauteuil* (m.)

around *autour de, vers*

arrive (to) *arriver*

   arrive (somewhere) (to) *arriver à (+ destination)*

   arrival time *heure* (f.) *de l'arrivée, d'arrivée*

art *art* (m.)

artist *artiste* (m./f.)

as *comme, aussi*

   as a result of ... (in a negative way) *à cause de...*

   as ... as *aussi... que*

   not as ... as *moins... que*

ashamed (to be) *avoir honte*

ask (for) (to) *demander*

   ask oneself (to) *se demander*

assistant *assistant / assistante* (m./f.)

at *à*

   at the *au / à la / à l' / aux* (m./f./m. or f. before a vowel or silent h/pl.)

   at someone's house/place *chez*

   at home *chez moi, à la maison*

   at what time? *à quelle heure ?*

   at any rate *de toute façon*

   at school *à l'école*

   at the office *au bureau*

   at work *au travail*

athletic *sportif / sportive* (m./f.)

ATM *guichet* (m.) *automatique, distributeur* (m.) *de billets*

attach a file (to) *envoyer un fichier en pièce jointe*

attachment *pièce* (f.) *jointe*

attend (a class) (to) *assister à (un cours)*

August *août*

aunt *tante* (f.)
Australia *Australie* (f.)
Australian *australien / australienne* (m./f.)
author *auteur / auteure* (m./f.)
auto racing *course* (f.) *automobile*
automobile *automobile* (f.)
autumn *automne* (m.)
  in autumn *en automne*
avenue *avenue* (f.)

B

baccalauréat (an exam for students wishing
  to continue their education beyond high
  school) *baccalauréat / bac* (m.)
baby *bébé* (m.)
  baby talk (baby language) *langage* (m.)
    enfantin
bachelor's degree *licence* (f.)
back *dos* (m.)
back-to-school *rentrée* (f.)
bad *mauvais / mauvaise* (m./f.), *mal*
  bad language *langage* (m.) *grossier*
badly *mal*
  It's going badly. *Ça va mal.*
bag *sac* (m.)
bakery *boulangerie* (f.)
ball *ballon (large – basketball, etc.)* (m.), *balle
  (small – tennis, etc.)* (f.)
ballet *ballet* (m.)
  ballet dancer *danseur / danseuse* (m./f.) *de
    ballet, ballerine* (f.)
banana *banane* (f.)
band *groupe* (m.) *de musique*
bandage *bandage* (m.), *pansement* (m.)
bank *banque* (f.), *quai (of a river)* (m.)
  bank clerk *employé / employée de banque*
    (m./f.)
banker *banquier / banquière* (m./f.)
banknote *billet* (m.)
baseball *baseball* (m.)
basket *panier* (m.)
  basket of strawberries *panier de fraises*
basketball *basket(-ball)* (m.)
bath towel *serviette* (f.) *de bain*
bathing suit/trunks *maillot* (m.) *de bain*
bathroom *salle* (f.) *de bains*
bathtub *baignoire* (f.)
be (to) *être*

be able to (to) *pouvoir*
be bored (to) *s'ennuyer*
be born (to) *naître*
be busy (to) *être occupé / occupée* (m./f.)
be called (to) *s'appeler*
be deaf (to) *être sourd / sourde* (m./f.)
be decided (to) *se décider*
be resolved (to do something) (to) *se décider*
be disabled (to) *être handicapé / handicapée*
  (m./f.)
be engaged (to) (to) *être fiancé / fiancée (à)*
  (m./f.)
be familiar with (to) *connaître*
be held (to) *avoir lieu*
be mistaken (to) *se tromper*
be necessary (to) *falloir*
be paralyzed (to) *être paralysé / paralysée*
  (m./f.)
be sick (to) *être malade*
be situated (to) *se trouver*
be sweating (to) *être en sueur, être en nage*
be unemployed (to) *être sans emploi, être
  sans travail, chômeur, chômeuse*
be afraid (to) *avoir peur*
be ashamed (to) *avoir honte*
be cold (to) *avoir froid*
be hot/warm (to) *avoir chaud*
be hungry (to) *avoir faim*
be thirsty (to) *avoir soif*
be sleepy (to) *avoir sommeil*
be right (to) *avoir raison*
be wrong (to) *avoir tort*
be ... years old (to) *avoir... ans*
be in the middle of (to), be in the process of
  (to) *être en train de*
beach *plage* (f.)
bean *haricot* (m.)
  green bean *haricot vert*
beautician *esthéticien / esthéticienne* (m./f.)
beautiful *beau / bel / belle* (m./m. before a vowel
  or silent h/f.)
  It's beautiful (outside). *Il fait beau.*
beauty parlor (beauty salon) *institut* (m.) *de
  beauté*
because *parce que*
  because of ... (in a negative way) *à cause de...*
become (to) *devenir*
bed *lit* (m.)

bedroom *chambre* (f.) *(à coucher)*
beef *bœuf* (m.)
beer *bière* (f.)
before *devant, avant (que), auparavant*
  the day before *veille* (f.) *de*
  before last *précédent / précédente* (m./f.),
    d'avant
beg (to) *prier*
begin (to) *commencer*
beginner *débutant / débutante* (m./f.)
  beginners' slope/hill *piste* (f.) *pour débutants*
behave (to) *agir*
behind *derrière*
beige *beige*
Belgian *belge*
Belgium *Belgique* (f.)
believe (to) *croire*
  I don't believe it! *Ce n'est pas possible !*
belly *ventre* (m.)
belongings *affaires* (f. pl.)
belt *ceinture* (f.)
best *meilleur / meilleure* (m./f.), *mieux*
  the best *le / la meilleur / meilleure*
better *meilleur / meilleure* (m./f.), *mieux*
  it is better (that), it would be better (that) *il*
    vaut mieux (que)
between *entre*
bicycle *bicyclette* (f.)
  go bike riding (to), ride a bike (to) *monter à*
    bicyclette
bidet *bidet* (m.)
big *grand / grande* (m./f.)
bike *vélo* (m.)
  go bike riding (to), ride a bike (to) *monter à*
    bicyclette
bill *billet (currency)* (m.), *addition (restaurant,*
  café, etc.) (f.)
  The bill, please. *L'addition, s'il vous plaît.*
billiards *billard* (m.)
billion *milliard*
billionaire *milliardaire* (m./f.)
biology *biologie* (f.)
birthday *anniversaire* (m.)
  Happy birthday! *Joyeux / Bon anniversaire !*
bisque (creamy soup) *bisque* (f.)
  lobster bisque *bisque de homard*
bite *morceau* (m.)
black *noir / noire* (m./f.)

black currant *cassis* (m.)
  black currant syrup *sirop* (m.) *de cassis*
bleach *eau* (f.) *de Javel*
blender *mixer* (m.)
blind *aveugle*
  be blind (to) *être aveugle*
blonde *blond / blonde* (m./f.)
blood *sang* (m.)
  blood transfusion *transfusion* (f.) *de sang*
blouse *chemisier* (m.), *blouse* (f.)
blue *bleu / bleue* (m./f.)
blush (to) *rougir*
boat *bateau* (m.)
body *corps* (m.)
  human body *corps humain*
  body parts *parties* (f. pl.) *du corps*
  body language *langage* (m.) *du corps*
bodybuilding *musculation* (f.)
  to do bodybuilding *faire de la musculation*
bone *os* (m.)
book *livre* (m.)
bookshelf *étagère* (f.), *bibliothèque* (f.)
bookstore *librairie* (f.)
border *bord* (m.)
  at the border of *au bord de*
bore (someone) (to) *ennuyer*
  be bored (to), get bored (to) *s'ennuyer*
  It's boring. *C'est ennuyeux.*
born (to be) *naître*
boss *patron / patronne* (m./f.), *chef* (m.)
bottle *bouteille* (f.)
  bottle of champagne *bouteille de*
    champagne
boulevard *boulevard* (m.)
boutique *boutique* (f.)
bowl *saladier* (m.), *bol* (m.)
box *boîte* (f.)
box office *guichet* (m.)
boxing *boxe* (f.)
boy *garçon* (m.)
boyfriend *copain* (m.), *petit ami* (m.)
bracelet *bracelet* (m.)
brain *cerveau* (m.)
brave *brave*
Brazil *Brésil* (m.)
Brazilian *brésilien / brésilienne* (m./f.)
bread *pain* (m.)
break (recess) *récré(ation)* (f.)

break (to) *casser, rompre*
  break one's arm/leg (to) *se casser le bras / la jambe*
breakfast *petit déjeuner* (m.)
  have breakfast (to) *prendre le petit déjeuner*
bridge *pont* (m.)
briefcase *serviette* (f.)
bring (to) *apporter*
brochure *brochure* (f.)
broom *balai* (m.)
brother *frère* (m.)
brown *brun / brune* (m./f.), *marron*
brush (to) *brosser*
  brush oneself (hair, teeth, etc.) (to) *se brosser*
buckwheat *sarrasin* (m.)
build (to) *bâtir*
  build a sandcastle (to) *faire un château de sable*
building *bâtiment* (m.), *immeuble (apartment, office)* (m.)
bundle, bunch *botte* (f.)
  bunch of asparagus *botte d'asperges*
bunny slope/hill *piste* (f.) *pour débutants*
burn *brûlure* (f.)
bus *bus* (m.), *autobus* (m.), *autocar* (m.)
  bus stop *arrêt* (m.) *de bus / d'autobus*
  bus tour *circuit* (m.) *en bus, excursion* (f.) *en autocar*
business *affaires* (f. pl.)
  businessman/woman *homme / femme d'affaires* (m./f.)
busy *occupé / occupée* (m./f.)
  be busy (to) *être occupé / occupée* (m./f.)
  The line is busy. *La ligne est occupée.*
but *mais*
butcher shop *boucherie* (f.)
butter *beurre* (m.)
butterfly *papillon* (m.)
buy (to) *acheter*
  a good buy (inexpensive) *bon marché*
by *par, d'ici*
  by foot *à pied*
  by heart *par cœur*
  by then *d'ici là*
  by the end of the week *d'ici la fin de la semaine*
Bye. *Salut.*

C

cab *taxi* (m.)
cabinet *armoire* (f.)
  medicine cabinet *armoire à pharmacie*
cable *câble* (m.)
café *café* (m.)
cafeteria *cafétéria (general term)* (f.), *cantine (school)* (f.)
cake *gâteau* (m.)
  chocolate cake *gâteau au chocolat*
calculus *calcul* (m.)
call (to) *appeler, téléphoner, donner / passer un coup de fil* (infml.)
  call back (to) *rappeler*
  Who's calling? (on the phone) *C'est de la part de qui ? / Qui est à l'appareil ?*
  call each other (to) *se téléphoner*
called (to be) *s'appeler*
calm *calme*
camera *appareil* (m.) *photo*
camp (to) *faire du camping*
camping *camping* (m.)
can (container) *boîte* (f.) *de conserve*
can (verb) *pouvoir*
  Can I help you? *Puis-je vous aider ?*
  can't wait (to look forward to) *avoir hâte*
  (I) can't wait for the end of the day! *Vivement la fin de la journée !*
Canada *Canada* (m.)
Canadian *canadien / canadienne* (m./f.)
candy *bonbons* (m. pl.)
  candy store *confiserie* (f.)
  pastry and candy store *pâtisserie-confiserie* (f.)
cane *canne* (f.)
  walk with a cane (to) *marcher avec une canne*
cantaloupe *melon* (m.)
cap *casquette* (f.)
capsule *capsule* (f.)
car *voiture* (f.), *automobile* (f.), *auto* (f.), *wagon (on a train)* (m.)
  car racing *course* (f.) *automobile*
caramel *caramel* (m.)
card *carte* (f.)
  playing cards *cartes* (pl.) *à jouer*
  card game *jeu* (m.) *de cartes*
care *soin* (m.)

carpenter *charpentier* (m.)

carpet *moquette* (f.)

carrot *carotte* (f.)

carry (to) *porter*

carton *boîte* (f.) *(en carton), carton* (m.), *brique* (f.)

  carton of orange juice *brique* (f.) *de jus d'orange*

cash *argent* (m.)

  cash register *caisse* (f.)

castle *château* (m.)

  sandcastle *château de sable*

casual *décontracté / décontractée* (m./f.)

cathedral *cathédrale* (f.)

  Notre Dame Cathedral *Cathédrale Notre-Dame*

CD player *lecteur* (m.) *de CD*

CD-ROM *CD-ROM* (m.)

  CD-ROM drive *lecteur* (m.) *de CD-ROM*

cease (to) *cesser*

ceiling *plafond* (m.)

celebrate (to) *célébrer*

celery *céleri* (m.)

cell phone *(téléphone) portable* (m.)

cellar *cave* (f.)

cello *violoncelle* (m.)

cent *cent* (m.)

center *centre* (m.)

  information center *centre d'informations*

  National Center of Art and Culture Georges-Pompidou (Pompidou Center) *Centre National d'Art et de Culture Georges-Pompidou (Centre Pompidou)*

certain *certain / certaine* (m./f.)

  it is certain that *il est certain que*

certainly *certainement*

chair *chaise* (f.)

champagne *champagne* (m.)

  bottle of champagne *bouteille* (f.) *de champagne*

  champagne with black currant liqueur *kir* (m.) *royal*

champion *champion / championne* (m./f.)

chance *hasard* (m.)

chandelier *lustre* (m.)

change *monnaie* (f.)

change (to) *changer*

  change channels (to) *changer de chaîne*

charming *charmant / charmante* (m./f.)

cheat (to) *tricher*

check *chèque* (m.), *addition (restaurant, café, etc.)* (f.)

  The check, please. *L'addition, s'il vous plaît.*

check in (to) *prendre une chambre*

check out (to) *régler sa note*

checkers *dames* (f. pl.)

checkup (medical) *examen* (m.) *médical*

cheek *joue* (f.)

cheese *fromage* (m.)

  slice of cheese *tranche* (f.) *de fromage*

  cheese sandwich *sandwich* (m.) *au fromage*

  ham and cheese sandwich *sandwich* (m.) *jambon-fromage*

  grilled ham and cheese sandwich *croque-monsieur* (m.)

  grilled ham and cheese sandwich with an egg on top *croque-madame* (m.)

chemistry *chimie* (f.)

cherry *cerise* (f.)

chess *échecs* (m. pl.)

chest *poitrine* (f.)

chestnut *marron* (m.)

  chestnut paste *crème* (f.) *de marrons*

  sugar-coated chestnuts *marrons* (pl.) *glacés*

chicken *poulet* (m.)

  chicken and fries *poulet frites*

  chicken/rooster cooked in wine *coq* (m.) *au vin*

child *enfant* (m./f.)

chin *menton* (m.)

China *Chine* (f.)

Chinese *chinois / chinoise* (m./f.)

  Chinese language *chinois* (m.)

chocolate *chocolat* (m.)

  chocolate cake *gâteau* (m.) *au chocolat*

  chocolate ice cream *glace* (f.) *au chocolat*

  chocolate mousse *mousse* (f.) *au chocolat*

  hot chocolate *chocolat* (m.) *chaud*

choice *choix* (m.)

choose (to) *choisir*

chop *côte* (f.)

  pork chop *côte de porc*

chopstick *baguette* (f.)

Christmas *Noël* (m.)

  Merry Christmas! *Joyeux Noël !*

Christmas Eve *réveillon* (m.) *de Noël, veille* (f.)

de Noël

church *église* (f.)

cider *cidre* (m.)

circus *cirque* (m.)

city *ville* (f.)

   city hall *mairie* (f.), *hôtel* (m.) *de ville*

civil servant *fonctionnaire / fonctionnaire* (m./f.)

clam *palourde* (f.), *clam* (m.)

clarinet *clarinette* (f.)

class *cours* (m.), *classe* (f.)

   French class *cours de français*

   dance class *cours de danse*

   to pass a class, to do well in a class *réussir à un cours*

classroom *salle* (f.) *de classe, classe* (f.)

clean *propre*

clean (to) *nettoyer*

   clean the house (to) *faire le ménage*

clerk *guichetier (at the window/counter)* (m.)

client *client / cliente* (m./f.)

climbing *alpinisme* (m.)

close *près*

   very close *tout près*

   close to here *près d'ici*

   the closest *le / la plus proche*

close (to) *fermer*

   close a file (to) *fermer un fichier*

closet *placard* (m.)

clothing/clothes *vêtements* (m. pl.)

   clothing store *magasin* (m.) *de vêtements*

   clothing size *taille* (f.)

cloud *nuage* (m.)

cloudy *nuageux / nuageuse* (m./f.)

   It's cloudy. *C'est nuageux.*

club (nightclub) *boîte* (f.) *(de nuit), discothèque* (f.), *centre* (m.)

   go out to clubs (to), go out clubbing (to) *sortir en boîte*

club (organization) *club* (m.), *cercle* (m.)

coach *entraîneur* (m.)

coast *côte* (f.)

coat *manteau* (m.), *blouse* (f.)

   white coat (doctor's coat) *blouse blanche*

coffee *café* (m.)

   coffee with cream *café-crème* (m.)

   coffee shop *café* (m.)

coffeemaker *cafetière* (f.)

coin *pièce* (f.)

coins *pièces* (pl.), *monnaie* (f.)

coincidence *coïncidence* (f.)

   What a coincidence! *Quelle coïncidence !*

cold *froid / froide* (m./f.)

   It's cold. *Il fait froid.*

   be cold (to) *avoir froid (person)*

cold (common cold) *rhume* (m.)

colleague *collègue / collègue* (m./f.)

collect (to) *collectionner*

collection *collection* (f.)

college *université* (f.)

   college degree *diplôme* (m.) *universitaire*

cologne *eau* (f.) *de cologne*

come (to) *venir*

   come back (to) *revenir*

   come back (in) (to), come home (to) *rentrer*

   come in (to) *entrer*

   come up (to) *monter*

   come down (to) *descendre*

   come out (to) *sortir*

comedy *comédie* (f.)

   romantic comedy *comédie romantique*

comfortable *confortable*

commercials *publicités* (f. pl.), *pubs* (f. pl.)

company *société* (f.), *firme* (f.)

competition *concours* (m.), *compétition* (f.)

complete (to) *compléter*

complicated *compliqué / compliquée* (m./f.)

computer *ordinateur* (m.)

   computer programmer *informaticien / informaticienne* (m./f.)

   computer science *informatique* (f.)

concert *concert* (m.)

Congratulations. *Félicitations.*

consommé (clear soup made from stock) *consommé* (m.)

   vermicelli pasta consommé (noodle soup) *consommé aux vermicelles*

construct (to) *construire*

construction worker *ouvrier / ouvrière en bâtiment* (m./f.)

consult (to) *consulter*

   consult a phone book (to) *consulter l'annuaire*

contest *concours* (m.), *compétition* (f.)

cook *cuisinier / cuisinière* (m./f.)

cook (to) *cuisiner, préparer, faire la cuisine*

cooking *cuisine* (f.)

do the cooking (to) *faire la cuisine*
cool (great) *sympa, cool*
corn *maïs* (m.)
corner *coin* (m.)
correct *exact / exacte* (m./f.)
cost (to) *coûter*
  That costs ... *Ça coûte...*
cotton *coton* (m.)
couch *canapé* (m.)
counter *bar* (m.), *comptoir* (m.), *guichet* (m.)
courageous *brave*
course *cours* (m.)
cousin *cousin / cousine* (m./f.)
cream, creamy dessert *crème* (f.)
  creamy dessert made with caramel *crème caramel*
  whipped cream (that is flavored and sweetened) *crème chantilly*
  shaving cream *crème à raser*
crêpe (tissue-thin pancake) *crêpe* (f.)
  crêpe Suzette (crêpe with sugar, orange, and liqueur) *Crêpe Suzette*
crime drama/film *film* (m.) *policier*
croissant *croissant*
cross (to) *traverser*
crowd *foule* (f.)
cruel *cruel, cruelle* (m./f.)
cruise ship *paquebot* (m.)
crutches *béquilles* (f. pl.)
  walk with crutches (to) *marcher avec des béquilles*
cucumber *concombre* (m.)
cup *tasse* (f.)
  cup of tea *tasse de thé*
cupboard *placard* (m.)
cure (to) *guérir*
currency *monnaie* (f.)
  currency exchange office *bureau* (m.) *de change*
curtain *rideau* (m.)
customer service department *service* (m.) *clientèle, service* (m.) *client*
cut *coupure* (f.)
cycling *cyclisme* (m.)

D

Dad/Daddy *papa*
daily *quotidien / quotidienne* (m./f.)
dance (to) *danser*
dance class *cours* (m.) *de danse*
dance/dancing *danse* (f.)
darling *chéri / chérie* (m./f.)
date (to) *sortir avec*
date *date* (f.), *rendez-vous* (m.)
daughter *fille* (f.)
daughter-in-law *belle-fille* (f.)
day *jour* (m.), *journée* (f.)
  the day after tomorrow *après-demain*
  the day before yesterday *avant-hier*
deaf *sourd / sourde* (m./f.)
dealer *marchand / marchande* (m./f.)
dear (adjective) *cher / chère* (m./f.)
dear (term of endearment) *chéri / chérie* (m./f.)
deceive (to) *tromper*
December *décembre*
decide (to) *décider*
decided (to be) *se décider*
defend (to) *défendre*
degree *degré* (m.)
degree (college) *diplôme* (m.) *universitaire*
delete (to) *supprimer*
delicatessen *charcuterie* (f.)
delicious *délicieux / délicieuse* (m./f.)
delighted *ravi / ravie* (m./f.)
demand (to) *exiger*
demonstrate (to) *manifester*
demonstration *manifestation* (f.)
demonstrator *manifestant / manifestante* (m./f.)
dentist *dentiste* (m./f.)
deodorant *déodorant* (m.)
depart (to) *quitter*
department *service* (m.)
  accounting department *service de comptabilité*
  IT department *service d'informatique*
  finance department *service financier*
  sales department *service des ventes*
  legal department *service juridique*
  marketing department *service de marketing*
  public relations (PR) department *service des relations publiques*
  shipping department (mail room) *service du*

courrier
customer service department *service clientèle, service client*
department store *grand magasin* (m.)
departure time *heure* (f.) *du départ*
descend (to) *descendre*
description *description* (f.)
desert *désert* (m.)
designer (fashion) *couturier* (m.)
desire *envie* (f.)
desire (to) *désirer*
desk *bureau* (m.)
dessert *dessert* (m.)
detective (adjective) *inspecteur/inspecteurice de police*
  detective drama/film *film* (m.) *policier*
detest (to) *détester*
device *appareil* (m.)
diagnosis *diagnostic* (m.)
diamond *diamant* (m.)
  diamond ring *bague* (f.) *en diamant*
die (to) *mourir*
different *différent / différente* (m./f.)
difficult *difficile*
  difficult subject *matière* (f.) *difficile*
Dijon mustard *moutarde* (f.) *de Dijon*
dine (to) *dîner*
dining room *salle* (f.) *à manger*
dinner *dîner* (m.)
  have dinner (to) *dîner*
  Dinner's ready! *À table !*
  late dinner *souper* (m.)
diploma *diplôme* (m.)
direction *direction* (f.)
director *directeur / directrice* (m./f.)
dirty *sale*
disabled *handicapé / handicapée* (m./f.)
discount *remise* (f.)
disease *maladie* (f.)
  Alzheimer's disease *maladie d'Alzheimer*
  Parkinson's disease *maladie de Parkinson*
dish *plat* (m.)
  side dish *plat d'accompagnement*
dishwasher *lave-vaisselle* (m.)
dishwashing detergent *liquide* (m.) *vaisselle*
disobey (to) *désobéir*
dispatch (to) *dépêcher*
dive (to) *plonger*

dive in(to) the pool (to) *plonger dans la piscine*
divorce *divorce* (m.)
  get a divorce (to) *divorcer*
do (to) *faire*
  do well (to) *réussir*
  do well on a test/in a class (to) *réussir à un examen / cours*
  do the cooking (to) *faire la cuisine*
  do the dishes (to) *faire la vaisselle*
  do the house cleaning (to) *faire le ménage*
  do the laundry (to) *faire la lessive*
  do the shopping (to) *faire les / des courses*
  do bodybuilding (to) *faire de la musculation*
  do strength training (to) *faire de la musculation*
  do horseback riding (to) *faire de l'équitation*
  do sports (to) *faire du sport*
  do yoga (to) *faire du yoga*
  do a tour (to) *faire un tour*
doctor *médecin* (m.), *docteur / doctoresse* (m./f.)
  doctor's office *cabinet* (m.) *médical*
  white coat (doctor's coat) *blouse* (f.) *blanche*
document *document* (m.)
documentary *documentaire* (m.)
dog *chien* (m.)
  seeing-eye dog *chien d'aveugle*
door *porte* (f.)
doubt (to) *douter*
downstairs, down below *en bas*
dozen *douzaine* (f.)
  dozen eggs *douzaine d'œufs*
drama *drame* (m.)
  period drama *drame d'époque*
drawer *tiroir* (m.)
drawing *dessin* (m.)
dress *robe* (f.)
dress (to) *habiller*
  get dressed (to), dress oneself (to) *s'habiller*
  dress code *code* (m.) *vestimentaire*
  dressing rooms *cabines* (f. pl.) *d'essayage*
drink (to) *boire*
drive (computer) *lecteur* (m.)
  CD-ROM drive *lecteur de CD-ROM*
drive (to) *conduire*
drugstore *pharmacie* (f.)
drums *batterie* (f.)
dry (alcohol) *brut / brute* (m./f.)

dryer *sèche-linge* (m.)
dubbed *doublé / doublée* (m./f.)
duck *canard* (m.)
  duck à l'orange, duck with orange
    sauce *canard à l'orange*
due to ... (in a negative way) *à cause de...*
during *pendant*
DVD player *lecteur* (m.) *de DVD*

E

each *chaque, chacun / chacune* (m./f.)
ear *oreille* (f.)
early *en avance, tôt*
earn (to) *gagner*
  earn money (to) *gagner de l'argent*
earring *boucle* (f.) *d'oreille*
easily *facilement*
east *est* (m.)
easy *facile*
eat (to) *manger*
éclair (type of cream-filled pastry) *éclair* (m.)
edge *bord* (m.)
  at the edge of *au bord de*
egg *œuf* (m.)
  egg whites *blancs* (m. pl.) *(d'œufs)*
  fried egg (over easy egg) *œuf au plat, œuf sur*
    le plat
  hard-boiled egg *œuf dur*
  poached egg *œuf poché*
  scrambled eggs *œufs* (pl.) *brouillés*
  soft-boiled egg *œuf à la coque*
Eiffel Tower *Tour* (f.) *Eiffel*
eight *huit*
eighteen *dix-huit*
eighth *huitième*
eighty *quatre-vingts*
either *ou bien*
elbow *coude* (m.)
elderly person *personne* (f.) *âgée*
electrician *électricien* (m.)
electronic game *jeu* (m.) *électronique*
electronics store *magasin* (m.) *d'électronique*
elegant *élégant / élégante* (m./f.)
elementary school *école* (f.) *primaire*
elephant *éléphant* (m.)
eleven *onze*
eleventh *onzième*
else *autre, d'autre*

elsewhere *ailleurs*
e-mail *mail* (m.), *mèl* (m.), *e-mail* (m.), *courriel*
  (m.), *courrier* (m.) *électronique*
emergency *urgence* (f.)
  emergency medical service *service* (m.)
    d'assistance médicale d'urgence
  emergency situations *cas* (m. pl.) *d'urgence*
employ (to) *employer*
employee *employé / employée* (m./f.)
employment *emploi* (m.)
end (to) *terminer*
  at the end of *au bout de*
end *fin* (f.)
  end of the game, end of the match *fin du*
    match
engaged (to) (to be) *être fiancé / fiancée (à)*
  get engaged (to each other) (to) *se fiancer*
engagement ring *bague* (f.) *de fiançailles*
engineer *ingénieur* (m.)
England *Angleterre* (f.)
English *anglais / anglaise* (m./f.)
  English language *anglais* (m.)
  in English *en anglais*
  English literature *littérature anglaise*
enjoy oneself (to) *s'amuser*
Enjoy your meal! *Bon appétit !*
enjoyable *agréable*
enormous *énorme*
enough *assez*
  That's enough. *Ça suffit.*
enter (to) *entrer*
entertain (to) *amuser*
entertainment *divertissement* (m.)
entrance *entrée* (f.)
equal *égal / égale* (m./f.)
errand *course* (f.)
escargots *escargots* (m. pl.)
especially *surtout*
essential *essentiel / essentielle* (m./f.)
  it is essential that *il est essentiel que*
euro *euro* (m.)
European *européen / européenne* (m./f.)
  European Union *Union* (f.) *européenne*
even *même*
  even more *bien plus*
evening *soir* (m.), *soirée* (f.)
  this evening *ce soir*
ever *jamais*

every *tout / toute / tous / toutes* (m./f./m. pl./f. pl.), *chaque*

everyday *quotidien / quotidienne* (m./f.)
   everyday language *langage* (m.) *courant*

everyone *tout le monde*

everywhere *partout*

exact *exact / exacte* (m./f.), *précis / précise* (m./f.)

exam *examen* (m.)
   baccalauréat (an exam for students wishing to continue their education beyond high school) *baccalauréat / bac* (m.)
   examine (to) *examiner*

excellent *excellent / excellente* (m./f.)

exchange (to) *changer (banking), échanger (store-bought items)*

exciting *passionnant / passionnante* (m./f.)

excuse (to) *excuser*
   Excuse me. *Pardon. / Excusez-moi.*

exit *sortie* (f.)

expect (to) *attendre*

expensive *cher / chère* (m./f.)

expression *expression* (f.)

extension (telephone) *poste* (m.)

exterior *extérieur* (m.)

extracurricular activities *activités* (f. pl.) *extra-scolaires / parascolaires*

eye (eyes) *œil* (m.) (*yeux*, pl.)
   blue/brown/green eyes *les yeux bleus / bruns / verts*

eyebrow *sourcil* (m.)

eyeglasses *lunettes* (f. pl.)

eyelash *cil* (m.)

F

face *visage* (m.), *figure* (f.)

facing *en face de*

factory *usine* (f.)

fail (a test/class) (to) *échouer à (un examen / cours), rater (un examen / cours)*

fall (season) *automne* (m.)
   in (the) fall *en automne*

fall (to) *tomber*

false *faux / fausse* (m./f.)

familiar language *langage* (m.) *familier*

familiar with (to be) *connaître*

family *famille* (f.)

famous *célèbre*

fan (sports) *supporteur / supportrice* (m./f.)

Fantastic. *Formidable.*

far *loin*
   far from here *loin d'ici*
   farther *plus loin*

farmer *fermier / fermière* (m./f.)

fashion *mode* (f.), *façon* (f.)
   high fashion *haute couture* (f.)
   fashion designer *couturier* (m.)

fat *gros / grosse* (m./f.)

father *père* (m.)

father-in-law *beau-père* (m.)

favorite *préféré / préférée* (m./f.), *favori / favorite* (m./f.)

fax machine *télécopieur* (m.)

fear *peur* (f.)

February *février*

feed (to) *nourrir*

feel like (to) *avoir envie de*

festival *fête* (f.)

fever *fièvre* (f.)

fewer *moins*

fiancé/fiancée *fiancé / fiancée* (m./f.)

fiddle with things (to) *bricoler*

field *champ* (m.)

fifteen *quinze*

fifteenth *quinzième*

fifth *cinquième*

fifty *cinquante*

figure *forme* (f.)

file *fichier* (m.)

fill (in) (to) *remplir*

filling (tooth) *plombage* (m.)

film *film* (m.)
   action film *film d'action*
   crime/detective film, crime/detective drama *film policier*
   original version of a film (not dubbed into French) *version* (f.) *originale (v.o.)*
   French version of a film (dubbed into French) *version* (f.) *française (v.f.)*

final *dernier / dernière* (m./f.)
   final score *score* (m.) *final*
   final year of high school *classe* (f.) *terminale*

finally *enfin, finalement*

finance department *service* (m.) *financier*

find (to) *trouver*

find oneself (somewhere) (to) *se trouver*
find that (to) *trouver que*
fine *bien*
finger *doigt* (m.)
fingernail *ongle* (m.)
finish (to) *finir, terminer*
fire *feu* (m.)
firm (company) *firme* (f.)
First ... *D'abord...*
first *premier / première (number)* (m./f.)
 first floor (one floor above ground
  floor) *premier étage* (m.)
 first base *première base* (f.)
first-aid kit *trousse* (f.) *de secours*
fish *poisson* (m.)
fishing *pêche* (f.)
fit (to be) *être en forme*
five *cinq*
fix things (to) *bricoler*
flag *drapeau* (m.)
flavor *parfum* (m.)
floor *étage (as in, second floor, third floor, etc.)*
 (m.), *sol (of a room)* (m.)
 ground floor *rez-de-chaussée* (m.)
flower *fleur* (f.)
flu *grippe* (f.)
flute *flûte* (f.)
fog *brouillard* (m.)
follow (to) *suivre*
food *nourriture* (f.)
foot *pied* (m.)
 on foot, by foot *à pied*
 at the foot of *au pied de*
football (American) *football* (m.) *américain*
for *pour, de / d', depuis, pendant*
 for a party of four, for four people *pour*
  quatre personnes
 for me *pour moi*
 for how long? *depuis combien de temps ?*
forehead *front* (m.)
foreign language *langue* (f.) *étrangère*
forest *forêt* (f.)
fork *fourchette* (f.)
form *forme* (f.)
formal language *langage* (m.) *soutenu*
formal (in formal dress/attire) *en tenue de*
 soirée
former *ancien / ancienne* (m./f.)

formerly *autrefois*
fortunately *heureusement*
forty *quarante*
forward (to) *faire suivre*
four *quatre*
fourteen *quatorze*
fourth *quatrième*
fragrance *parfum* (m.)
France *France* (f.)
frankly *franchement*
free *libre*
 free time *temps* (m.) *libre*
French *français / française* (m./f.)
 French language *français* (m.)
 French version of a film (dubbed into
  French) *version* (f.) *française (v.f.)*
 in French *en français*
french fries *frites* (f. pl.)
frequently *fréquemment*
Friday *vendredi*
friend *ami / amie* (m./f.)
friendly *amical / amicale* (m./f.), *sympathique*
fries *frites* (f. pl.)
 chicken and fries *poulet* (m.) *frites*
 mussels and fries *moules* (f. pl.) *frites*
 steak and fries *steak* (m. pl.) *frites*
from *de / d'*
 from here *d'ici*
 from (someone) *de la part de*
 from me *de ma part*
 from time to time *de temps en temps*
front *devant*
 in front (of) *devant*
fruit *fruit* (m.)
 fruit salad *salade* (f.) *de fruits*
full-time *à plein temps*
funny *amusant / amusante* (m./f.), *drôle*
 so funny *si drôle*
furniture *meubles* (m. pl.)
 a piece of furniture *meuble* (m.)

G

gain weight (to) *grossir*
gallery *galerie* (f.)
game *jeu* (m.), *match* (m.)
garage *garage* (m.)
garbage *poubelle* (f.)
garden *jardin* (m.)

gastronomy *gastronomie* (f.)
general *général / générale* (m./f.)
generally *généralement, en général*
generous *généreux / généreuse* (m./f.)
genre *genre*
gentle *doux / douce* (m./f.)
gentlemen *messieurs*
gently *doucement*
geometry *géométrie* (f.)
German *allemand / allemande* (m./f.)
Germany *Allemagne* (f.)
get a divorce (to) *divorcer*
get a shot (to) *recevoir une piqûre*
get a tan (to) *bronzer*
get along with (to) *s'entendre bien avec*
get better (to) *guérir*
get bored (to) *s'ennuyer*
get dressed (to) *s'habiller*
get engaged (to each other) (to) *se fiancer*
get married (to each other) (to) *se marier*
get sick (to) *tomber malade*
get somewhere (to) *arriver*
　get to (a destination) (to) *arriver à (+ destination)*
get up (to) *se lever*
girl *fille* (f.)
girlfriend *copine* (f.), *petite amie* (f.)
give (to) *donner*
　give in to (to) *se rendre à (+ evidence, an argument, etc.)*
glass *verre* (m.)
　glass of milk *verre de lait*
glasses *lunettes* (f. pl.)
glove *gant* (m.)
go (to) *aller*
　Let's go. *Allons-y. / On y va.* (infml.)
　Go on!/Go ahead!/Go there! *Vas-y !* (infml.)
　go across (to) *traverser*
　go away (to) *partir*
　go out (to) *partir, sortir*
　go out clubbing (to), go out to clubs (to) *sortir en boîte*
　go out with (to) (to date) *sortir avec*
　go down (to) *descendre*
　go up (to) *monter*
　go home (to), go in (to) *rentrer*
　go (past) (to) *passer*
　go to (to) *se rendre à (+ location)*

go shopping (to) *faire des / les courses*
go sightseeing (to) *aller visiter*
go to bed (to) *se coucher*
go swimming (to) *faire de la natation*
go hiking (to) *faire de la marche*
go camping (to) *camper, faire du camping*
go bike riding (to) *monter à bicyclette*
go horseback riding (to) *faire de l'équitation, monter à cheval*
go jogging (to) *faire du jogging*
go on a picnic (to) *faire un pique-nique*
go scuba diving (to) *faire de la plongée sous-marine*
go skiing (to) *faire du ski*
go water-skiing (to) *faire du ski nautique*
goal *but* (m.)
god *dieu* (m.)
　My god! *Mon dieu !*
gold *or* (m.)
golf *golf* (m.)
　golf course *parcours* (m.) *de golf, terrain* (m.) *de golf*
good *bon / bonne* (m./f.), *bien, sympa, brave*
　very good *très bien, très bon / bonne* (m./f.), *très sympa*
　Good luck. *Bonne chance.*
　Good day. *Bonjour.*
　Good evening. *Bonsoir.*
　Good night. *Bonne nuit.*
　Good-bye. *Au revoir.*
　I'm having a good time. *Je m'amuse.*
　a good buy (inexpensive) *bon marché*
grade *note (score)* (f.), *classe (year)* (f.)
gram *gramme* (m.)
grammar *grammaire* (f.)
grandfather *grand-père* (m.)
　grandfather clock *pendule* (f.)
grandmother *grand-mère* (f.)
grandparent *grand-parent* (m.)
grape(s) *raisin* (m.)
great *formidable, extra, super*
　Great! *Super !*
　It's great. *C'est extra.*
Greece *Grèce* (f.)
Greek *grec / grecque* (m./f.)
green *vert / verte* (m./f.)
　green bean *haricot* (m.) *vert*
　green salad *salade* (f.) *verte*

grocery store *épicerie* (f.)
grow (to) *grandir, pousser*
growing (to be) *être en pleine expansion* (business)
grown-up *adulte* (m./f.)
guide *guide* (m.)
guided tour *visite* (f.) *guidée*
guitar *guitare* (f.)
gym *gym(nastique) (physical education)* (f.), *gymnase (place)* (m.)
gymnastics *gymnastique* (f.)

H

hail *grêle* (f.)
  It's hailing. *Il grêle.*
hair *cheveux* (m. pl.)
  hair (single strand) *cheveu* (m.)
  brown/blond/red/black hair *les cheveux bruns / blonds / roux / noirs*
half *demi / demie* (m./f.)
  half past ... *... et demie*
  half hour *demi-heure* (f.)
halftime *mi-temps* (f.)
hall *salle* (f.) *(for public events), entrée* (f.) *(foyer of a house)*
hallway *couloir* (m.)
ham *jambon* (m.)
  ham and cheese sandwich *sandwich* (m.) *jambon-fromage*
  ham sandwich *sandwich* (m.) *au jambon*
  grilled ham and cheese sandwich *croque-monsieur* (m.)
  grilled ham and cheese sandwich with an egg on top *croque-madame* (m.)
hand *main* (f.)
handkerchief *mouchoir* (m.)
handsome *beau / bel / belle* (m./m. before a vowel or silent h/f.)
hang up (to) *raccrocher*
Hanukkah *Hanoukka* (f.), *Hanoucca* (f.)
happen (to) *arriver*
happily *heureusement*
happy *heureux / heureuse* (m./f.)
  to make oneself happy *se rendre heureux / heureuse*
  Happy birthday!/Happy anniversary! *Joyeux / Bon anniversaire !*

Happy Holidays! *Joyeuses / Bonnes Fêtes !*
  Happy New Year! *Bonne Année !*
hard *dur / dure* (m./f.), *difficile*
  hard-boiled egg *œuf* (m.) *dur*
hardware store *quincaillerie* (f.)
haste *hâte* (f.)
hasten (to) *hâter*
hat *chapeau* (m.)
hate (to) *détester*
hatred *haine* (f.)
have (to) *avoir*
  have (food/drink) (to) *prendre*
  have a drink (to) *prendre un verre*
  have breakfast (to) *prendre le petit déjeuner*
  have lunch (to) *déjeuner*
  have dinner (to) *dîner*
  have a late dinner (to) *souper*
  have a good time (to) *s'amuser*
  have fun (to) *s'amuser*
  have a party (to) *organiser une fête*
  have (the) time (to) *avoir le temps*
  have to (to) *devoir*
  have a sore (something) (to) *avoir mal à*
  have pain in (to) *avoir mal à*
  have trouble (doing something) (to) *avoir du mal à*
  have an accident (to) *avoir un accident*
  have an interview (to) *avoir une entrevue*
hazelnut *noisette* (f.)
he *il*
head *tête* (f.)
health *santé* (f.)
  To your health! *À votre santé !*
  health club *club/centre* (m.) *de remise (en forme), club* (m.) *de forme*
healthy *en bonne santé*
hear (to) *entendre*
heart *cœur* (m.)
  heart attack *crise* (f.) *cardiaque*
heartbeat *battement* (m.) *de cœur*
held (to be) *avoir lieu*
Hello. *Bonjour. / Salut.*
  Hello. (on the phone) *Allô.*
helmet *casque* (m.)
help (to) *aider*
her *son / sa / ses* (m./f./pl.), *elle, la / l'* (direct object pronoun)

to her *lui* (indirect object pronoun)
herbal tea *tisane* (f.)
here *ici, ci*
  from here *d'ici*
  here is/are, here it is/they are *voici, voilà*
hero/heroine *héros / héroïne* (m./f.)
herself *se / s'* (reflexive pronoun)
Hey! *Tiens ! (surprise)*
Hi. *Salut.*
hide and seek *cache-cache* (f.)
  to play hide and seek *jouer à cache-cache*
high *haut / haute* (m./f.)
  high fashion *haute couture*
  high-speed train *train* (m.) *à grande vitesse*
  (TGV)
high school *lycée* (m.)
  high school student *lycéen / lycéenne* (m./f.)
hill *colline* (f.)
him *lui, le / l'* (direct object pronoun)
  to him *lui* (indirect object pronoun)
himself *se / s'* (reflexive pronoun)
his *son / sa / ses* (m./f./pl.)
history *histoire* (f.)
hobby *passe-temps* (m.)
hockey *hockey* (m.)
  ice hockey *hockey sur glace*
hold (to) *tenir*
  Hold on, please. *Ne quittez pas, s'il vous plaît.*
holiday *fête* (f.)
home *maison* (f.), *foyer* (m.)
homemade *maison*
homemaker *homme / femme au foyer* (m./f.)
homework *devoirs* (m. pl.)
honestly *franchement*
honey *miel* (m.)
honey (term of endearment) *chéri / chérie*
  (m./f.)
hope (to) *espérer*
horrible *horrible*
horror movie *film* (m.) *d'épouvante*
horse *cheval* (m.)
horseback riding *équitation* (f.)
  go horseback riding (to) *faire de l'équitation,*
  monter à cheval
hose (stocking) *bas* (m.)
hospital *hôpital* (m.)
hot *chaud / chaude* (m./f.)
  It's hot./It's warm. *Il fait chaud.*

be hot/warm (to) *avoir chaud (person)*
hot chocolate *chocolat* (m.) *chaud*
hotel *hôtel* (m.)
hour *heure* (f.)
house *maison* (f.)
  at someone's house/place *chez*
  house cleaning *ménage* (m.)
  do the house cleaning (to), clean the house
   (to) *faire le ménage*
how *comment, comme*
  how many, how much *combien*
  How? *Comment ?*
  How's it going?/How are you? *(Comment)*
  ça va ?
  How are you? *Comment vas-tu ?* (infml.) /
   Comment allez-vous ? (pl./fml.)
  (for) how long? *depuis combien de temps ?*
hug (each other) (to) *s'embrasser*
human being *être* (m.) *humain*
human body *corps* (m.) *humain*
human resources *personnel* (m.)
  human resources manager *directeur* (m.) *du*
  personnel
hundred *cent*
hunger *faim* (f.)
  hungry (to be) *avoir faim*
hunting *chasse* (f.)
hurdle *haie* (f.)
hurricane *ouragan* (m.)
hurry (to) *se dépêcher*
hurt (to) *blesser, faire mal*
  hurt oneself (to) *se blesser*
husband *mari* (m.)

I

I *je / j'*
  I am called ... (My name is ...) *Je m'appelle...*
  I don't understand. *Je ne comprends pas.*
  I'm fine. *Ça va.*
  I'm very well. *Je vais très bien.*
  I want ... *Je veux...*
  I would like ... *Je voudrais...*
ice *glace* (f.)
  ice hockey *hockey* (m.) *sur glace*
  ice skate, ice skating *patin* (m.) *à glace*
  ice skating *patinage* (m.) *sur glace*
ice cream *glace* (f.)
  chocolate ice cream *glace au chocolat*

strawberry ice cream *glace à la fraise*
vanilla ice cream *glace à la vanille*
idea *idée* (f.)
if *si*
if necessary, if needed *s'il le faut*
Île de la Cité (City Island) *Île* (f.) *de la Cité*
illness *maladie* (f.)
important *important / importante* (m./f.)
  it is important that *il est important que*
impoverished *pauvre*
in *à, dans, en*
  in the *au / à la / à l' / aux* (m./f./m. or f. before a
    vowel or silent h/pl.)
  in front (of) *devant*
  in general *en général*
  in the middle of *au milieu de*
  be in the middle of (to), be in the process of
    (to) *être en train de*
  in college *à l'université*
  in high school *au lycée*
  in middle school *au collège*
  in my opinion *à mon avis*
  in order that *afin que, pour que*
indeed *en effet*
India *Inde* (f.)
Indian *indien / indienne* (m./f.)
individual *individu* (m.)
inexpensive *bon marché*
infection *infection* (f.)
inflammation *inflammation* (f.)
informal language *langage* (m.) *familier*
information center *centre* (m.) *d'informations*
information technology (IT) *informatique* (f.)
  IT department *service* (m.) *d'informatique*
inherit (to) *hériter*
injection *piqûre* (f.), *injection* (f.)
inn *auberge* (f.)
instant message *message* (m.) *instantané*
instructions *instructions* (f. pl.)
insurance *assurance* (f.)
intelligent *intelligent / intelligente* (m./f.)
interesting *intéressant / intéressante* (m./f.)
Internet *Internet* (m.)
interrupt (to) *interrompre*
intersection *intersection* (f.)
interview *entrevue* (f.)
into *dans, en*
introduce (to) *présenter*

Let me introduce ... *Je te présente...* (infml.) /
  Je vous présente... (pl./fml.)
invite (to) *inviter*
Ireland *Irlande* (f.)
Irish *irlandais / irlandaise* (m./f.)
  an Irishman *un Irlandais*
iron *fer* (m.) *à repasser*
ironing board *planche* (f.) *à repasser*
Is that all? *C'est tout ?*
isn't it?/isn't that so? ... *n'est-ce pas ?*
it *ça / c', il / elle / ils / elles* (m./f./m. pl./f. pl.), *le
  / la / l' / les* (direct object pronoun) (m./f./m. or f.
  before a vowel or silent h/pl.)
  to it *lui* (indirect object pronoun)
  It rains. *Il pleut.*
it is *c'est*
  isn't it? *n'est-ce pas ?*
  It's going well. *Ça va bien.*
  It's not going well./It's going badly. *Ça va
    mal.*
  It's beautiful (outside). *Il fait beau.*
  It's hot./It's warm. *Il fait chaud.*
  It's cold. *Il fait froid.*
  It's sunny. *Il fait (du) soleil. / Il y a du soleil.*
  It's windy. *Il fait du vent. / Il y a du vent.*
  It's hailing. *Il grêle.*
  It's snowing. *Il neige.*
  It is time to .../Now is the time to ... *Il est
    temps de...*
  It's not serious./It's not a problem./It's not a
    big deal. *Ce n'est pas grave.*
  it's necessary to *il faut*
  it's necessary that *il faut que*
  it is better *il vaut mieux*
  it is better that *il vaut mieux que*
  it is certain that *il est certain que*
  it is true that *il est vrai que*
  it is possible that *il est possible que*
  it is probable that *il est probable que*
  it seems that *il semble que*
  it is urgent that *il est urgent que*
  it is essential that *il est essentiel que*
  it is important that *il est important que*
  it is necessary that *il est nécessaire que*
  it is preferable that *il est préférable que*
Italian *italien / italienne* (m./f.)
Italy *Italie* (f.)
its *son / sa / ses* (m./f./pl.)

itself *se / s'* (reflexive pronoun)

J

jacket *veste* (f.), *veston* (m.)
jam *confiture* (f.)
January *janvier*
Japan *Japon* (m.)
Japanese *japonais / japonaise* (m./f.)
jeans *jean* (m.)
jelly *confiture* (f.)
jewel *bijou* (m.)
 jewelry *bijoux* (m. pl.)
job *boulot* (m.), *emploi* (m.), *travail* (m.)
joint (of meat) *rôti* (m.)
journalist *journaliste* (m./f.)
juice *jus* (m.)
July *juillet*
jump (to) *sauter*
June *juin*
junior high school *collège* (m.)
just *juste*
 just as ... *aussi...*

K

keyboard *clavier* (m.)
kick (to) *donner un coup de pied*
kilo *kilo* (m.)
kind (nice) *gentil / gentille* (m./f.), *aimable*
kind (type) *genre*
kiss (each other) (to) *s'embrasser*
kitchen *cuisine* (f.)
 kitchen sink *évier* (m.) *de la cuisine*
knee *genou* (m.)
knife *couteau* (m.)
knitting *tricot* (m.)
know (to) *savoir, connaître*
 I don't know. *Je ne sais pas.*
 know each other (to) *se connaître*

L

laboratory *laboratoire* (m.)
lady
 ladies *dame* (f.), *mesdames*
lake *lac* (m.)
lamb *agneau* (m.)
lamp *lampe* (f.)
lamppost *réverbère* (m.)
land *terre* (f.)

lane *voie* (f.)
language *langue* (f.), *langage* (m.)
 informal language, familiar
  language *langage familier*
 formal language *langage soutenu*
 everyday language *langage courant*
 bad language *langage grossier*
 body language *langage du corps*
 baby talk (baby language) *langage enfantin*
 sign language *langage des signes*
 programming language *langage de
  programmation*
 legal language, legal terminology *langage
  juridique*
 foreign language *langue étrangère*
large *grand / grande* (m./f.)
last *dernier / dernière* (m./f.)
 last Monday *lundi dernier*
 last month *mois* (m.) *dernier*
 last summer *été* (m.) *dernier*
 last night *hier soir, nuit* (f.) *dernière*
 last year *année* (f.) *dernière*
 the last time *la dernière fois*
late *en retard, tard*
 late dinner *souper* (m.)
latest *dernier / dernière* (m./f.)
laundry detergent *lessive* (f.)
lawyer *avocat / avocate* (m./f.)
lay down (to) *coucher, allonger*
lead (to) *mener*
learn (to) *apprendre*
 learn by heart (to) *apprendre par cœur*
 I'm learning French. *J'apprends le français.*
the least ... *le / la moins...*
leather *cuir* (m.)
leave (to) *partir, sortir, laisser*
leek *poireau* (m.)
left *gauche* (f.)
 on the left, to the left, at the left *à gauche*
 left bank *rive* (f.) *gauche*
leg *jambe* (f.)
legal (related to the law) *juridique*
 legal department *service* (m.) *juridique*
 legal language, legal terminology *langage
  (m.) juridique*
leisure activities *loisirs* (m. pl.)
lemon *citron* (m.)
lens *verre* (m.), *lentille* (f.)

contact lenses *verres / lentilles* (pl.) *de contact*
less *moins*
  less ... than *moins... que*
lesson *leçon* (f.)
let (someone do something) (to) *laisser*
let go (to) *laisser*
Let me introduce ... *Je te présente...* (infml.) / *Je vous présente...* (pl./fml.)
Let's go. *Allons-y. / On y va.* (infml.)
letter *lettre* (f.)
lettuce *laitue* (f.)
library *bibliothèque* (f.)
lie down (to) *se coucher, allonger*
life *vie* (f.)
lifeguard *maître-nageur* (f.), *sauveteur* (m.)
lift (to) *lever*
  lift a dumbbell (to) *soulever un haltère*
  lift weights (to) *faire de la musculation*
light *léger / légère* (m./f.)
lightly *légèrement*
lightning *éclair* (m.)
like *comme*
like (to) *aimer*
  like each other (to) *s'aimer*
  I like ... *J'aime...*
  I do not like ... *Je n'aime pas...*
lime *citron vert* (m.)
line *queue* (f.)
  wait in line (to) *faire la queue*
link *liaison* (f.)
listen (to) (to) *écouter*
literature *littérature* (f.)
little *petit / petite* (m./f.)
  a little *un peu*
live (to) *habiter*
living room *salon* (m.)
lobster *homard* (m.)
  lobster bisque *bisque* (f.) *de homard*
lonely *seul / seule* (m./f.)
long *long / longue* (m./f.), *longtemps*
  a long time ago *il y a longtemps*
look at (to) *regarder*
  look at each other (to) *se regarder*
look for (to) *chercher*
look forward to (to) (can't wait) *avoir hâte*
look great on someone (to) *aller à ravir à quelqu'un*
lose (to) *perdre*

lose weight (to) *maigrir*
lose a game/match (to) *perdre un match*
lost *perdu / perdue* (m./f.)
  I'm lost. *Je suis perdu / perdue.*
Louvre *Louvre* (m.)
  Louvre museum *musée* (m.) *du Louvre*
love (to) *aimer, adorer*
  love each other (to) *s'aimer*
low *bas / basse* (m./f.)
luck *chance* (f.)
  No luck! *Pas de chance !*
  Good luck! *Bonne chance !*
lunch *déjeuner* (m.)
  have lunch (to) *déjeuner*
lung *poumon* (m.)
Lutetia (old name for Paris) *Lutèce* (f.)

M

ma'am/madam *madame*
magazine *magazine* (m.), *revue* (f.)
magnificent *magnifique*
mail *poste* (f.)
  mail room *service* (m.) *du courrier*
mail (to) *mettre à la poste*
main *principal / principale* (m./f.)
  main course/dish *plat* (m.) *principal*
make (to) *faire, préparer*
  make a phone call (to) *téléphoner, donner (or passer) un coup de fil* (infml.)
  make a mistake (to) *se tromper, faire une faute / erreur*
  make a reservation (to) *faire une réservation*
  make an appointment (to) *prendre rendez-vous*
  make up one's mind (to) *se décider*
  to make oneself happy (to) *se rendre heureux / heureuse* (m./f.)
  to make oneself sick (to) *se rendre malade*
  to make oneself aware (to) *se rendre compte (de)*
  make a sandcastle (to) *faire un château de sable*
  That makes ... *Ça fait...*
mall *centre commercial* (m.)
man *homme* (m.)
  Oh man! (disappointment, anger) *Ce n'est pas possible !*
  Man! (lit., Say so!) *Dis donc !*

manage to (do something) (to) *arriver à (+ verb)*

management *direction* (f.)

manager *gérant / gérante* (m./f.), *directeur / directrice* (m./f.)

  personnel manager, human resources manager *directeur / directrice* (m./f.) *du personnel*

many *beaucoup de, beaucoup*

  as many as *autant de*

map *plan* (m.), *carte* (f.)

  map of the city *plan* (m.) *de la ville, carte* (f.) *de la ville*

  map of the subway *plan* (m.) *du métro, carte* (f.) *du métro*

March *mars*

march (to) *défiler*

market *marché* (m.)

marketing department *service* (m.) *de marketing*

marmalade *confiture* (f.)

married *marié / mariée* (m./f.)

  get married (to each other) (to) *se marier*

marry (someone) (to) *épouser (quelqu'un)*

master's degree *maîtrise* (f.), *master* (m.)

match (in sports) *match* (m.)

math *maths* (f. pl.), *mathématiques* (f. pl.)

matter (to) *importer*

May *mai*

maybe *peut-être*

mayor *maire* (m.)

me *moi, me / m'* (direct object pronoun)

  to me *me / m'* (indirect object pronoun)

meal *repas* (m.)

meat *viande* (f.)

medical checkup *examen* (m.) *médical*

medical student *étudiant / étudiante* (m./f.) *en médecine*

medicine *médecine* (f.)

  medicine cabinet *armoire* (f.) *à pharmacie*

meet (a person/someone) (to) *rencontrer (une personne/quelqu'un), faire connaissance*

meeting *rendez-vous* (m.), *réunion* (f.)

  meeting room *salle* (f.) *de réunion*

melon *melon* (m.)

member *membre* (m.)

  be a member of (to) *faire partie de, être membre de*

memory *mémoire* (f.)

menu *menu* (m.), *carte* (f.)

  The menu, please. *Le menu / La carte, s'il vous plaît.*

merchant *marchand / marchande* (m./f.)

meringue cookie *macaron* (m.)

metro *métro* (m.)

  metro station *station* (f.) *de métro*

Mexican *mexicain / mexicaine* (m./f.)

Mexico *Mexique* (m.)

microwave (oven) *micro-ondes* (m.)

middle *milieu* (m.)

  in the middle of *au milieu de*

  be in the middle of (to) *en train de*

  middle school *collège* (m.)

midnight *minuit* (m.)

milk *lait* (m.)

million *million*

millionaire *millionnaire* (m./f.)

mineral water *eau* (f.) *minérale*

mint *menthe* (f.)

minus *moins*

mirror *miroir* (m.)

miss *mademoiselle (Mlle)*

  misses *mesdemoiselles*

mistake *faute* (f.), *erreur* (f.)

  spelling mistake *faute d'orthographe*

mistaken (to be) *se tromper*

modem *modem* (m.)

mole *grain* (m.) *de beauté*

Mom/Mommy *maman*

moment *moment* (m.)

Mona Lisa *Joconde* (f.)

Monday *lundi*

money *argent* (m.)

monitor *écran* (m.)

month *mois* (m.)

  next month, in one month *dans un mois*

  next month *mois prochain*

  last month *mois dernier*

  two months before *deux mois auparavant*

  two months before *deux mois avant*

  months of the year *mois* (pl.) *de l'année*

monument *monument* (m.)

moon *lune* (f.)

mop (to) *éponger*

moped *solex* (m.), *vélomoteur* (m.)

more *plus, encore*

even more, much more *bien plus*
more ... than *plus... que*
morning *matin* (m.), *matinée* (f.)
Moroccan *marocain / marocaine* (m./f.)
Morocco *Maroc* (m.)
mosque *mosquée* (f.)
the most ... *le / la plus...*
mostly *surtout*
mother *mère* (f.)
mother-in-law *belle-mère* (f.)
motorcycle *motocyclette* (f.), *moto* (f.)
mountain *montagne* (f.)
  mountain climbing *alpinisme* (m.)
mouse *souris* (f.)
mousse *mousse* (f.)
  chocolate mousse *mousse au chocolat*
mouth *bouche* (f.)
move out (to) *déménager*
movie *film* (m.)
  movie theater, the movies *cinéma* (m.)
Mr. *M. (Monsieur)*
Mrs. *Mme (Madame)*
Ms. *Mme (Madame)*
much *beaucoup*
  much more *bien plus*
municipal building *mairie* (f.), *hôtel* (m.) *de ville*
muscle *muscle* (m.)
muscular *musculaire (medical), musclé / musclée* (m./f.) *(person)*
museum *musée* (m.)
  Louvre museum *musée du Louvre*
  Orsay museum *musée d'Orsay*
mushroom *champignon* (m.)
music *musique* (f.)
musical *comédie* (f.) *musicale*
musician *musicien / musicienne* (m./f.)
mussel *moule* (f.)
  mussels and fries *moules* (pl.) *frites*
must *devoir*
mustard *moutarde* (f.)
  Dijon mustard *moutarde de Dijon*
my *mon / ma / mes* (m./f./pl.)
  My name is ... *Je m'appelle...*
myself *me / m'* (reflexive pronoun)
mysterious *mystérieux / mystérieuse* (m./f.)

N

name *nom* (m.)

under what name? *sous quel nom ?*
napkin *serviette* (f.)
nation *nation* (f.)
national *national / nationale* (m./f.)
  national holiday *fête nationale* (f.)
nationality *nationalité* (f.)
natural *naturel / naturelle* (m./f.)
naturally *naturellement*
near *près*
  very near *tout près*
  nearby, near here *près d'ici*
  the nearest *le / la plus proche*
necessary *nécessaire*
necessary (to be) *falloir*
  it's necessary to *il faut*
  it's necessary that *il faut que, il est nécessaire que*
neck *cou* (m.)
necklace *collier* (m.)
need *besoin* (m.)
need (to) *avoir besoin de, avoir besoin que*
  need for (to) *avoir besoin de*
needle *aiguille* (f.)
neighborhood *quartier* (m.), *coin* (m.)
nephew *neveu* (m.)
never *jamais, ne... jamais*
new *nouveau / nouvel / nouvelle* (m./m. before a vowel or silent h/f.)
  New Year *Nouvel An* (m.)
  New Year's Day *jour* (m.) *de l'An*
  New Year's Eve *Saint-Sylvestre* (f.), *réveillon* (m.) *(du jour de l'An)*
newborn *nouveau-né* (m.)
news (the news) *nouvelles* (f. pl.)
newspaper *journal* (m.)
next *prochain / prochaine* (m./f.), *ensuite*
  next part, what happens next *suite* (f.)
  Can't wait for what happens next! *Vivement la suite !*
  next to *à côté de*
  next month *dans un mois, mois prochain*
  next week *dans une semaine, semaine prochaine*
nice *gentil / gentille* (m./f.), *sympa, joli / jolie* (m./f.), *beau / bel / belle* (m./m. before a vowel or silent h/f.), *sympathique, aimable*
  Nice to meet you. *Enchanté. / Enchantée.* (m./f.)

niece *nièce* (f.)

night *nuit* (f.), *soir* (m.), *soirée* (f.)

nightclub *boîte* (f.) *de nuit, discothèque* (f.)
   go out to clubs (to), go out clubbing
   (to) *sortir en boîte*

nine *neuf*

nineteen *dix-neuf*

ninety *quatre-vingt-dix*

ninth *neuvième*

no *non*
   no longer, no more *ne... plus*
   No way! *Oh là là !*
   no one, nobody *ne... personne*

noodle soup (vermicelli pasta
   consommé) *consommé* (m.) *aux vermicelles*

noon *midi* (m.)

north *nord* (m.)

nose *nez* (m.)

not *ne / n'... pas, pas*
   not at all *pas du tout*
   not yet *ne... pas encore*
   Not bad. *Pas mal.*
   Not a lot. *Pas grand-chose.*
   not as good *moins bon / bonne* (m./f.)
   not as bad *moins mauvais / mauvaise* (m./f.)

note *note* (f.)

notebook *cahier* (m.)

nothing *rien, ne... rien*
   nothing else *ne... rien d'autre*
   It's nothing. *De rien.*
   Nothing much. *Rien de particulier.*
   Nothing new. *Rien de neuf.*

notice (to) *se rendre compte (de)*

November *novembre*

now *maintenant*

nowhere *nulle part*

number *nombre* (m.), *numéro* (m.)
   phone number *numéro de téléphone*

nurse *infirmier / infirmière* (m./f.)

nursery school *école* (f.) *maternelle*

O

obey (to) *obéir*

occasionally *de temps en temps*

ocean *océan* (m.)
   ocean liner *paquebot* (m.)

October *octobre*

of *de / d'*

of it, of them *en*

of which, of whom *dont*

of the *du / de la / de l' / des* (m./f./m. or f. before
   a vowel or silent h/pl.)

Of course. *Bien sûr. / Bien entendu.*

office *bureau* (m.)
   office building *immeuble* (m.)

often *souvent*

Oh okay ... *Ah bon...*

Oh really ... *Ah bon...*

Oh well ... *Eh bien..., Ben...* (infml.)

oil *huile* (f.)

Okay. *D'accord.*
   Oh okay ... *Ah bon...*

old *vieux / vieil / vieille* (m./m. before a vowel or
   silent h/f.), *ancien / ancienne* (m./f.)
   oldest child *aîné / aînée* (m./f.)

omelet *omelette* (f.)
   mushroom omelet *omelette aux champignons*

on *sur*
   on top *dessus*
   on behalf of *de la part de*
   on my behalf *de ma part*
   on foot *à pied*
   on one's own *seul / seule* (m./f.)
   on the left/on the right *à gauche / à droite*
   on the other side of *de l'autre côté de*
   on time *à l'heure*
   on strike *en grève*

once *une fois*

one (number) *un / une* (m./f.)

one (pronoun) *on*

oneself *se / s'* (reflexive pronoun)

one-way *aller simple* (m.)

onion *oignon* (m.)
   onion soup *soupe* (f.) *à l'oignon*

only *juste, seul / seule* (m./f.), *seulement*
   only child *fils / fille unique* (m./f.)

open (to) *ouvrir*
   open a file (to) *ouvrir un fichier*

opera *opéra* (m.)

or *ou*
   or even, or else *ou bien*

orange *orange, orange* (f.)

order (to) *commander*

organize (to) *organiser*

origin *origine* (f.)

original *original / originale* (m./f.)

original version of a film (not dubbed into French) *version* (f.) *originale (v.o.)*
other *autre*
our *notre / nos* (m. or f./pl.)
ourselves *nous* (reflexive pronoun)
outdoor activities *activités* (f. pl.) *de plein air*
outfit *ensemble* (m.), *tenue* (f.)
outside *hors, dehors, extérieur* (m.)
oven *four* (m.)
over there *là-bas*
owe (to) *devoir*
own *propre*
own (to) *posséder*
oyster *huître* (f.)

P

pain *douleur* (f.)
paint (to) *peindre*
painting *tableau* (m.), *peinture* (f.)
pair *paire* (f.)
That's three euros per pair. *Ça coûte trois euros la paire.*
pajamas *pyjama* (m.)
pants *pantalon* (m.)
paper *papier* (m.)
paralyzed *paralysé / paralysée* (m./f.)
Pardon (me). *Pardon.*
parent *parent* (m.)
Paris *Paris*
Parisian *parisien / parisienne* (m./f.)
park *parc* (m.)
parlor *salon* (m.)
part (in a play, movie, etc.) *rôle* (m.)
partner *partenaire / partenaire* (m./f.)
part-time *à temps partiel*
party *soirée* (f.), *fête* (f.), *partie* (f.)
pass (to) *passer*
pass a test/class (to) *réussir à un examen / cours*
passport *passeport* (m.)
past *passé* (m.)
in the past *autrefois*
pastry *pâtisserie* (f.)
pastry shop *pâtisserie* (f.)
pastry and candy store *pâtisserie-confiserie* (f.)
pastime *passe-temps* (m.)
path *chemin* (m.)

patient *patient / patiente* (m./f.)
pay (to) *payer*
peach *pêche* (f.)
peaches with ice cream *pêche Melba*
pear *poire* (f.)
peas (green) *petits pois* (m. pl.)
people *gens* (m. pl.)
people in general *on* (pronoun)
pepper *poivre (condiment)* (m.), *poivron (vegetable)* (m.)
per *par*
perfect *parfait / parfaite* (m./f.)
It's perfect. *C'est parfait.*
perform (to) *jouer*
perfume *parfum* (m.)
permit (to) *permettre*
person *personne* (f.)
personnel manager *directeur / directrice du personnel* (m./f.)
pharmacist *pharmacien / pharmacienne* (m./f.)
pharmacy *pharmacie* (f.)
phone *téléphone* (m.)
cell phone *portable* (m.)
phone number *numéro* (m.) *de téléphone*
answer the phone (to) *répondre au téléphone*
telephone extension *poste* (m.)
phone (to) *téléphoner*
photo *photo* (f.)
Can you take our picture (photo)? *Pourriez-vous nous prendre en photo, s'il vous plaît ?*
phrase *phrase* (f.)
physical education *gym(nastique)* (f.), *éducation physique*
physics *physique* (f.)
pick up (the phone) (to) *décrocher, ramasser (object), prende (passenger)*
pie *tarte* (f.)
apple pie *tarte aux pommes*
pumpkin pie *tarte à la citrouille*
strawberry pie *tarte aux fraises*
piece *pièce* (f.), *morceau* (m.)
pig *porc* (m.), *cochon* (m.)
pill *pilule* (f.), *comprimé* (m.)
pink *rose*
pitcher *carafe* (f.)
pitcher of wine *carafe de vin*
pitcher of water *carafe d'eau*
place *place* (f.), *lieu* (m.), *endroit* (m.)

take place (to) *avoir lieu*
plan *plan* (m.)
plan (to) *projeter*
plant *plante* (f.)
plastic *plastique* (m.)
  made of plastic *en plastique*
plate *assiette* (f.)
platform *quai* (m.)
play (theater) *pièce* (f.) *(de théâtre)*
play (to) *jouer*
  play a sport (to) *faire du sport*
  play a game/match (to) *jouer un match*
  play hide and seek (to) *jouer à cache-cache*
  play soccer (to) *faire du foot(ball)*
player *joueur / joueuse (games, sports, etc.)*
  (m./f.), *lecteur (CDs, DVDs, etc.)* (m.)
  soccer player *footballeur / footballeuse* (m./f.)
  CD player *lecteur de CD*
  DVD player *lecteur de DVD*
playground *cour* (f.) *de récréation*
playing cards *cartes* (f. pl.) *à jouer*
pleasant *agréable*
please *s'il te plaît* (infml.) / *s'il vous plaît* (pl./fml.)
  Pleased to meet you. *Enchanté. / Enchantée.*
  (m./f.)
pleasure *plaisir* (m.)
  With pleasure. *Avec plaisir.*
plum *prune* (f.)
plumber *plombier* (m.)
poem *poème* (m.)
police (adjective) *policier / policière* (m./f.)
  police station *poste* (m.) *de police,*
   commissariat (m.)
policeman/woman *policier / femme policier*
  (m./f.), *agent / agente de police* (m./f.)
polite *poli*
politely *poliment*
politics *politique* (f.)
Pompidou Center *Centre* (m.) *Pompidou*
pond *étang* (m.), *mare* (f.)
pool *piscine (swimming)* (f.), *billard (billiards)*
  (m.)
poor *pauvre*
pork *porc* (m.)
  pork chop *côte* (f.) *de porc*
Portugal *Portugal* (m.)
Portuguese *portugais / portugaise* (m./f.)
possible *possible*

it is possible that *il est possible que*
It's not possible! (disappointment,
  anger) *Ce n'est pas possible !*
possibly *peut-être*
post office *poste* (f.), *bureau* (m.) *de poste*
potato *pomme* (f.) *de terre*
  boiled potatoes in their skins, baked
   potatoes *pommes* (pl.) *de terre en robe des*
   champs
  mashed potatoes *purée* (f.) *de pommes de*
   terre
poultry *volaille* (f.)
pound *livre* (f.)
  pound of butter *livre de beurre*
powder *poudre* (f.), *talc* (m.)
practice (to) *pratiquer*
precise *précis / précise* (m./f.)
prefer (to) *préférer, aimer mieux*
preferable *préférable*
  it is preferable that *il est préférable que*
prepare (to) *préparer*
preschool *école* (f.) *maternelle*
prescription *ordonnance* (f.)
present (to) *présenter*
pretty *joli / jolie* (m./f.)
primary school *école* (f.) *primaire*
principal *principal / principale* (m./f.)
printer *imprimante* (f.)
probable *probable*
  it is probable that *il est probable que*
probably *probablement*
produce (to) *produire*
profession *profession* (f.)
professor *professeur / professeure* (m./f.), *prof*
  (m./f.) (infml.)
programmer (computer) *informaticien /*
  informaticienne (m./f.)
programming language *langage* (m.) *de*
  programmation/informatique
progress *progrès* (m.)
protect (to) *protéger*
protest *manifestation* (f.)
protest (to) *manifester*
protestor *manifestant / manifestante* (m./f.)
proud *fier / fière* (m./f.)
public relations (PR) department *service* (m.)
  des relations publiques
pull (a tooth) (to) *arracher (une dent)*

pull a muscle (to) *se faire une élongation*
pull-ups *tractions* (f. pl.)
pumpkin *citrouille* (f.)
  pumpkin pie *tarte* (f.) *à la citrouille*
punish (to) *punir*
pupil *élève* (m./f.)
purée *purée* (f.)
purple *violet / violette* (m./f.)
purse *sac* (m.)
push-ups *pompes* (f. pl.)
put (to) *mettre*
  put in the mail (to) *mettre à la poste*
  put away (to) *ranger*
  put someone to bed (to) *coucher*

Q

quarter *quart* (m.), *quartier* (m.)
  quarter after/past ... *... et quart*
  quarter to ... *... moins le quart*
quay *quai* (m.)
question *question* (f.)
quiche *quiche* (f.)
quick *rapide*
quickly *vite, rapide*
quiet *calme*
quit (to) *quitter*
quite *assez, bien*
  quite the opposite, quite the contrary *bien au contraire*

R

race *course* (f.)
rack (of meat) *carré* (m.)
  rack of lamb *carré d'agneau*
radish *radis* (m.)
  rosette-cut radishes served with butter on top (lit., radishes in butter) *radis* (m. pl.) *au beurre*
rain *pluie* (f.)
rain (to) *pleuvoir*
  It's raining./It rains. *Il pleut.*
raincoat *imperméable* (m.)
raise (to) *lever*
Ramadan *Ramadan* (m.)
rarely *rarement*
raw *cru / crue* (m./f.)
  crudités (French appetizer of raw, mixed vegetables) *crudités* (f. pl.)

razor *rasoir* (m.)
reach (to) *arriver*
read (to) *lire*
reading *lecture*
ready *prêt / prête* (m./f.)
real *vrai / vraie* (m./f.)
realize (to) *se rendre compte (de)*
really *vraiment, en effet, bien*
  I (do) like ... *J'aime bien...*
  I (do) want ... *Je veux bien...*
reason *raison*
recent *dernier / dernière* (m./f.)
reception desk *réception* (f.)
recess *récré(ation)* (f.)
recipe *recette* (f.)
recommend that (to) *recommander que*
recreation *loisirs* (m. pl.)
red *rouge*
  red wine *vin* (m.) *rouge*
redden (to) *rougir*
reflect (to) *réfléchir*
refrigerator *réfrigérateur* (m.)
reject (to) *rejeter*
relative *parent* (m.)
relax (to) *se reposer*
relief *soulagement* (m.)
  What a relief! *Quel soulagement !*
remember (to) *se souvenir*
remove (to) *enlever*
repair things (to) *bricoler, réparer (around the house)*
repeat (to) *répéter*
  Repeat (that), please. *Répétez, s'il vous plaît.*
reply (to) *répondre*
report card *bulletin* (m.) *scolaire*
reservation *réservation* (f.)
  to make a reservation *faire une réservation*
  to make reservations *faire des réservations*
reserve (to) *réserver*
resolved (to do something) (to be) *se décider*
respond (to) *répondre*
rest (what's left) *reste* (f.), *suite* (f.)
  Can't wait for the rest! *Vivement la suite !*
rest (to) *reposer*
  rest (oneself) (to) *se reposer*
restaurant *restaurant* (m.)
restroom *toilettes* (f. pl.)
  Where is the restroom? *Où sont les toilettes ?*

results *résultats* (m. pl.)
retired *à la retraite*
retirement *retraite* (f.)
return (to) *revenir, rentrer, rendre, retourner*
reunion *réunion* (f.)
rib (meat) *côte* (f.)
rice *riz* (m.)
rich *riche*
ride a bike (to) *monter à bicyclette*
ride a horse (to) *monter à cheval*
ride a stationary bike (to) *faire du vélo d'appartement*
right (opposite of left) *droite* (f.)
  be right (to) *avoir raison*
  right? *n'est-ce pas ?*
  right bank *rive* (f.) *droite*
ring *bague* (f.), *anneau* (m.)
  engagement ring *bague de fiançailles*
  diamond ring *bague en diamant*
  wedding ring *alliance* (f.)
ring (to) *sonner*
rise (to) *monter, se lever*
river *rivière* (f.)
roast (of meat) *rôti* (m.)
  roast beef *rôti de bœuf*
roast(ed) *rôti / rôtie* (m./f.)
  roast rack of lamb *carré* (m.) *d'agneau rôti*
rock *rocher* (m.)
role *rôle* (m.)
roll the dice (to) *lancer les dés*
romantic *romantique*
  romantic comedy *comédie* (f.) *romantique*
room *pièce* (f.), *salle* (f.), *place* (f.)
rooster *coq* (m.)
rose *rose* (f.)
rosé (wine) *vin* (m.) *rosé*
round-trip *aller-retour* (m.)
  I would like a round-trip ticket. *Je voudrais un billet aller-retour.*
rug *tapis* (m.)
rugby *rugby* (m.)
  rugby team *équipe* (f.) *de rugby*
run *course* (f.)
run (to) *courir*
  run errands (to) *faire des achats*
  run the marathon (to) *courir le marathon*
running *course* (f.) *à pied*
rural *rural / rurale* (m./f.)

rush (to) *se hâter*
Russia *Russie* (f.)
Russian *russe*

S

sad *triste*
sailing *voile* (f.)
salad *salade* (f.)
  fruit salad *salade de fruits*
green salad *salade verte*
salary *salaire* (m.)
sales department *service* (m.) *des ventes*
salesman/woman *vendeur / vendeuse* (m./f.)
salt *sel* (m.)
same *même*
sand *sable* (m.)
  sandcastle *château* (m.) *de sable*
  make/build a sandcastle (to) *faire un château de sable*
sandwich *sandwich* (m.)
  ham sandwich *sandwich au jambon*
  ham and cheese sandwich *sandwich jambon-fromage*
  grilled ham and cheese sandwich *croque-monsieur* (m.)
  grilled ham and cheese sandwich with an egg on top *croque-madame* (m.)
sardines *sardines* (f. pl.)
  sardines in tomato sauce *sardines sauce tomate*
Saturday *samedi*
sauce *sauce* (f.)
sausage *saucisse* (f.)
sauté (to) *sauter*
save a document (to) *sauvegarder un document*
savory *salé / salée* (m./f.)
saxophone *saxophone* (m.)
say (to) *dire*
  Say! *Tiens !* (surprise)
You don't say!/Say! (lit., Say so!) *Dis donc !*
say to each other (to) *se dire*
scallops *coquilles* (f. pl.) *Saint-Jacques*
scarf *foulard (fashion)* (m.), *écharpe (long)* (f.)
scary *effrayant / effrayante* (m./f.)
schedule *horaire* (m.)
school *école* (f.)
  at school *à l'école*
  high school *lycée* (m.)

in high school *au lycée*
high school student *lycéen / lycéenne* (m./f.)
final year of high school *classe* (f.) *terminale*
secondary school, junior high school,
   middle school *collège* (m.)
in middle school *au collège*
elementary school, primary school *école
   primaire*
nursery school, preschool *école maternelle*
school cafeteria *cantine* (f.)
back-to-school *rentrée* (f.)
schoolyard *cour* (f.) *de récréation*
science *science* (f.)
score *score* (m.)
   final score *score final*
score (to) *marquer*
Scotland *Écosse* (f.)
Scottish *écossais / écossaise* (m./f.)
screen *écran* (m.)
sculpture *sculpture* (f.)
sea *mer* (f.)
seat *place* (f.)
seated *assis / assise* (m./f.)
second *deuxième, second / seconde* (m./f.)
   second base *deuxième base* (f.)
secondary school *collège* (m.)
secretary *secrétaire* (m./f.)
see (to) *voir*
   See you later! *À tout à l'heure ! / À plus tard !
   / Salut ! / À la prochaine !*
   See you soon! *À bientôt !*
   see each other (to) *se voir*
seeing-eye dog *chien* (m.) *d'aveugle*
seem (to) *sembler*
   it seems that *il semble que*
sell (to) *vendre*
send (to) *envoyer*
   send a file (to) *envoyer un fichier*
   send an e-mail (to) *envoyer un mail / mèl /
   e-mail / courriel / courrier électronique*
September *septembre*
series (TV) *feuilleton* (m.) *(télévisé)*
serious *grave, sérieux / sérieuse* (m./f.)
   It's not serious. *Ce n'est pas grave.*
server *serveur / serveuse* (m./f.)
seven *sept*
seventeen *dix-sept*
seventh *septième*

seventy *soixante-dix*
several *plusieurs*
sewing *couture* (f.)
shame *honte* (f.)
   be ashamed (to) *avoir honte*
shampoo *shampooing* (m.)
shape *forme* (f.)
   be in shape (to) *être en forme*
   be in good shape (to) *être en pleine / bonne
   forme*
sharp *précis / précise* (m./f.)
   at noon sharp *à midi précis*
shave (to) *se raser*
shaving cream *crème* (f.) *à raser*
she *elle*
shelf *étagère* (f.)
ship *bateau* (m.)
shipping department (mail room) *service* (m.)
   du courrier
shirt *chemise* (f.)
shoe *chaussure* (f.)
   shoe store *magasin* (m.) *de chaussures*
   shoe size *pointure* (f.)
shop (small) *boutique* (f.)
shop (to) *faire des / les courses*
short *petit / petite* (m./f.), *court / courte* (m./f.)
shot *piqûre* (f.), *injection* (f.)
should *devoir*
shoulder *épaule* (f.)
show (to) *montrer, présenter, donner*
shower *douche* (f.)
   shower gel *gel* (m.) *douche*
shrimp *crevettes* (f. pl.)
sick *malade*
   make oneself sick (to) *se rendre malade*
   be sick (to) *être malade*
side *côté* (m.)
   at the side of (next to) *à côté de*
   at the side, on the side, to the side *à côté*
   on the other side of *de l'autre côté de*
   side dish *plat* (m.) *d'accompagnement*
   side effect *effet* (m.) *secondaire*
sidewalk *trottoir* (m.)
sign language *langage* (m.) *des signes*
silk *soie* (f.)
silver *argent* (m.)
since *depuis*
   since when? *depuis quand ?*

sincere *sincère*
sing (to) *chanter*
singer *chanteur / chanteuse* (m./f.)
single *célibataire*
sink *lavabo* (m.), *évier* (m.)
sir *monsieur*
sister *sœur* (f.)
sitcom *comédie* (f.) *de situation*
sitting (down) *assis / assise* (m./f.)
situated (to be) *se trouver*
sit-ups *abdominaux* (m. pl.)
six *six*
sixteen *seize*
sixth *sixième*
sixty *soixante*
size (clothing) *taille* (f.)
size (shoe) *pointure* (f.)
skate/skating *patin* (m.)
skateboard *planche* (f.) *à roulettes, skateboard* (m.)
ski (to) *faire du ski, skier*
ski resort *station* (f.) *de sports d'hiver*
ski slope *piste* (f.)
skiing *ski* (m.)
 go skiing (to) *faire du ski*
skin *peau* (f.)
skirt *jupe* (f.)
sky *ciel* (m.)
sleep *sommeil* (m.)
sleeping car/sleeper car *wagon-lit* (m.)
sleepy (to be) *avoir sommeil*
slice *tranche (bread, cheese)* (f.), *part (cake, pie, pizza)* (f.), *rondelle (round - cucumber, banana, sausage, etc.)* (f.)
 slice of cheese *morceau de fromage*
slope (ski) *piste* (f.)
slow *lent / lente* (m./f.)
slowly *lentement*
small *petit / petite* (m./f.)
 small shop *boutique* (f.)
smile *sourire* (m.)
snails *escargots* (m. pl.)
sneaker *basket* (m./f.), *chaussure* (f.) *de basket / tennis*
snow *neige* (f.)
snow (to) *neiger*
 It's snowing. *Il neige.*
snowboarding *surf* (m.) *sur neige*

snowman *bonhomme* (m.) *de neige*
so *alors, donc*
 so that *afin que, pour que*
soak up (to) *éponger*
soap *savon* (m.)
soccer *foot(ball)* (m.)
 soccer player *footballeur / footballeuse* (m./f.)
 soccer stadium *stade* (m.) *de foot*
social *social / sociale* (m./f.)
sock *chaussette* (f.)
sofa *canapé* (m.)
soft *doux / douce* (m./f.)
 soft drink *boisson* (f.) *gazeuse*
softly *doucement*
software *logiciel* (m.)
sojourn *séjour* (m.)
sole (fish) *sole* (f.)
 sole covered in flour and sautéed in butter *sole meunière*
some *du / de la / de l' / des* (m./f./m. or f. before a vowel or silent h/pl.), *en*
someone, somebody *quelqu'un*
 someone else *quelqu'un d'autre*
something *quelque chose*
 something else *autre chose*
sometimes *quelquefois, parfois*
son *fils* (m.)
son-in-law *beau-fils* (m.)
song *chanson* (f.)
soon *bientôt*
 See you soon! *À bientôt !*
sorrow *douleur* (f.)
sorry *désolé / désolée* (m./f.)
 I am sorry. *Je suis désolé / désolée.*
So-so. *Comme ci, comme ça.*
sound system *chaîne* (f.) *hi-fi*
soup *soupe* (f.), *potage* (m.)
 onion soup *soupe à l'oignon*
 consommé (clear soup made from stock) *consommé* (m.)
 vermicelli pasta consommé (noodle soup) *consommé aux vermicelles*
sour *aigre*
south *sud* (m.)
souvenir, memory *souvenir* (m.)
Spain *Espagne* (f.)
Spanish *espagnol / espagnole* (m./f.)
 Spanish language *espagnol* (m.)

speak (to) *parler*
  speak to each other (to) *se parler*
  Speak slower/more slowly, please. *Parlez plus lentement, s'il vous plaît.*
  I speak a little French. *Je parle un peu français.*
specialty *spécialité* (f.)
spectator *spectateur / spectatrice* (m./f.)
spelling *orthographe* (f.)
spend time (to) *passer du temps*
spinach *épinards* (m. pl.)
spoon *cuillère* (f.), *cuiller* (f.)
sport *sport* (m.)
sprain one's ankle (to) *se fouler la cheville*
spring *printemps* (m.)
  in (the) spring *au printemps*
square *carré* (m.)
stadium *stade* (m.)
  soccer stadium *stade de foot*
staff *personnel* (m.)
stairs *escaliers* (m. pl.)
stamp *timbre* (m.)
standing (up) *debout*
star *étoile* (f.)
start (to) *commencer*
station *station* (f.)
  subway/metro station *station* (f.) *de métro*
stationary bike *vélo* (m.) *d'appartement*
  ride a stationary bike (to) *faire du vélo d'appartement*
statue *statue* (f.)
stay *séjour* (m.)
stay (to) *rester*
  stay in shape (to) *rester en forme*
steady job *emploi* (m.) *régulier*
steak *steak* (m.)
  steak and fries *steak frites*
stepdaughter *belle-fille* (f.)
stepfather *beau-père* (m.)
stepmother *belle-mère* (f.)
stepson *beau-fils* (m.)
still *toujours, encore*
stocking (hose) *bas* (m.)
stomach *estomac* (m.)
stop *arrêt* (m.)
  bus stop *arrêt de bus / d'autobus*
stop (to) *cesser*
store *magasin* (m.)

candy store *confiserie* (f.)
pastry and candy store *pâtisserie-confiserie* (f.)
grocery store *épicerie* (f.)
hardware store *quincaillerie* (f.)
storm *orage* (m.)
story *histoire* (f.)
stove *cuisinière* (f.)
straight *droit*
  straight ahead *tout droit*
strange *étrange, bizarre*
  It's strange. *C'est bizarre. / C'est étrange.*
strawberry *fraise* (f.)
  strawberry ice cream *glace* (f.) *à la fraise*
  strawberry pie *tarte* (f.) *aux fraises*
street *rue* (f.)
streetlight *lampadaire* (m.)
strength training *musculation* (f.)
  do strength training (to) *faire de la musculation*
strike *grève* (m.)
  on strike *en grève*
strike (to) *faire (la) grève*
stroke *attaque* (f.) *cérébrale*
strong *fort / forte* (m./f.)
strongly *vivement*
student *étudiant / étudiante* (m./f.), *élève* (m./f.)
  medical student *étudiant / étudiante en médecine*
  high school student *lycéen / lycéenne* (m./f.)
study (to) *étudier*
subject *sujet* (m.), *matière* (f.)
subtitle *sous-titre* (m.)
suburban *de banlieue*
suburbs *banlieue* (f.)
subway *métro* (m.)
  subway station *station* (f.) *de métro*
succeed (to) *réussir*
suddenly *soudain*
  all of a sudden *tout à coup/tout d'un coup*
sugar *sucre* (m.)
suggest (to) *suggérer*
suit (man's) *costume* (m.), *complet* (m., fml.)
  three-piece suit *complet-veston*
  suit (woman's) *tailleur* (m.)
suit someone well (to) *aller à ravir à quelqu'un*
summer *été* (m.)
  in (the) summer *en été*

summer vacation *grandes vacances* (f. pl.)
summer job *emploi* (m.) *saisonnier*
sun *soleil* (m.)
  It's sunny. *Il y a du soleil. / Il fait soleil.*
sunbathe (to) *prendre un bain de soleil*
Sunday *dimanche*
sunglasses *lunettes* (f. pl.) *de soleil*
super *super*
superficial injury *blessure* (f.) *superficielle*
supermarket *supermarché* (m.)
surfing *surf* (m.), *planche à voile* (f.)
surprise (to) *surprendre*
surrender (to) *se rendre*
sweater *pull(-over)* (m.), *tricot* (m.)
sweat *sueur* (f.)
  be sweating (to) *être en sueur, être en nage*
sweet *sucré / sucrée* (m./f.), *doux / douce* (m./f.)
  sweet bun *brioche* (f.)
sweetly *doucement*
swim (to) *nager, faire de la natation*
swimming *natation* (f.)
  go swimming (to) *faire de la natation*
Swiss *suisse*
Switzerland *Suisse* (f.)
synagogue *synagogue* (f.)

T

table *table* (f.)
  table for two *table pour deux*
  table setting *couvert* (m.)
tablecloth *nappe* (f.)
tablet *cachet* (m.), *comprimé* (m.)
tail *queue* (f.)
take (to) *prendre*
  take a bath (to) *prendre un bain*
  take a shower (to) *prendre une douche*
  take a tour (to) *faire un tour*
  take a walk (to) *faire une promenade, se promener*
  take someone or something for a walk (to) *promener*
  take (someone) along (to) *emmener*
  take off (to) *enlever*
  take a picture (to) *prendre une photo*
  Can you take our picture? *Pourriez-vous nous prendre en photo, s'il vous plaît ?*
  take oneself to (a place) (to) *se rendre à (+ location)*

take (a class) (to) *suivre (un cours), assister à (un cours)*
take (a test) (to) *passer (un examen)*
tale *histoire* (f.)
talented *talentueux / talentueuse* (m./f.)
talk (to) *parler*
tall *grand / grande* (m./f.)
tan (color) *beige*
tan (to) *bronzer*
tan (from the sun), tanned *bronzé / bronzée* (m./f.)
tart *tarte* (f.)
taste *goût* (m.)
taxi *taxi* (m.)
  taxi driver *chauffeur* (m.) *de taxi*
tea *thé* (m.)
  herbal tea *tisane* (f.)
  cup of tea *tasse* (f.) *de thé*
  teakettle, teapot *théière* (f.)
teach (to) *enseigner*
teacher *professeur / professeure* (m./f.), *prof* (infml., m./f.), *enseignant / enseignante* (m./f.)
team *équipe* (f.)
  rugby team *équipe de rugby*
teenager *adolescent / adolescente* (m./f.)
telephone *téléphone* (m.), *appareil* (m.)
  telephone extension *poste* (m.)
  cell phone *portable* (m.)
  phone number *numéro* (m.) *de téléphone*
  to answer the phone *répondre au téléphone*
  to make a phone call, to phone *téléphoner*
television *télé(vision)* (f.)
  television program *émission* (f.)
  TV series *feuilleton* (m.) *(télévisé)*
tell (to) *dire*
  tell each other (to) *se dire*
teller *guichetier* (m.)
temperature *température* (f.)
temple *temple* (m.)
ten *dix*
tendon *tendon* (m.)
tennis *tennis* (m.)
  tennis shoe *basket* (m./f.), *chaussure* (f.) *de basket / tennis*
tenth *dixième*
test *examen* (m.)
  fail (a test) (to) *rater (un examen)*
  pass (a test) (to) *réussir à (un examen)*

textbook *livre* (m.) *scolaire*
than *que*
  more ... than *plus... que*
  less ... than *moins... que*
  as ... as *aussi... que*
thank you *merci*
  Thank you very much. *Merci bien.*
thanks to ... *grâce à...*
that *ce / cet / cette* (m./m. before a vowel or silent h/f.), *ça / c', que, qui*
  that one, that one there *celui-là / celle-là* (m./f.)
  that way *par là*
  That doesn't interest me. *Ça ne m'intéresse pas.*
  That interests me. *Ça m'intéresse.*
  That makes ... /That is ... *Ça fait...*
  that is *c'est*
  That's bad. *C'est mauvais.*
  Is that all? *C'est tout ?*
  That's all. *C'est tout.*
the *le / l' / la / les* (m./m. before a vowel or silent h/f./pl.)
theater *théâtre* (m.)
  movie theater *cinéma* (m.)
their *leur / leurs* (m. or f./pl.)
them *eux / elles* (m./f.), *les* (direct object pronoun)
  to them *leur* (indirect object pronoun)
themselves *se / s'* (reflexive pronoun)
then *alors, donc, ensuite, puis*
there *là, là-bas, y*
  over there *là-bas*
  there is/are *il y a, voilà*
  there was/were *il y avait*
  there it is/they are *voilà*
therefore *donc*
these *ces*
  these ones, these ones here *ceux-ci / celles-ci* (m./f.)
they *ils / elles* (m./f.)
thin *mince*
thing *chose* (f.)
think (to) *penser, réfléchir*
  think that (to) *trouver que, penser que*
third *troisième*
  third base *troisième base* (f.)
thirst *soif* (f.)
  be thirsty (to) *avoir soif*

thirteen *treize*
thirty *trente*
this *ce / cet / cette* (m./m. before a vowel or silent h/f.), *ça / c', ci*
  this is *c'est*
  this way *par ici*
  this one, this one here *celui-ci / celle-ci* (m./f.)
those *ces*
  those ones, those ones there *ceux-là / celles-là* (m./f.)
thousand *mille*
threaten (to) *menacer*
three *trois*
thriller *film* (m.) *à suspense, thriller* (m.)
throat *gorge* (f.)
through *à travers*
throw (to) *envoyer, jeter*
  throw out/away (to) *jeter*
thunder *tonnerre* (m.)
Thursday *jeudi*
ticket *billet* (m.), *place* (f.)
  ticket window *guichet* (m.)
  I would like a round-trip ticket. *Je voudrais un billet aller-retour.*
tie *cravate* (f.)
tie (in a game/match) (to) *faire match nul*
time *fois* (f.), *temps* (m.)
  at what time? *à quelle heure ?*
  What time is it? *Quelle heure est-il ?*
  arrival time *heure* (f.) *de l'arrivée*
  one time (once) *une fois*
  I don't have (the) time. *Je n'ai pas le temps.*
tinker (to) *bricoler*
tire *pneu* (m.)
tissue *mouchoir* (m.)
to *à, pour, en, jusqu'à*
  to the *au / à la / à l' / aux* (m./f./m. or f. before a vowel or silent h/pl.)
  next to *à côté de*
  To your health! *À votre santé !*
  to the left/to the right *à gauche / à droite*
today *aujourd'hui*
toe *doigt* (m.) *de pied, orteil* (m.)
toenail *ongle* (m.) *de pied*
together *ensemble*
toilet *toilettes* (f. pl.)
  toilet paper *papier* (m.) *hygiénique*
tomato *tomate* (f.)

tomorrow *demain*
tongue *langue* (f.)
tonight *ce soir*
too *aussi (also), trop (much)*
tooth *dent* (f.)
touchdown *essai* (m.)
tour *tour* (m.)
tourist *touriste* (m./f.)
towel *serviette* (f.)
  bath towel *serviette de bain*
tower *tour* (f.)
  Eiffel Tower *Tour Eiffel*
town *ville* (f.)
  town hall *hôtel* (m.) *de ville*
track *voie* (f.), *piste* (f.)
track (and field) *athlétisme* (m.)
traffic *circulation* (f.)
trail *piste* (f.)
train *train* (m.)
  train station *gare* (f.)
  high-speed train *train à grande vitesse (TGV)*
train (to) *s'entraîner*
training *entraînement*
transportation *transport* (m.)
trash can *poubelle* (f.)
travel *voyage* (m.)
travel (to) *voyager*
traveler's check *chèque* (m.) *de voyage*
treadmill *tapis* (m.) *de course / de jogging*
tree *arbre* (m.)
trillion *trillion*
trip *voyage* (m.), *séjour* (m.)
  round-trip *aller-retour*
trout *truite* (f.)
  trout cooked in wine and vinegar *truite au bleu*
truck *camion* (m.)
true *vrai / vraie* (m./f.)
  it is true that *il est vrai que*
truly *vraiment*
try (to) *essayer*
  try on/out (to) *essayer*
T-shirt *T-shirt* (m.)
Tuesday *mardi*
turn *tour* (m.)
turn (to) *tourner*
TV *télé(vision)* (f.)
  TV series *feuilleton* (m.) *(télévisé)*

twelve *douze*
twentieth *vingtième*
twenty *vingt*
twice *deux fois*
two *deux*
  two dozen *deux douzaines*
  two months before *deux mois auparavant, deux mois avant*
  two times *deux fois*
type *genre*

U

ugly *laid / laide* (m./f.)
umbrella *parapluie* (m.)
uncle *oncle* (m.)
under *sous*
  under what name? *sous quel nom ?*
underneath *dessous*
underpants *caleçon* (m.)
undershirt *maillot* (m.) *de corps*
understand (to) *comprendre*
  I don't understand. *Je ne comprends pas.*
  Completely understood. *Bien entendu.*
  understand each other (to) *se comprendre*
underwear *sous-vêtements* (m. pl.)
unemployed *au chômage, sans emploi, sans travail, chômeuse, chômeur*
unemployment *chômage* (m.)
unfortunate *malheureux / malheureuse* (m./f.), *pauvre*
unfortunately *malheureusement*
unfriendly *peu amical / peu amicale* (m./f.)
unhappily *malheureusement*
unhappy *malheureux / malheureuse* (m./f.)
United States *États-Unis* (m. pl.)
university *université* (f.)
unless *à moins que... ne*
until *jusqu'à, jusqu'à ce que, d'ici*
upstairs, up above *en haut*
up until, up to *jusqu'à*
urban *urbain / urbaine* (m./f.)
urgent *urgent / urgente* (m./f.)
  it is urgent that *il est urgent que*
us *nous*
  to us *nous* (indirect object pronoun)
use (to) *employer, utiliser*
  use sign language (to) *utiliser le langage des signes*

usually *normalement, d'habitude, en général*

V

vacation *vacances* (f. pl.)
  summer vacation *grandes vacances* (f. pl.)
  winter vacation *vacances* (f. pl.) *d'hiver*
    400
vaccine *vaccin* (m.)
vain *vain / vaine* (m./f.)
vanilla *vanille* (f.)
  vanilla ice cream *glace* (f.) *à la vanille*
veal *veau* (m.)
vegetable *légume* (m.)
vendor *marchand / marchande* (m./f.)
vermicelli pasta *vermicelle* (m.)
  vermicelli pasta consommé (noodle
    soup) *consommé* (m.) *aux vermicelles*
version *version* (f.)
very *très, bien*
  very good *très bien, très bon / bonne* (m./f.)
  very well *très bien*
veterinarian *vétérinaire* (m.)
video game *jeu* (m.) *vidéo*
Vietnamese *vietnamien / vietnamienne* (m./f.)
village *village* (m.)
violet (purple) *violet / violette* (m./f.)
violin *violon* (m.)
virus *virus* (m.)
visit (a person) (to) *rendre visite à*
visit (a place) (to) *visiter*
vocabulary *vocabulaire* (m.)
volleyball *volley(-ball)* (m.)
voyage *voyage* (m.)

W

waffle *gaufre* (f.)
wait (for) (to) *attendre*
  wait in line (to) *faire la queue*
  can't wait (to look forward to) *avoir hâte*
  (I) can't wait for the end of the
    day! *Vivement la fin de la journée !*
waiter/waitress *serveur / serveuse* (m./f.)
wake (someone) (to) *réveiller*
  wake up (to), wake oneself up (to) *se réveiller*
walk (to) *marcher*
  take a walk (to) *se promener*
  take someone or something for a walk
    (to) *promener*

walk with a cane (to) *marcher avec une canne*
walk with crutches (to) *marcher avec des
  béquilles*
wall *mur* (m.)
want (to) *vouloir, désirer*
  I want … *Je veux…*
  I would like … *Je voudrais…*
wardrobe *armoire* (f.)
warm *chaud / chaude* (m./f.)
  It's warm./It's hot. *Il fait chaud.*
  be warm/hot (to) *avoir chaud*
wash (to) *laver*
  wash up (to), wash oneself (to) *se laver*
washing machine *machine* (f.) *à laver, lave-linge*
  (m.)
washroom *salle* (f.) *de bains*
waste (to) *perdre*
  waste time (to) *perdre du temps*
  waste your time (to) *perdre votre / ton temps*
watch *montre* (f.)
watch (to) *regarder*
  watch each other (to) *se regarder*
water *eau* (f.)
  mineral water *eau minérale*
  pitcher of water *carafe* (f.) *d'eau*
water-ski (to) *faire du ski nautique*
water-skiing *ski* (m.) *nautique*
way *direction* (f.), *chemin* (m.)
  this way *par ici*
  that way *par là*
we *nous, on* (infml.)
weak *faible*
wear (to) *porter*
  wear contact lenses (to) *porter des verres de
    contact, porter des lentilles de contact*
weather *temps* (m.)
  What's the weather today? *Quel temps fait-il
    aujourd'hui ?*
webpage *page* (f.) *web*
website *site* (m.) *web*
wedding ring *alliance* (f.)
Wednesday *mercredi*
week *semaine* (f.)
  in one week *dans une semaine*
  next week *semaine prochaine, dans une
    semaine*
  the week before last *semaine précédente,
    semaine d'avant*

the week after next *semaine d'après, semaine suivante, dans deux semaines*

days of the week *jours* (m. pl.) *de la semaine*

weekend *week-end* (m.)

weigh (to) *peser*

weightlifting *haltérophilie* (f.), *musculation* (f.)

lift weights (to) *faire de la musculation*

Welcome. *Bienvenue.*

You're welcome. *De rien. / Il n'y a pas de quoi. / Je vous en prie.* (fml.)

well *bien*

very well *très bien*

It's going well. *Ça va bien.*

Well done. *Bravo.*

Well ... *Eh bien... / Ben...* (infml.) */ Alors... / Alors là...*

well-dressed *bien habillé / habillée* (m./f.)

west *ouest* (m.)

western *western* (m.)

what *qu'est-ce que, quel / quelle* (m./f.), *quoi, que, qu'est-ce qui*

what happens next *suite* (f.)

what?/of what? *de quel / quelle ?* (m./f.)

at what time? *à quelle heure ?*

What is this/that? *Qu'est-ce que c'est ?*

What is the weather today? *Quel temps fait-il aujourd'hui ?*

What time is it? *Quelle heure est-il ?*

What's your name? *Comment vous appelez-vous ?* (pl./fml.) */ Comment t'appelles-tu ?* (infml.)

What's up?/What's new? *Quoi de neuf ?*

whatever *n'importe quoi*

wheelchair *chaise* (f.) *roulante*

when *quand*

since when? *depuis quand ?*

where *où*

Where is ... ? *Où se trouve... ? / Où est... ?*

Where is the restroom? (lit., Where are the toilets?) *Où sont les toilettes ?*

wherever *n'importe où*

which *que, quel / quelle* (m./f.), *lequel / laquelle / lesquels / lesquelles* (m./f./m. pl./f. pl.)

of which *dont*

while *pendant que*

whipped cream (that is flavored and sweetened) *crème* (f.) *chantilly*

white *blanc / blanche* (m./f.)

white wine *vin* (m.) *blanc*

white wine with black currant liqueur *kir* (m.)

white coat (doctor's coat) *blouse* (f.) *blanche*

who *qui*

Who is it? *Qui est-ce ?*

Who's calling? (on the phone) *C'est de la part de qui ? / Qui est à l'appareil ?*

whoever *n'importe qui*

whom *que*

of whom *dont*

whose *dont*

why *pourquoi*

wide *large*

wife *femme* (f.)

win (to) *gagner*

win a game/match (to) *gagner un match*

wind *vent* (m.)

It's windy. *Il fait du vent. / Il y a du vent.*

window *fenêtre* (f.), *guichet (ticket)* (m.)

wine *vin* (m.)

red/white/rosé/sparkling wine *vin rouge / blanc / rosé / mousseux*

white wine with black currant liqueur *kir* (m.)

type of French sparkling wine *crémant* (m.)

wine list *carte* (f.) *des vins*

winter *hiver* (m.)

in (the) winter *en hiver*

winter vacation *vacances* (f. pl.) *de neige*

wish (to) *désirer, souhaiter, vouloir*

with *avec*

With pleasure. *Avec plaisir.*

without *sans, sans que*

wolf *loup* (m.)

woman *femme* (f.)

wonder (to) *se demander*

wood *bois* (m.)

Bois de Vincennes (Vincennes Wood) *Bois de Vincennes (a large park in Paris)*

Bois de Boulogne (Boulogne Wood) *Bois de Boulogne (a large park in Paris)*

wooden *en bois*

word *mot* (m.)

work *travail* (m.), *boulot* (m.), *emploi* (m.)

work (to) *travailler*

work hard (to) *travailler dur*

worker *employé / employée* (m./f.)

Glossary ④⁰¹

workout *entraînement* (m.)

world *monde* (m.)

worried *inquiet / inquiète* (m./f.)

  Don't worry about it. *Ce n'est pas grave.*

worse *pire, plus mauvais / mauvaise* (m./f.)

  the worst *le / la pire, le / la plus mauvais / mauvaise*

worth (to be) *valoir*

  be worth the trouble (to) *valoir la peine*

wounded *blessé / blessée* (m./f.)

Wow! *Oh là là !*

wrestling *lutte* (f.)

wrist *poignet* (m.)

write (to) *écrire*

writer *écrivain* (m.) (sometimes: *écrivaine*, f.)

wrong *faux / fausse* (m./f.), *mal, tort*

  be wrong (to) *avoir tort*

X

x-ray *radio(graphie)* (f.)

Y

year *année* (f.), *an* (m.)

  be ... years old (to) *avoir... ans*

  final year of high school *classe* (f.) *terminale*

yellow *jaune*

yes *oui, si (negative)*

yesterday *hier*

yield to (to) *se rendre à* (+ evidence, an argument, etc.)

yoga *yoga* (m.)

you *tu* (infml.), *vous* (pl./fml.), *toi* (infml.), *te / t'* (direct object pronoun) (infml.), *vous* (direct object pronoun) (pl./fml.)

  to you *te / t'* (infml.), *vous* (pl./fml.) (indirect object pronoun)

  you have to/need to/must *il faut*

  You're welcome. *De rien. / Je vous en prie.* (fml.)

young *jeune*

  youngest child *cadet / cadette* (m./f.)

your (infml.) *ton / ta / tes* (m./f./pl.)

your (pl./fml.) *votre / vos* (m. or f./pl.)

yourself *te / t'* (infml.), *vous* (fml.) (reflexive pronoun)

yourselves *vous* (reflexive pronoun)

youth hostel *auberge* (f.) *de jeunesse*

Z

zero *zéro*